THE DUTCH LANGUAGE
A Survey

*The following books for learners of Dutch are also
available from Stanley Thornes (Publishers) Ltd:*
Schoenmakers PRAATPAAL — Dutch for Beginners
Smit and Meijer DUTCH GRAMMAR AND READER
Williams A DUTCH READER
*Donaldson DUTCH REFERENCE GRAMMAR
*Shetter INTRODUCTION TO DUTCH — A Practical Grammar
†Donaldson A DUTCH VOCABULARY

Also available from Stanley Thornes (Publishers) Ltd:
Meijer LITERATURE OF THE LOW COUNTRIES

*Published by Martinus Nijhoff; distributed in the UK by
Stanley Thornes (Publishers) Ltd

†Published by Australian Educa Press; distributed in the UK by
Stanley Thornes (Publishers) Ltd

THE DUTCH LANGUAGE
A Survey

Pierre Brachin

Professor Emeritus, Université de Paris-Sorbonne

Translated from the French
by
Paul Vincent

STANLEY THORNES (PUBLISHERS) LTD

First published 1977 by Didier Hatier S A, Brussels

English translation first published 1985 by
Stanley Thornes (Publishers) Ltd
Old Station Drive
Leckhampton
CHELTENHAM GL53 0DN

British Library Cataloguing in Publication Data

Brachin, Pierre
 The Dutch language.
 1. Dutch language
 I. Title II. La langue néerlandaise. *English*
 439.3'1   PF73

 ISBN 0-85950-246-5

Typeset in 10/11 Paladium by Setrite Typesetters, Hong Kong
Printed and bound in Great Britain at The Pitman Press, Bath

Contents

Preface to The Original Edition

The present work aims to make a new contribution, less in its detailed contents than in its overall conception.

It is not a grammar and does not presume to compete with any of the methods currently in use. Neither is it a full-scale academic study, but rather a modest **essay**, in both senses of the word.

I have tried to sketch as succinctly as possible the origins and development of Dutch, to highlight some of the language's essential characteristics and underlying tendencies, and finally to answer once and for all a number of questions which I have been constantly asked over the last quarter of a century.

This short survey is obviously addressed in the first instance to students, but has also been written with a wider educated public in mind, including all those who are interested in varying degrees in the problems of language. It is hoped that they will read this book with pleasure and profit. Indeed, technical jargon has been as far as possible avoided, in an attempt to reconcile scholarly rigour with simplicity of presentation.

For the same reason, references have been reduced to a minimum, and are usually given in only three cases: where there is quotation; where a specific work is alluded to; where mention is made of a particular discovery or hypothesis to which a scholar has attached his name.

I am most indebted to Professors Emeriti C. B. van Haeringen and J. L. Pauwels for their critical reading of the manuscript and for their comments.

P.B.

NOTE TO THE ENGLISH EDITION

With the author's agreement, the translation has been adapted, where necessary, to the needs of English-speaking readers, and on some points of detail the original has been amended and updated.

For most geographical and place names in the text the official spelling in the country or area concerned has been used (see the map on p. ix). Exceptions have been made for, e.g. Antwerp, Brussels and

The Hague, and the Rivers Meuse, Rhine and Scheldt, where it was felt that departure from current English usage would be distracting.

I am grateful to my colleague Dr Theo Hermans, of University College London, for his helpful advice.

Note: Examples marked with an asterisk indicate ungrammatical sentences.

Key

- - - · - - -   National Frontier
· · · · · · · · · · · · ·   Provincial Boundary
━━━━━━━   Linguistic Frontier

GRONINGEN
• Emden
Leeuwarden
• Groningen
FRIESLAND
• Assen
DRENTHE

NOORD-HOLLAND
• Enkhuizen
NORTH SEA
• Alkmaar
Zaandam
• Zwolle
Haarlem ■ AMSTERDAM
OVERIJSSEL
• Bentheim

ZUID-HOLLAND
• Leiden
Utrecht
GELDERLAND
's-Gravenhage ■
Gouda
UTRECHT
• Delft
Arnhem
Rotterdam
Culemborg
Dordrecht
Nijmegen
• Emmerich
Kleve
W. GERMANY
's-Hertogenbosch
ZEELAND
Breda
NOORD
Geldern
R. Rhine
• Middelburg
Tilburg
BRABANT
Mörs
Venlo
Turnhout
(DUTCH)
Antwerpen
LIMBURG
• Düsseldorf
Brugge •
OOST-
ANTWERPEN
(BELGIAN)
WEST-
Gent
Mechelen
LIMBURG
Köln •
VLANDEREN
Aalst
Aarschot
Hasselt Genk
Bergues •
Ieper
Kortrijk
Brussel
Leuven
Hoeselt
Boulogne •
Comines
Oudenaarde
Tienen
Maastricht
Cassel •
Warneton
Mouscron Ronse
BRABANT
Tongeren
Hazebrouck •
Lille •
Halle
Wavre
Liège
Eupen •
Waterloo
R. Scheldt
LIEGE
Mons •
HAINAULT
Namur
R. Meuse
• Arras
Bavay
NAMUR
Cambrai •

LUXEMBOURG
FRANCE
Arlon •

The Netherlands and Belgium

General Points

Definition

Dutch is the language used: 1) in the Netherlands (*Noord-Nederland* or, more frequently, simply *Nederland*), which has some fourteen million inhabitants;[1] 2) in the northern part of Belgium (*Zuid-Nederland*, population approximately six million). The dividing line between Germanic and Romance speech in Belgium, proceeding from west to east, passes north of Warneton, Comines, Mouscron and Dottignies, south of Ronse, north of Enghien, south of Halle, north of Waterloo and Wavre, south of Hoegaarden, Tienen and Tongeren, veering south-eastwards a little further on to leave Eupen in Germanic territory, and from there runs in a southerly direction, separating German proper and Romance.[2]

If one does not limit oneself to *ABN*,[3] the equivalent of Standard English or the German *Hochsprache*, but takes in the dialects, then the area defined above proves too narrow. In the north-east the transition from Dutch to Low German is an imperceptible one: the 'German' dialect of Bentheim turns out to be closer to *ABN* than the 'Dutch' dialects of Maastricht or Tongeren. To the west, in the part of French Flanders around Hazebrouck, Cassel and Bergues (sometimes called, rather oddly, *Zuid-Vlaanderen*), an estimated 100,000 country people still use a dialect of Dutch in their everyday lives. But whereas in Belgium the dividing-line between Dutch and French has remained remarkably stable since early medieval times, in France the domain of Dutch has shrunk progressively over the centuries.

Dutch, then, spills over slightly at both extremities into foreign territory. On the other hand, it does not have a monopoly either in the Netherlands or in northern Belgium. It is subject to three restrictions:

1) In the province of Friesland, the Frisian language (quite distinct from Dutch, and with an ancient pedigree of its own) is still very much alive. While it is true in principle that all Frisian-speakers (some 350,000 of them) have a command of Dutch, Frisian is accorded a place in education, local government and the administration of justice.

2) The Brussels conurbation, situated slightly north of the linguistic frontier, is at present, despite its designation as a bilingual area, populated by a large majority of French-speakers, most of whom speak no Dutch, or have only a very rudimentary passive knowledge. (This has come about in roughly the last eighty years, and the process has accelerated since 1958, when Brussels became the administrative centre of the European Economic Community.) Complex official provisions attempt to ensure that everyone is able to use his own language in all circumstances.

3) In the Dutch-speaking part of Belgium there are still some groups who wish to retain French as their means of communication. Since

Belgian legislation has been strictly based on monolingualism, the numerical importance of these *franskiljons* (as they have been dubbed by their opponents) is constantly diminishing, but their presence is still not negligible.

Outside Europe, Dutch is used in the Netherlands Antilles (the principal island being Curaçao) by the administration and, in a more or less bastardised form, by a section of the population. The same applies to former Dutch Guyana, or Surinam, which gained independence in 1975. In Indonesia, Dutch still enjoys some status in intellectual circles, but the long shadow which the New Guinea affair cast over relations between Djakarta and The Hague has been harmful to its retention as a foreign language in the face of fierce competition from English. South Africa is a special case: Afrikaans (see Appendix) has gained such a degree of autonomy from Dutch that the latter is no longer spoken at all, although many Afrikaans-speakers are still able to understand Dutch. In the universities, the study of Dutch language and literature is a compulsory part of degree courses in Afrikaans.

Names

The English word 'Dutch', like German *deutsch*, is related to the old forms *dietsch* (Flanders), *duutsch* (Brabant) and the subsequently generally used *duitsch*.[4] Originally the term, which was Latinised as *theodiscus* and later Gallicised as *thiois*, had no national connotations, but simply meant the vernacular as opposed to Latin. Although it appears to have originated in what is today Belgium, its meaning was eventually extended to apply to the whole Germanic area. In the first text in which it is found, dating from 781, *theodiscus* refers to the Germanic dialects of Britain.

The term *Nederlandsch* first appeared in an incunable of 1482, and rapidly gained currency. Undoubtedly a need was felt to differentiate the language from German. For the same reason, by the middle of the 16th century *Nederduitsch* had almost completely ousted *duitsch*. There ensued a protracted, up-and-down struggle for ascendancy between *Nederlandsch* and *Nederduitsch*. Although the latter retained a degree of ambiguity (since it could also apply to the dialects of Northern Germany), *Nederlandsch* did not finally emerge triumphant until the beginning of the 19th century in the Netherlands and the beginning of the 20th century in Flanders.[5]

There is certainly nothing odd about a linguistic frontier not coinciding with a political one: French, for example, is spoken in Wallonia and German in Austria. But what is striking is that on neither side of the border separating the two kingdoms has the term *Nederlands* been as yet entirely accepted into everyday usage. For some speakers, it continues to have slightly administrative, scholarly or official overtones. In the north *Hollands*, and in the south *Vlaams* (Flemish), retains some widespread currency in informal discourse. Both are obvious misnomers, since the first term applies properly only to the dialects spoken in the provinces of North Holland (capital Haarlem) and South Holland (capital The Hague). Similarly 'Flemish' in the strict sense designates the speech of West Flanders (capital Brugge) and East Flanders (capital Gent). But the fact of this usage remains, and it is still persistent among older, less educated and dialect speakers in North and South, even though since 1940 *Nederlands* has gained considerable ground. Writing in the 1950s, a distinguished Dutch linguist went so far as to claim that '90% of novel-readers, if asked whether they have read such and such English or French work in the original, will answer, assuming that this is not the case: "No, in *Hollands*" or "No, in a *Hollands* translation".'[6] It is doubtful whether the same sweeping claim could be made today. In Belgium the use of *Nederlands* in official documents was not made compulsory until the issue of a royal decree on 10th December 1973. A year previously, the venerable Flemish Academy (*Koninklijke VLAAMSE Academie voor Taal- en Letterkunde*) had become the *Koninklijke Academie voor NEDERLANDSE Taal- en Letterkunde*. A further difference between North and South is that whereas someone from Groningen or Breda may, despite his spontaneous use of the term, often be loth to admit that he speaks *Hollands*, for every Dutch-speaking Belgian, though he may be from Brabant or Limburg, the national language is popularly known as *Vlaams*.

It remains to be seen whether the signing in 1980 of the *Nederlandse Taalunie* (Dutch Language Union), which enshrined *Nederlands* as the official designation of the language in the constitutions of both the Netherlands and Dutch-speaking Belgium, together with its consistent use and propagation in education and the media, will lead to the eventual demise of the particularist terms.

Dutch as a Germanic Language

The great 'Indo-European' family of languages is, as we know, as far as Europe is concerned, made up of various branches: Celtic, Slavonic, Romance, Germanic, etc. 'Common Germanic' split over the course of the centuries into three groups. One of these, East Germanic, has not survived in any modern language (though a translation of the Bible into Gothic, made in the 4th century by Bishop Ulfilas, gives us a good impression). The Scandinavian languages belong to the North Germanic group. West Germanic, which concerns us here, can be further subdivided. From it emerged on the one hand English and Frisian, on the other German and Dutch. Dutch occupies third place among Germanic languages, with more native-speakers than those of Danish, Swedish, Norwegian and Icelandic put together.

'Dutch has a number of features which distinguish it from the other Germanic languages, for example:
1) *Sch* at the beginning of a syllable is pronounced $[\chi]$[7]: cf. Du. *school*, Eng. *school*, Germ. *Schule*, Swed. *skola*.
2) The consonantal group *ft* has often become *cht*: Du. *kracht* cf. Eng. *craft*, Germ. *Kraft*, Swed. *kraft*.

3) The consonantal group *ks* (spelt either *chs* or *x*) has become *s* through assimilation: Du. *zes* and *os* correspond to Eng. *six* and *ox*, Germ. *sechs* and *Ochs*, Swed. *sex* and *oxe*.

4) The consonantal group *al, ol* + *d,t* has become *ou* + *d,t*[8]: Du. *oud* and *goud* cf. Eng. *old* and *gold*, Germ. *alt* and *Gold*, Swed. *äldre* (comparative) and *guld*.

5) Before the ending *-er*, Dutch often inserts *d* after *l, n* and *r*: Du. *kelder* corresponds to Eng. *cellar*, Germ. *Keller*, Swed. *Källare*.

6) Long vowels are generally not palatalised: Du. *horen* and *groen* as opposed to Eng. *hear* and *green*, Germ. *hören* and *grün*, Swed. *höra* and *grön*.

7) The subordinating conjunction *dat* cannot be implied: *Ik denk dat hij morgen komt* cannot be replaced by **Ik denk hij komt morgen*, whereas Eng. *I think (that) he'll come tomorrow*, Germ. *Ich glaube, dass er morgen kommt* or *Ich glaube, er kommt morgen*, or Swed. *Jag tror (att) han kommer i morgon* are all interchangeable.

8) Diminutives may be formed not only from nouns, but also from adverbs: *zachtjes* (softly), *eventjes* (just for a moment), *netjes* (nicely), *kalmpjes* (calmly), etc.

Dutch occupies an intermediate position between the most closely related Germanic languages, German and English, as a few examples will show:

1) The infinitive ending: German *hören* (*n* voiced), Du. *horen* (*n* often silent), Eng. *hear* (no ending);

2) The conjugation of the present tense:

German	Dutch	English
ich höre	*ik hoor*	*I hear*
du hörst	*jij hoort*	*you hear*
er/sie hört	*hij/zij hoort*	*he/she hears*
wir hören	*wij horen*	*we hear*
ihr hört	*jullie horen*	*you hear*
sie hören	*zij horen*	*they hear*

3) Gender: Germ. has three definite articles (*der, die, das*), Du. two (*de, het*), Eng. only one (*the*);

4) Noun plurals: Germ. has quite a large number of forms (*-e, -en, -er, Umlaut*, etc.), Du. two (*-en* and *-s*) and Eng. only *-s*, allowing for a number of irregularities in the latter two cases.'[9]

We shall have occasion, in Chapter IV, to return in greater detail to the parallels between Dutch and German.

The Dialects

Leaving aside Friesland, a distinction is traditionally made between **Saxon** and **Franconian** dialects, and this distinction may be retained (provided it is not confused with the historical division into different tribes). The former are found above a line running from north-west to south-east which links the IJsselmeer (formerly the Zuiderzee) with the German frontier, passing slightly north of Arnhem. They are charac-

terised especially by the fact that final n is not dropped in speech.[10]
The Franconian dialects, by far the most important in all respects,
break down approximately as follows:
1) 'Hollands', which for dialectologists includes not only the two provinces of Holland, but also that of Utrecht;
2) the dialects of Zeeland (capital Middelburg) and West Flanders;
3) 'Brabants', spoken in North Brabant (Netherlands, capital 's-
Hertogenbosch), the province of Antwerp, the northern part of Belgian
Brabant and East Flanders;
4) 'Limburgs', Dutch Limburg (capital Maastricht) and Belgian
Limburg (capital Hasselt).

---

1 Given the ambiguity of the English term 'Netherlands', it is essential not to confuse
Nederland (singular), i.e. the present-day 'Kingdom of the Netherlands', with de
Nederlanden (plural). The latter is used historically to denote the vast political conglo-
merate which was at its largest under Charles V (1515–1555) and comprised the present-
day Netherlands, Belgium (except for the prince-bishopric of Liège) and parts of
northern France (the county of Artois and the bishopric of Cambrai). The term was
revived to designate the short-lived state which from 1815 to 1830 reunited what are
now the Netherlands and Belgium under the rule of King Willem I. As can be seen, in
both cases 'the Netherlands' (de Nederlanden) in the wider sense embraced very significant
French-speaking areas. At present, it is true, the term is occasionally used synonymously
with the Dutch language-area, hence excluding Wallonia. On the other hand, although
cut in half by the Belgian Revolution of 1830, the Dutch state has retained as its official
title 'Het Koninkrijk der Nederlanden'.
2 At least this is its official course. For further details, see the Grote Winkler Prins
Encyclopedie (Amsterdam, 1967), III, pp. 454–455.
3 An abbreviation of Algemeen Beschaafd Nederlands, or 'General Educated Dutch'.
Whatever the merits of the term (often shortened to Algemeen Beschaafd), the initials
'ABN' have come to acquire a generally-accepted meaning, though the more neutral
standaardtaal is gaining currency, at least among linguists.
4 Down to the 15th and 16th centuries 'Dutch' was widely used in English as a synonym
of 'German' and 'Germanic'. Even after the Revolt of the Netherlands its more general
use persisted in such expressions as 'High and Low Dutch', while 'Pennsylvania Dutch'
refers to an immigrant community in the USA which in fact originated from the Rhine
Palatinate and Switzerland. cf. The Oxford English Dictionary (Compact Edition), 2 vols
(London, 1979), I, pp. 819–820.
5 Diets[ch], a doublet of Duits[ch], still survives, but its use is sporadic and artificial,
though it remains dear to those wishing to stress the cultural unity of the Netherlands
and Flanders. It was this ideal which inspired the setting up, in 1855, of the magazine
Dietsche Warande (which has since become D. W. en Belfort). Nowadays, however, the
term is generally avoided, because of the misuse made of it before and during the
Second World War by certain Fascist-inspired organisations. In any case, it has not been
applied to the **language** for centuries.
6 C. B. van Haeringen, Nederlands tussen Duits en Engels (Den Haag, n. d.), p. 18.
7 [χ] represents the sound heard both in German and in Dutch in, for example, laCHen
or noCH.
8 Note that ou and au represent the same sound in Modern Dutch, though relating to
historically distinct diphthongs.
9 J. de Rooij, Inleiding tot de geschiedenis van de Nederlandse taal (Københavns Univer-
sitetet, Offset Afdelingen, n. d.), pp. 1–3. [Notes 7 and 8 have been added, P. B.]
10 This of course refers to the final n in words of more than one syllable ending in
unstressed en, and not to the n of gaan, veen or loon.

CHAPTER I

History in Broad Sweeps

1. THE MISTS OF TIME

At the time of its conquest by Caesar, a little before the start of the Christian era, the territory of what is now Belgium was probably, like the rest of Gaul, inhabited by Celts. Further north, around the mouth of the Rhine, the Romans encountered barbarian tribes of whom little is known. Some decades later, they appealed to a Germanic tribe, the Batavi, for help and installed them as allies in the *insula Batavorum*, which probably included the Betuwe area and part of South Holland. That these regions were previously inhabited by Celts is proved by certain place-names: a Celtic root, for example, can be detected in Nijmegen (Noviomagus). But of course place-names of Celtic origin are decidedly more common south of the River Meuse. Gent, Tongeren, names ending in -*ik* like Doornik (Tournai) or Kamerijk (Cambrai), may be cited as examples. Certain common nouns also date back to the Celtic period: *duin* (dune), *ambt* (office), *eed* (oath), M. Du. *gisel* (hostage), and patronyms in -*rijc*. All in all, a fairly meagre harvest. As for the language of the Batavi, it would appear that almost nothing is left.

One thing is certain: the profound impact made by Gallo-Roman civilisation, and hence by Latin. The influence emanating from Noviomagus over three centuries was felt as far north as Friesland. As farmers, the Germanic peoples learned from the Romans how to use the flail (*vlegel* < flagellum) and the fork (*vork* < furca), how to grow fruit (*vrucht* < fructus), and even how to make butter (*boter* < butyrum) and cheese (*kaas* < caseus). As soldiers, they marched along the military roads (*straat* < via strata), mounted guard on ramparts (*wal* < vallum) and may have made the acquaintance of a prison cell (*kerker* < carcer). Roman merchants taught them the use of coins as money (*munt* < moneta) and units of measure like the hectolitre (*mud* < modius) and the pound (*pond* < pondus). Rough wooden huts gave way to houses surrounded by a wall (*muur* < murus) and equipped with a loft (*zolder* < solarium). A number of Dutch words of Latin origin are not found in German, which seems to imply an even deeper penetration than in other regions: *oogst* (< augustus, 'harvest'), *lemmet* (< lamina, 'blade'), *zaterdag* (< Saturni dies, 'Saturday'). Of course, it is impossible to date such borrowings precisely. Nevertheless, *keizer* (< caesar), *kelder* (< cellarium), *kist* (< cista) and *wijn* (< vinum) are definitely very old, as they predate the shift in Latin from *k* to *s* and from *w* to *v*.[1]

From the 4th century onwards, the Roman Empire began to disintegrate, and barbarian tribes gradually came to dominate the area. Among these were the Franks, whose name first appears in 250 A.D.: Ripuarians on the Mid-Rhine, Salians on the Lower Rhine. In 358, the Emperor Julian succeeded in confining the Salians, under the name of *foederati*, in Toxandria, in what is now North Brabant, but the pressure resumed, and finally exploded. In 486 Clovis founded his Frankish kingdom with Paris as its capital.

It is basically from the language of the Salians, Lower Franconian, that Dutch derives.

However, in the north, other tribes emerged. For a while, the Frisians occupied a very extensive territory; the *lex Frisonum* held sway from the Weser to the Zwin in Flanders. This state of affairs has been preserved in one geographical detail; to the west of the IJsselmeer the region around Alkmaar and Enkhuizen is still called West Friesland, although the Frisian language has long since died out there. The Saxons, for their part, originating from the mouth of the Elbe, reached the Flemish coast by sea, from where, in the 5th century, some of them crossed over into Britain. Other Saxons drove out the Frisians from Groningen and the Eastern Netherlands, and pushed as far as Utrecht.

Frisian and Saxon have not been without influence on Dutch. From Frisian derive *fuik* (fish-trap), *terp* (mound) and many of the words beginning with *sj-*, like *sjorren* (to lash down) and *sjouwen* (to lug), or in *tj-*, like *tjalk* (sailing barge) and *tjotter* (small ship). Forms of Saxon origin are often marked by their vowel mutations; *scheper, sneu* and *geneugte* are the equivalents of Franconian *schaper* (shepherd), *snood* (wicked) and *genoegen* (pleasure) respectively. Also from Saxon comes the adverb *vaak* (often).

In addition, among all those coastal peoples, from Gaul to Jutland, there existed certain linguistic peculiarities which are generally designated as Inguaeonic, a term used by Tacitus, though in a completely different context. Very clear traces of Inguaeonic are found in Dutch, as in English, but to a lesser degree. Primitive *n*, which survives, for example, in Germ. *fünf*, has disappeared from Du. *vijf* and Eng. *five*. The same phenomenon of denasalisation is found in *Diks-muide, IJ-muiden* (and *Portsmouth*), as opposed to *Dender-monde* and *Rupel-monde*. Also Inguaeonic are the second person personal pronouns *jij, je* and *jou* (cf. Eng. *you*, as opposed to Germ. *du*) and certain plurals in *-s* (the only productive form in English, but very rare in German).[2] To these must be added, in the field of vocabulary, a number of very common words, such as *ladder* (ladder), *eiland* (island), *wiel* (wheel), etc., as well as place-names ending in *-drecht* (*Dordrecht, Loosdrecht*).

But interesting as the joint impact in the north of Franconian, Saxon and Frisian may be, it is in the south of the language-area that the most important and most vexing problem is raised: that of the origin of the linguistic frontier between Germanic and Romance. What led to the existence of this almost straight line which crosses the Belgian plain and whose course, at first sight, is singularly arbitrary?

Eighty years ago, the thesis of the historian C. Kurth that between the 3rd and 5th centuries the Franks of Toxandria had invaded and colonised Northern Belgium, was generally accepted. Their failure to penetrate further was due partly to the huge tract of woodland known as the 'Kolenwoud' (Forêt Charbonnière) which covered part of present-day Brabant, and partly to a line of Roman defensive positions protecting the strategic route which ran from Boulogne to Cologne via Arras, Bavay, Tongeren and Maastricht. Subsequently, it is true, these defences succumbed, but by that time the cultural and linguistic situation was fixed once and for all. Beginning in 1926, two German scholars, F. Steinbach and F. Petri, observed that the Kolenwoud had 'neither the size nor the right location to act as a barrier', and that the line of the Roman road, quite apart from the fact that Frankish tombs are still being uncovered on both sides of it, 'corresponds only very vaguely to that of the linguistic frontier'.[3] Kurth's static theory was replaced by a dynamic hypothesis. On the basis of archaeological finds and toponymy, Petri believes that gradual Frankish penetration into Gaul gave way at the time of the great migrations to a massive influx. Gaul, he claims, was widely Germanised as far south as the Loire, but this was followed by a reaction, a 're-Romanisation' from south to north. According to this theory, the linguistic frontier simply marks the point where this process stopped. The theory has hardly any currency today; certainly it is accepted that the Romans never considered the Boulogne–Cologne highway as the frontier of the Empire and that they never seriously fortified it. But Petri's positive arguments have never carried conviction. He has been accused of ascribing to Frankish settlement 'a numerical importance, a geographical extension and an intensity which it never achieved', as Petri himself, moreover, was subsequently forced partially to admit.[4] If, therefore, 'the existence of the linguistic frontier between Flemish and Walloon is not attributable to the action of the Salian Franks',[5] the whole problem needs looking at afresh.

Most recent historians stress the particularly inhospitable nature of the areas in question: in the first centuries of the Christian era, the land east of the River Scheldt was covered in dense forests, and to the west there were nothing but heaths and marshlands. From all the evidence, these regions did not begin to be colonised until long after the period of the migrations, under the Carolingians, and then only very gradually. The line marking the **limit** of Romance only became a **frontier** when there were sufficient people on the other side. 'The linguistic frontier, therefore, does not have the simple and almost catastrophic origin that is still too often attributed to it. It is the result of population trends, and as such the work of centuries.'[6]

*   *   *   *   *

As in the case of English and German, it is customary to distinguish three stages in the history of the language: from the 8th century to the

beginning of the 11th century; from the 12th to the 16th century; and
from the 16th century to the present day. The first period is that of Old
Dutch, the second of Middle Dutch, and the third of Modern Dutch.

But unlike the situation for English and German, there are scarcely
any traces of Old Dutch in black and white. To be more exact, this is
somewhat a matter of definition. We do, in fact possess a partial
translation of the psalms in Lower Franconian, made in the
Carolingian period. These are the *Wachtendonckse psalmen,* called after
the canon of Liège in whose house the Renaissance scholar Justus
Lipsius discovered the manuscript. But this translation is in **East**
Lower Franconian, in other words Lower Rhenic. Those who believe
that the language of Gelderland, Mörs and Kleve should be included in
Dutch make a great deal of the Wachtendonck psalms.[7] Most specialists, however, limit the area of Medieval Dutch to a triangle formed by
the North Sea, the linguistic frontier with Romance and 'a line (or
rather, a broad band) which runs from the Limburg Meuse to the
former Zuiderzee'. In other words, it would comprise only 'Flanders,
Brabant, Limburg, Zeeland, Holland and the bishopric of Utrecht'.[8] If
one takes this point of view, 'our knowledge of the oldest forms of
Dutch has been more or less reconstructed on the basis of a few old
glosses and the odd Dutch word in Latin texts, and especially on the
basis of numerous personal names and place-names which have come
down to us from the 7th century onwards, without forgetting an
appreciable number of names taken from Lower Franconian in
northern France'.[9]

Fortunately, we have the famous *probatio pennae.* In 1931, a British
scholar discovered on the back of an old English manuscript in the
Bodleian Library the following few words:

> *Hebban olla vogala nestas hagunnan hinase hi(c)*
> *(e)nda thu...*

What follows is less clear. Most probably, it should read: *wat umbidan
we nu.* The whole means: 'All the birds have begun their nests, except
for me and you: what are we waiting for?'

These two lines have provoked a veritable flood of ink. What can
have been in the mind of the scribe when he wrote them down to try
out his pen? Are they taken from some love song? Are they an exile's
sigh of melancholy? A call to monastic life in the spirit of Saint
Bernard? Or simply an exercise in formal virtuosity, as the Dutch text
is accompanied by a Latin version to which it conforms word for
word?[10] Whatever the answer, we possess in it a quite invaluable
document for the linguist. The text of the *probatio* is of West Flemish
origin — as is proved by the form *olla* — and dates at the latest from
the second half of the 11th century.

The formation of Old Dutch coincides with the spread of
Christianity. In the mid-7th century Saint Amand converted the Gent
region, Saint Lieven that of Oudenaarde and Aalst. Bishoprics were
founded at Cambrai, Tournai, Arras and Liège. In the north, Saint
Willibrord worked among the Frisians, and the episcopal seat of

Utrecht became a great centre of religious life. The evangelisation process brought with it the emergence of a new vocabulary. Sometimes attempts were made to assimilate certain indigenous terms, giving them a new content, such as *boete* ('penance', associated with the notion of 'better', cf. *beter*), *doop* ('baptisim', starting from the idea of immersion), and *bekering* (a loan-translation of *conversio*). But mostly, Latin or Greek terms were Germanised, as with *bijbel* (< biblia), kerk (< kuriakon), *engel* (< angelos) and *zegen* (< signum). Included in this category are many words denoting functions: *priester* (< presbyteros), *bisschop* (< episcopus), *koster* (< *custor < custos), and *leek* (< laïcus), as well as many architectural terms: *dom* (< domus), *portaal* and *crypt*. Borrowing naturally extended to verbs: *vieren* (< feriari), *offeren* (< offerre), and *jubelen* (< jubilare).

Monasteries had gardens containing hitherto unknown flowers and fruits: lilies (*lelie*, < lilia), parsley (*peterselie*, < petroselinum) and chervil (*kervel*, < caerefolium). They were also intellectual centres, where writing was practised (*schrijven*, related to *scribere*) to produce, among other things, letters (*brief*, < breve), which were sealed with a *zegel* (< sigillum). In the schools (*school*, < scola) the use of ink (*inkt*, < enkaustum) and parchment (*perkament*, with its echo of Pergamum) was taught.

With certain words, such as *natuur*, *kroon* or *purper*, it is difficult to say whether they were taken directly from Latin or via French. Certainly, French influence, notably in Flanders, was from early times very great on the upper classes. There were constant relations with the aristocracy of Hainault and Artois. Chrétien de Troyes (1135–1183) spent his last years at the court of Philip of Alsace, Count of Flanders. As French was also the language of international trade, a town like Ieper quite quickly found itself more or less Gallicised. The French terms in which the first Middle Dutch texts abound, had been adopted as early as the 12th century or before. This conclusion is based not only on various phonetic features, but also on the frequency of suffixes of French origin, such as *-ier*, *-ië*, *-age* and *-eren*, combined by analogy with Germanic roots, as for example in: *halveren* (to halve) and *minnares* (mistress). Such a phenomenon presupposes that a sufficient number of French words including these suffixes had already been in circulation for quite some time.

2. MIDDLE DUTCH: *E meridie lux*

Transposed into Middle Dutch, the *probatio pennae* would yield: 'Hebben alle vogele neste begonnen het en si ic ende du'. From a comparison of the two texts, a crucial difference emerges: in the unstressed final syllables of nouns and verbs, the vowels have been muted to *-e*. Another change of less significance is that the *th* (pronounced as in English) has become *d*.[11] Finally, although in this

case the written form does not reveal it, the *u* is henceforth pronounced with lip-rounding as in the *uu* of *minuut*, and no longer as in
the *oe* of *zoet*.

Such, in broad outline, is the look of the language in its second
stage. However, its unity was still only very relative. From a literary
point of view, interest focuses in the first instance on Limburg, with
Hendrik van Veldeke's *Sint Servaes* of about 1170. Then, in the 13th
century, it turns to Flanders with Jacob van Maerlant, 'father of all the
Dutch poets', and *Van den vos Reinaerde*, a Dutch version of the *Roman
de Renart*. Brabant, which in the 13th century had already produced
the lofty mystical poetry of Hadewych, sees a century later, with
Ruusbroec, the emergence of religious prose; and it was in the
language of Brabant that at the end of the Middle Ages the two
dramatic masterpieces, *Elckerlijc* and *Marieken van Nieumeghen*, were to
be written. In the north, Holland only began to count for anything
from 1400 onwards, but to the east of the Zuiderzee there developed
the so-called school of the 'Modern Devotion' (*Devotio moderna*),
founded by Geert Groote (1340–1384). From this emerged (at first in
Latin) the *Imitation of Christ* by Thomas à Kempis. The 'devotees'
wrote a great deal, in a language often coloured by Saxon. They were
also copyists renowned both for their zeal and their conscientiousness.
It is nonetheless true that during the Middle Ages it was in the
Southern Netherlands that civilisation shone most brilliantly. Hence
the prestige and the tenacious influence of the Flemish and Brabant
dialects.

To determine the nuances which separate the dialects, we also have
at our disposal extra-literary documents such as charters, accounts and
chronicles. The vernacular is used more and more in this area: the
magistrates of Boechout (East Flanders) stopped using Latin from 1249,
though those of Mechelen waited until 1465. These documents have
the advantage of being precisely located in time and place, although
they do not always reflect the local idiom faithfully. The scribe may
not be a local, or may have his own idiosyncrasies.

The popular language is known to us through *Van den vos Reinaerde*,
through numerous farces and also through the very curious *Livre des
Mestiers* from Brugge (14th century), a kind of conversation manual for
the use of foreigners.

The invention of printing, or its principles at any rate, have been
ascribed by some to Laurens Janszoon Coster of Haarlem (1405–1484).
Whatever the case, it enjoyed rapid success in the Netherlands.
Printing-houses sprung up virtually everywhere, but after 1500 some
concentration took place, in Amsterdam and particularly in Antwerp,
which was to become one of the principal centres of the European
book-trade.

Addressing a much wider public than the copyists, the printer can
be expected in general to be at pains to minimise dialectal differences.
But even earlier, certain tendencies had emerged, notably in the area
of orthography. The proliferation of redundant letters (*icK*, *gHi*) may

perhaps be seen as an echo of the exuberance of the Late Gothic. On the other hand, one felicitous habit is the spelling of a long vowel in a closed syllable, i.e. one ending in a consonant, with a double letter. In this way any possible confusion between, for example, *veel* (much, many) and *vel* (skin) is obviated. Sometimes, as in this example or in *ii, ij*, the letter is repeated, sometimes it is followed by an *e* (*jaer*, 'year') or by an *i* (*poirter*, 'burgher'). The *ae* group, representing the long *a*, was to survive for a very long time. As for the *ij*-group, it still exists today, but for more than three centuries has represented not a long *i* but a diphthong (cf. p. 17).

The most surprising things for a modern reader are the phenomena of proclisis and enclisis. 'Under the influence of sentence stress, certain words (such as articles and pronouns) lose all accent of their own and are subordinated to the accented word (noun, verb, preposition), becoming part of it.'[12] Examples of proclisis are: *tlaken* or *dlaken*, for *dat laken*, 'that sheet'; *tens* for *het en is*, 'it is not'; *entie man* for *ende die man*, 'and that man'. And of enclisis: *hi sachti* for *hi sach di*, 'he saw you'; *wattet ware* for *wat het ware*, 'what it was'; *in weet* for *ic en weet*, 'I do not know'. Proclisis and enclisis are good illustrations of the fact that written Middle Dutch is keen to stay as close as possible to everyday usage. This is true not only of word-forms, but also of syntax and vocabulary, and is found even in narrative and didactic works. The rift between the literary language and the colloquial language came about in the Renaissance (which does not mean that older graphic traditions died out overnight).

During the Middle Dutch period the influence of French increased still further. In Flanders, the situation remained as previously sketched, with the urban bourgeoisie being increasingly won over. In Brabant, except of course for the French-speaking part of the duchy south of Brussels, French was less widespread. However, it made enormous advances from the 15th century onwards, when Brabant came under the sovereignty of the Dukes of Burgundy. In 1429 Philip the Good transferred his capital from Dijon to Brussels, and henceforward French became the language of the court, at which resided the chronicler Georges Chastellain, from Aalst, and later Jean Lemaire de Belges, the librarian of Margaret of Austria. It was also, at least at the higher levels, the language of the administration. But long before that, French terms had been adopted relating to furnishings (*tapijt, couverture*), food (*fazant, taart*), warfare (*eskader, kapitein*) and music (*refrein, fluit*). Still more important are words describing states of mind or moral attitudes (*aise, joye, ennoi*), some of which survive to this day: *grief* (grievance), *spijt* (regret) < despit. The total amounts to several hundred words, but their use remained restricted to certain circles, for 'had French really profoundly penetrated to all classes, the Flemish that ultimately emerged would have had, like English, the characteristics of a hybrid language, half Germanic and half Romance'.[13]

From 1354 to 1435, the county of Holland was ruled by a dynasty of Bavarian origin. There ensued something of a vogue for German among the poets of the area. But it turned out to be a flash in the pan, and virtually the only thing one can point to as dating from this period is the breakthrough of the reflexive pronoun *zich*, which in fact did not gain ascendancy until much later, in the 18th century.

It is in a quite different field that relations between German and Middle Dutch are most fruitful: that of mysticism. Certainly Dutch mysticism had from the outset its own originality. In Hadewych's work one finds terms unique to her, such as *abolghe* (anger) and *orewoet* (fervour). But subsequently the works of Meister Eckhart, as well as those of Tauler and Suso, were widely read, and their vocabulary assimilated. However, since the new terms are invariably based on Latin, one is often hard put to it to say whether a given word, found for example in Ruusbroec, was coined by him or found in his reading of Eckhart. Whatever the case, mysticism is even more important for the history of the language than literature proper, as the new terms soon pass into sermons and thence into current usage. Many have become a permanent part of the language, albeit with the loss of their religious sense: *oorzaak* (cause), *wezen* (essence), *indruk* (impression), *neiging* (tendency), *werkelijk* (real), etc.

3. THE 16TH CENTURY: *Turmoil and Split*

'The 16th century, viewed as the transition from medieval to modern times, is a period of ferment but also of germination. In the Low Countries, in the political and economic as well as the intellectual field, it is a time of upheaval', in which there take place 'decisive events, of the utmost importance for the development of the language: besides the impact of the Reformation and the Renaissance, felt all over Europe, it sees a shift in the centre of gravity from the Southern to the Northern Netherlands.'[14]

In some respects the transition was a slow one. This is shown in particular by the proliferation in the 16th century of the Chambers of Rhetoric, which are a typical product of the last phase of the Middle Ages. A small town like Bergues (French Flanders) had no less than four chambers. The Rhetoricians have been much maligned, for while it is true that they were over-fond of complexity, indeed verbal acrobatics, and in order to satisfy this passion made exaggerated use of diminutives, padding and contorted syntax, they nevertheless contributed to the purification of the language. In their own way, the Chambers also fostered the taste for good style, particularly through their famous contests. And as they proved adaptable, there were not always the kind of conflicts between Rhetoricians and advocates of the new poetry which were found elsewhere. Matthijs de Casteleyn's *Conste van Rhetoriken* (Art of Rhetoric), the bible of the old school, written in 1548 and first published in 1555, was to be reprinted in Rotterdam in 1612 and 1616, and left its mark even on the great writers of the Golden Age.

That Catholics were not without interest in translating the Scriptures is particularly evident from the 'Delft Bible' (1477), one of the very first books printed in the Netherlands, and the 'Leuven Bible' of 1548. But naturally the Protestants applied themselves to the task with an especial zeal. To begin with, Luther's Bible was adapted, first in the Liesveldt Bible (1526–1542), which was subsequently reworked to become the so-called 'Deux-Aes' Bible of 1562, the authoritative version for Protestants for the next three-quarters of a century. There is more originality in certain translations of the New Testament; that published in Delft in 1542 by C. Lettersnijder and that attributed to H. Rode of Utrecht, which appeared in 1525. Both aimed at being comprehensible in the whole Dutch-speaking area. Even more ambitious was the project of the Fleming J. Utenhove, who for his translation of the New Testament, which was aimed at the motley group of refugees at Emden (1553–1556), undertook to create a language which he considered could be understood as far as the Baltic. A Utopian idea certainly, but perhaps less strange than it seems. For one finds a similar attempt among the Anabaptists of the period, the Frisian Menno Simons and the German Melchior Hoffmann, to create a language partaking of both Eastern Dutch and Low German. However, the majority of Protestants considered the Southern dialects preferable, as appears from the translation of Luther's *Gesangbuch* which appeared in Frankfurt in 1565, and the following year P. Dathenus, from Cassel, translated the Psalms into pure Flemish for a Calvinist audience. The need for a common language for the Low Countries as a whole was, however, still strongly felt and in 1592 the States of Holland entrusted to Marnix van Sint-Aldegonde the task of translating the whole Bible 'using the **most general**, clear and correct language'. Marnix was not able to bring this project to fruition, but it was to be taken up and realised a little later, as we shall see, in the *Statenbijbel*.

As in Italy and France, Humanists in the Low Countries fall into two groups. Some, in the footsteps of Erasmus, write only in Latin, and occasionally in Greek. Others, equally well versed in the Classical languages, have in addition a passionate love for their mother tongue. They are anxious (in Du Bellay's words) to defend it by showing it as not inherently inferior to any other, and to 'illustrate', i.e. purify and enrich it. A writer like Jan van Hout (1542–1609), a close friend of Douza and other Leiden neo-Latin poets, did not hesitate to give an address in Dutch when opening the University session.

Certainly such men did not always escape the double danger of concerning themselves exclusively with the intellectual élite and of basing themselves too much on Classicial models. On occasion also their enthusiasm takes on naïve forms. Johannes Goropius Becanus, in his *Origines Antwerpianae* (1569) asserts that Dutch was the language of the first man, for is not *duyts* the same as *douts* (the oldest)? The great mathematician and engineer Simon Stevin, in his *Uytspraeck van de Weerdigheyt der duytsche tael* (Statement on the Dignity of the Dutch Language) (1586), invokes in support of the excellence and originality of Dutch the large number of monosyllables, the ease with which compound words may be formed, its great flexibility, and its capacity to convince and move. But the quality of the arguments is immaterial: what counts is the attitude they show, and the consequences of that attitude were not long in coming. From the middle of the century on, works in the vernacular on botany, astronomy, medicine, etc., begin to appear. Along with this, interest awakens in questions of spelling, vocabulary and grammar.

The spelling-reformers are interesting in their own right, but also because of their phonetic observations and their ideas on the unity or diversity of Dutch. The majority are only concerned with their local dialect, whether it be Joos Lambrecht of Gent (*Nederlandsche Spellijnghe*, 1550), A. Sexagius from Brabant (*De orthographia linguae belgicae*, 1576), or the Amsterdammer H. L. Spiegel in the *Twe-spraak* (Dialogue) of 1584. The only dissenter is Pontus de Heuiter (*Nederduitse Orthographie*, 1581). A native of Delft, he had travelled widely, and on spelling questions his position is an individual one: he is neither an advocate, like Lambrecht or Sexagius, of the introduction of new characters, nor too conservative like Spiegel, and proposed reasonable simplifications. Unfortunately his work did not have the success it deserved.

Since 1470 there had appeared numerous glossaries, vocabularies and lists of terms. These works were eclipsed by the *Thesaurus Theutonicae Linguae*, published in 1573 by the famous French printer Plantin, based in Antwerp. But even more noteworthy is the *Dictionarium Teutonico-Latinum* by Cornelis Kiliaan, one of Plantin's assistants, published in 1574, which was to become known to posterity under the name *Etymologicum*, the title of the third edition (1599). This was no longer a tool for the learning of foreign languages, but a scholarly description of the Dutch vocabulary. Archaic terms were marked '*vetus*', and for non-Brabant words, Kiliaan indicated the origin as precisely as possible. The *Etymologicum* is a treasure-house on which scholars are still drawing.

Renaissance man wanted a language which was not only rich but elegant and pure. And so, war was declared on Latin and French intruders. In 1553 the Antwerp jurist Jan van de Werve published *Het Tresoor der Duytscher talen*, on the principle of: 'don't say this, but this'. In his preface to the *Tresoor*, the printer Jan de Laet suggested that in the absence of an adequate equivalent one should have recourse to German as a sister-language. A similar linguistic Pan-germanism is found in the *Twe-spraak*, whose author also has in mind Danish, Frisian and English. By far the most influential purist was Simon Stevin, who in the last years of the century successfully introduced a whole new mathematical vocabulary: *middellijn* (diameter), *driehoek* (triangle), *aftrekken* (subtract), *wortel* (root), etc. But more even than these isolated terms, his example has left its mark on the language. By an odd paradox, although in other aspects so accommodating, Dutch-speakers (especially in the South) are to this day

somewhat resistant to the international scientific vocabulary, preferring *scheikunde* to *chemie, natuurkunde* to *fysica* and *aardrijkskunde* to
geografie.

Together with a purified vocabulary goes a renewed grammar. H. L.
Spiegel's *Twe-spraak van de Nederduytsche Letterkunst* of 1584, written
on behalf of the Amsterdam Chamber of Rhetoric, has already been
mentioned.

The author starts from the idea, then current, that the richness of a
language depends on the richness of its forms. Except for fixed expressions, there were already no longer any declensions in Dutch. Notably,
no distinction was made any longer between accusative and nominative. In the North at any rate the definite article for non-neuter
nouns was *de*. In the South the same thing had happened with certain
nouns (*de man, de muur*) and the others were always preceded by *den*
(*den boer, den appel*). Spiegel wants to bring some order to matters and
prescribes the following uniform declension:

N.	*de heer*	*de vrouw*	*het dier*
G.	*des heers*	*des vrouws*	*des diers*
D.	*den here*	*den vrouwe*	*den diere*
Acc.	*de(n) heer*	*de(n) vrouw*	*het dier*
Abl.	*vande(n) heer*	*vande(n) vrouw*	*van het* } *dier*
			vant

The tendency is clear: to stick to Latin by reinstating the case-system.
It also emerges from this table that even where Spiegel might have
relied on Middle Dutch he does not do so: the authentic form of the
genitive was for the weak masculine *des heren* and for the feminine *der
vrouwe*. The method of proceeding was to have long-lasting and grave
consequences almost down to our own day. For if the norms of the
Twe-spraak can scarcely be said to have been followed in detail,
grammarians long continued to prefer the Classical tradition to
national usage. The fact remains that Spiegel's codification was com-
mendable and that it can easily bear comparison with what was being
done at the same period in England or Germany.

*   *   *   *   *

The revolt against Spain which broke out in 1568 had disastrous
consequences for the Southern Netherlands. It involved, especially
after the fall of Antwerp in 1585, a massive exodus of Protestants into
Holland and Zeeland: one sixth of the population, it would appear.
The refugees included a good number of intellectuals, merchants and
industrialists. They were very quickly integrated, so much so as to
irritate some native Hollanders (cf. Bredero's comedy *Spaanschen
Brabander* of 1617). By 1611, they accounted for more than half of the
310 most prominent merchants in Amsterdam. They provided the
young Dutch Republic with numerous diplomats, civil servants,
officers and of course, clergymen. Among them or their children there
were teachers, renowned professors like C. van Baerle (Barleus), or

simple schoolmasters, poets like Carel van Mander, Daniël Heinsius and the great Joost van den Vondel. This, then, is the moment at which the North takes off politically and economically. Modern Dutch is to be formed on a basis of *Hollands*, but not without *Flemish* and *Brabants* making a large contribution, with the multifarious personal influences of the refugees adding to the cultural prestige of the South and the Southern written language.

4. THE GOLDEN AGE

The 'Holland expansion' in the 17th century is easily explained. Of the seven Northern provinces, Holland was far and away the most populous and the most prosperous. Between 1585 and 1685 the built-up area of Amsterdam increased from 106 to 726 hectares. Leiden was proud of its University, founded in 1575, which for a time was the only one in the country and remained the most prestigious. The Hague was the seat of the Prince of Orange and of the court. The language of the province of Holland won the day without imperialist designs on the one hand or resistance on the other. In this process one sees the final disappearance of the pronoun *du*, dear to Easterners, from good usage and the demise of that compromise between Franconian and Saxon which at the time of the Hansa and of the *devotio moderna* had seemed to have a chance of survival. 'The war welds Gelderland and Groningen to Holland and the powerful influence of Holland erodes little by little the marked differences in the language and customs of the eastern provinces; after 1600 the language written by a Groningen syndic, or a Gelderland chancellor loses its eastern stamp.'[15] Frisian resists more successfully, although in the language of the towns (*stadfries*) *Hollands* is henceforward to have the lion's share.

At the moment when *Hollands* is about to acquire its full historical importance, it is still neither fixed nor homogeneous. It even undergoes, in the first decade of the century, a profound phonetic transformation: the diphthongisation of the long vowels *u* and *i*, which become *ui* and *ij* respectively, so that *huus* gives way to *huis* and *crigen* to *krijgen*. The first phenomenon appears in the language of Amsterdam society around 1600; the second, unknown to the author of *Twespraak*, is attested around 1620 in the polished speech of The Hague. Both win over the whole province step by step. Since diphthongisation had been accomplished in Brabant by the end of the Middle Ages in the first case and the 14th century in the second, it is hard to avoid the conclusion that it took place in Holland under Southern influence.[16]

There can be no hesitation, at least, as far as the Southern contribution to the vocabulary is concerned. But in this case something very odd happened. Terms introduced into Holland by 'Brabanters', which for the latter had a very common meaning, retained in the

North something 'alien', in the sense that they were reserved for the written language, elevated style and metaphor. And so it has remained to this day. There is, of course, nothing to prevent one writing: *ik zal een brief ZENDEN* (I shall send a letter), but in speaking, a Hollander will always say: *ik zal een brief STUREN*. The current equivalent of 'today' is *vandaag* but in a notification of a death one regularly reads: *HEDEN overleed*...Here are a few more examples, with the elevated word, of southern origin, on the left and the current term on the right:

fraai	*mooi*	'beautiful'	*spoedig*	*gauw*	'quick'
wenen	*huilen*	'to cry'	*werpen*	*gooien*	'to throw'
reeds	*al*	'already'	*gelijk*	*zoals*	'like, as'
gaarne	*graag*	'willingly'	*lieden*	*lui*	'people'

But the most characteristic case is that of *gij*; this second-person pronoun has assumed an exalted role in the North, the only living form being *jij* (later supplemented with the polite form *U*).

To sum up, 'the geographical opposition led to a stylistic opposition'.[17]

The *Hollands* which in this way took on more or less the function of a national language is based, as might have been expected, on the usage of the large towns. Amsterdammers liked to poke fun at the inhabitants of Enkhuizen, whom they regarded as backward, while at the same time defending themselves against those of The Hague, whom they saw as pretentious. On the one hand, the perfecting of the language is the work of a particular élite and it is achieved only gradually. One still finds here and there in an as accomplished writer as Hooft, traces of dialect, such as *deur* for *door, leit* for *ligt* or *zel* for *zal*. But a consensus is finally established among those called to debate in public assemblies, administer justice or speak from the pulpit. In his *Aenleidinge ter Nederduitsche dichtkunste* (Remarks on Dutch Poetry, 1650), Vondel is able to affirm: 'This language is at present spoken most perfectly in The Hague, at the States-General and at the court of the Stadholder, and in Amsterdam, the most powerful commercial centre in the world, by people of good education (at least if one excludes non-Dutch terms from the language of courtiers, lawyers and merchants), for old *Amsterdams* is too ridiculous and pure *Antwerps* is too coarse and insufficiently clear.'[18]

At the same time as it is being refined, the language is being enriched. This enrichment may be spontaneous, as when, for example, it results from contact with new countries or cultures. In this way the names of materials and substances enter the language from Asia, and more specifically from Malay: *katoen, koffie, thee*, as do animal names such as *papagaai* (parrot) and *jakhals* (jackal) and terms familiar to seamen like *soebatten* (to cajole) and *bakkeleien* (to fight). There are also spontaneous borrowings from German: large numbers of weavers, artists, mercenaries and students had come from across the Rhine, and to them Dutch owes abstract words (*beantwoorden* 'to answer', *beramen* 'to plan'), commercial terms (*achterstallig* 'in arrears') and, in particular, military vocabulary (*ruiterij* 'cavalry', *spits* 'vanguard', *zoetelaar* 'sutler', *wer da*? 'who goes there?'). Even Vondel sometimes goes so far as to use the adjective *rustig*, not in its usual sense of 'peaceful', but with the same meaning as Germ. *rüstig*, i.e. 'solid'.

However, German influence, compared to French, is as a trickle to a torrent. A long tradition of borrowings is continued, sometimes unconscious, but mostly systematic. French is more than ever the vehicle of intellectual and international relations. Children of good family attend the 'French school' and young people complete their education with a trip to France. As the century goes on, the greater the impact of the fashion becomes.[19] Letters and conversations are interlarded with French words. In their fields, administrators multiply the borrowings ad lib, and these so-called *stadhuiswoorden* or 'town hall words' have not all disappeared from the modern language, as *resolveren, permissie, annexeren* and many others testify. More generally, the French of the period has left indelible traces on Dutch, especially in the shape of loan-translations: *staat van beleg* (état de siège), *staat van zaken* (état de choses), *staat van genade* (état de grâce), *dank weten* (savoir gré), *het hof maken* (faire la cour), *partij trekken* (tirer parti), *rekening houden met* (tenir compte de) — these are all expressions which have long since ceased to be felt as foreign. Gallomania progressively descends the social scale, but one can observe how, as they become more widespread (not without becoming corrupted in many cases), the French terms tend to become debased. *Krek* (coming from 'correct', but meaning 'precisely'), *astrant* (< assurant, i.e. 'shameless'), *navenant* (< à l'avenant, 'in proportion'), and *mankement* (defect) are regarded as vulgar; *magnifiek, abuis* (< abus, 'misunderstanding') and *apart* (unusual), are more familiar than high style.

This vogue for French, which is often carried to extremes, greatly concerns some writers. One remembers the restriction Vondel made above in his praise of courtiers and of Amsterdam merchants and lawyers, and in the field of law especially his views were shared by Grotius.[20] No one was a greater advocate of purism than Hooft (except, that is, in his official correspondence). Certainly many of his suggestions were not taken up: no one has ever used *vernufteling* for *ingenieur* (engineer), *zaaierij* for *seminarie* (seminary), or *wondheler* for *chirurg* (surgeon). But we owe to him *boekerij*, which, although a little old-fashioned nowadays, was for a long time a rival to *bibliotheek* (library), as well as *redenaar* (speaker) and *beroep* (appeal), which have replaced *orateur* and *appellatie*.

This purism is only one side of the coin. It goes without saying that in many other fields too, the great writers had an influence on the language through their ideas, and even more through their example. Some, like Jacob Cats (1577–1660) and Bredero (1585–1618) drew extensively on the language of the common people. Bredero, a shoemaker's son, was an Amsterdammer heart and soul. In his farces he takes his cue from beggars as well as kings and is equally at home rummaging among dustbins as in the most sumptuous treasure-houses. Past Rhetoricians and present grammarians leave him completely cold. The Zeelander Cats, 'Father Cats' as he is called, whose long moralistic poems adorned many a home down to the middle of the 19th century, makes it a point of honour to use a language which is accessible, simple, straightforward and quite current, as far as possible identical to our everyday speech'.[21] In such a case, spelling and rules count for little. The great variety of forms presented by Cats' work is less the effect of negligence than of an attitude which is more reminiscent of the Middle Ages than the Renaissance.

The case of the three 'great names' of the Golden Age seems more complicated. Constantijn Huygens (1596–1687) is a specialist in Marinistic preciosity, who as early as 1622 wrote to his parents (in French): 'The difficulty people find in my work just makes me laugh.' But the same Huygens, a Brabanter on his mother's side, is able to give the farce *Trijntje Cornelisdr*, a rich Antwerp flavour, and from his garden at Hofwijck eavesdrops on the conversations of fishermen and peasants. P. C. Hooft (1581–1647), bailiff of Muiden, who in all respects occupies first place among Dutch historians, is not averse on occasion to rehabilitating certain 'disreputable' words, or to slipping a shocking, familiar expression into some train of argument worthy of Tacitus. As early as 1616 his *Warenar* had transposed the *Aulularia* of Plautus into 17th-century Amsterdam: it represented no more than a gentleman's pastime, but was an unexpected success. Joost van den Vondel (1587–1679), the man of the grandiose baroque, has Joseph's brothers speak with a quite rustic simplicity in one of his plays, and at a time when Racine was making subtle use of the restricted vocabulary of Versailles, Vondel was off questioning tradesmen, farmhands, carpenters and sailors.

Having said this, it is without question that whereas Cats and Bredero were unconcerned with linguistic matters, either with practical improvement or theoretical speculation, both concerns were present to a high degree in Huygens, Hooft and Vondel. From 1623 onwards the latter two met regularly, together with the jurist De Hubert and the diplomat Reael, to discuss linguistic topics. They were concerned to establish sound principles concerning 'syntax, word-formation, gender distinctions, declension and the spelling of every word'.[22] Before publishing the first part of his *Nederlandsche Historiën*, Hooft thoroughly revised the text, eliminating grammatical inconsistencies and simplifying the spelling. Vondel did the same with his own works, retouching them from edition to edition. The work did not, however, proceed without a considerable number of hitches. Hooft, who in theory distinguished two forms of the third-person masculine singular pronoun (dative *hum*, accusative *hem*) and two reciprocal pronouns (*elkander* (each other) for two and *elkanderen* for three or more), never ventured to put these odd notions into practice. Vondel adapted his spelling as well as he could to current usage, but was afraid that too radical a reform would cause some latterday Cadmos to over-expand the alphabet. And the linguistic deliberations had in the last analysis left everyone a free hand, 'seeing', in Vondel's own words, 'that we have not yet found anything which satisfies us'.[23] Their failure could not be put more neatly: Vondel and his friends were well aware of the nature of the problems posed by a language still in the process of development. What they failed to see was that in instinctively resorting, like the author of the *Twe-spraak* before them, to the categories of Latin, they were excluding *a priori* any satisfactory solution.

The same can be said of many grammarians, whose echo may be heard in the *Taelbericht* (Essay on Language) of the Rev. Ampzing of 1628. He speaks out strongly against 'the confusion of [grammatical] genders and the blurring of cases'. He calls for a strict set of rules, not based on 'the custom of the masses', since 'it is among the learned that the best and soundest judgement is to be found'. Nevertheless, as has been pointed out by later commentators, there were linguists of merit, 'a succession of obscure, modest toilers, whose names are rarely quoted today, but whose work survives'.[24] In 1635 P. Montanus founded the sciences of phonetics and dialectology, and ten years later D. L. Kok coined a felicitous Dutch linguistic terminology, which was eventually to become the standard one: *klinker* (vowel), *medeklinker* (consonant), *lettergreep* (syllable), *zelfstanding naamwoord* (noun), etc. P. Leupenius, writing in 1653, insists that Dutch is a language in its own right, based 'on its own foundation'. At the very end of the century David van Hoogstraten, in his *Aenmerkingen* (Critical Comments) of 1700, suggests that the question of genders be settled by a meticulous examination of the great authors. He defends himself, moreover, against the charge of trying to 'prescribe rules', while hoping, particularly with education in mind, for the establishment of a broad consensus. Given the intelligence of its approach and the modesty of its argumentation, it is fortunate that Van Hoogstraten's work should have served as the starting-point for more than one later theoretician.

The public reached by the grammarians was a limited one, and their impact, when they had any at all, slow-working. It was very different with the translation of the Bible, the initiative for which was taken at the Synod of Dordrecht in 1618 and which was published in 1637. This translation (made from the original Greek and Hebrew texts) was financed by the States-General, from which it derives its name of *Statenbijbel*. The principal concern, to arrive at a text usable in all regions, is evident from the choice of translators: two came from Friesland, two from West Flanders, one from Zeeland and one from Holland, while the 'revisors' came from all parts of the Low Countries. It is therefore a work of compromise, whose consistency occasionally leaves much to be desired, especially in the inevitable matter of genders and declensions. Broadly speaking, the Southern element (recognisable, for example, in the form *de HeerE*) clearly has the edge. Can the *Statenbijbel, mutatis mutandis*, be put in the same class as Luther's translation? Certainly it was not as original, and it has been pointed out that, as far as the stylistic quality is concerned, the 'Deux-Aes' Bible was by no means its inferior. This does not detract from its historical importance. Adopted by almost all Protestants, it remained in use until 1951. Read and reread for three centuries in churches, schools and homes, it made a significant contribution to the unification of the language. It also enriched it with Hebrew and Greek borrowings and a host of expressions which have passed into proverbial usage: *met twee maten meten* (to apply a double standard), *met zijn talenten woekeren* (to use one's talents wisely), *op twee gedachten hinken* (to hesitate between two opinions), etc. In the field of grammar too it represented a landmark, among other things through its exclusion of the pronoun *du* and of double negation.[25] It should be added, though, that either because of Luther's influence or prevailing ideas, the authors of the *Statenbijbel* have drawn liberally on High German. In this way, not only words like *heftig* (vehement) and *verschaffen* (to obtain), whose origin is clear, but also *beledigen* (to insult) and *bouwvallig* (tumbledown), entered the language.

*   *   *   *   *

What happened to Dutch during this time in the part of the area which had remained under Spanish rule? Cut off from the Northern provinces (in reality from about 1580, officially from 1648), devastated by eighty years of war, weakened by the emigration of a part of its élite, economically strangled by the closing of the Scheldt estuary, the Southern Netherlands went through a difficult period in the 17th century. Of course one should not paint too black a picture: this is the age of Rubens and Jordaens, and also the time of the building of the Place Royale in Brussels. But as for writers, one is hard put to mention a couple of honourable names per generation.

Despite this, for a time, the Southerners did not have any kind of inferiority complex with regard to Hollanders. The satirical poets of Brugge, Brussels and Antwerp were to give Coster and Bredero as good as they got. As for the purists in the North, they are told to put their own house in order, since they are constantly talking of *Reformatie, Predestinatie, Excellentie* and *Consistorie!* Brabanters and Flemings who stayed put are not responsive to the need for refinement and discipline which was making itself felt in the North. With some rare exceptions, the only Northern writers who interest them are precisely those who lack a sense of this need. In his comedies, Willem Ogier (1618—1689) takes his inspiration from Bredero, and the very popular preacher Adriaan Poirters (1605—1674) is an avid reader of Cats. Everyone speaks and writes as he thinks fit. G. Bolognino of Antwerp did, in 1657, propose a standardisation of spelling and pronunciation (on the basis, of course, of his own dialect), but his attempt, made without much conviction, bore no fruit. Generally speaking, the Southern Netherlands tend towards conservatism. People quite happily continue using the article *den* in the nominative,

and the old negative particle *en* (which in Holland was fast dis-
appearing) instead of *niet*.[26]

*   *   *   *   *

Let us look, in conclusion, at the international diffusion of Dutch in
the Golden Age. The question is an obvious one, since economically, if
not politically and militarily, the Republic was a great power. Likewise
culturally: one need think only of the jurist and theologian Grotius, of
Christiaan Huygens, whom Louis XIV made the founding president of
his Academy of Sciences, and in the medical field of Boerhaave. The
percentage of foreign students at Dutch universities was high. Certainly the prestige of **Dutch** did not entirely match that of **the** Dutch,
and also varied from country to country, but it unquestionably
reached its high-point during this period.

In some cases, it is only a matter of technical terms. In the case of
France, a long-standing tradition was continued (cf. p. 47, n. 13).
Bâbord (< bakboord, 'portside') is attested from the 16th century, *foc*
(< fok, 'forecastle') from 1702. Dutch engineers called in to drain the
marshes of the Vendée introduced *polder*, or rather re-introduced it,
since 'pouldres' had been known in France since the 13th century. In
1665, at the request of Colbert, Van Robaais from Zeeland set up a
linen factory at Abbeville, where the terms *bosse* (< bos, 'length of
material') and *striquer* (< strijken, 'to iron') came into use. England,
too, had a long history of visits and immigration from Flanders and
Holland, and its textile industry had been founded by Flemings. In the
16th and 17th centuries painters such as Van Dyck worked at the
English court. All of this gave rise to countless borrowings which both
Dutch and English bibliographers have assiduously listed.[27] A random
sample provides some indication of the impact of Dutch in many
fields: beleaguer (< *belegeren*), brandy (< *brandewijn*), dock (< *dok*),
landscape (< *landschap*), ledger (< *ligger*), yacht (< *jacht*). The
renown of Dutch technical expertise penetrated as far as Russia, as is
illustrated by the incognito visit of Czar Peter the Great to the shipbuilding centre of Zaandam in 1697. There followed the adoption into
Russian of a number of nautical words, such as *matros* (< matroos,
'seaman'), *botsman* (< bootsman, 'boatswain') and *forstewen*
(< voorsteven, 'prow'). As for Germany, areas bordering on the
Netherlands like Bentheim, Emmerich and Kleve, had always been
particularly subject to Dutch influence. But a quirk of history was to
give the limelight to East Friesland, the area of Germany situated
between the mouth of the Ems and the Bay of the Jade, where from the
Middle Ages on Frisian had been largely superseded by Low German.
In the 16th century large numbers of exiles from Flanders and Holland
sought sanctuary there and founded communities which prospered, or
at least survived. Though they gradually became Germanised, these
communities, Calvinist, Anabaptist and so on, continued to pray, sing
and read in Dutch (the only exception being the Lutherans). Budding

ministers received their training across the border. In the long run, no doubt, the High German propagated by the authorities was bound to win the day, but Dutch sermons were preached in Emden as late as 1879. Further east, from the Elbe to Dantzig, Dutch owed its impact to the Republic's merchants and its marine technology. At the beginning of the 19th century, instruction was still given in Dutch at the Hamburg School of Navigation, and this has left traces which are as obvious as they are numerous on the language of the German navy.

Perhaps Scandinavia presents the most remarkable instance of all. Danish makes considerable borrowings from Dutch, not only in the area of shipbuilding, commerce and warfare, but also 'in scientific vocabulary and even more so in the everyday language. Dutch influence can even be detected in the stress-system of Danish. Most of this has been preserved to the present day'.[28] A whole book has been written on the intellectual links between Sweden and the Netherlands at this period.[29] In 1644 the Elseviers considered setting up a book-shop in Uppsala and in 1652 a printing-house in Stockholm. Theatrical troupes from Holland were much appreciated: proof that there was a public of some kind which understood their language. According to the catalogue of the exhibition devoted to her some years ago at the National Museum in Stockholm, Queen Christina knew 'most of the modern cultural languages: French, German, Italian and **Dutch**',[30] and Swedish scholars sometimes had recourse to Dutch in their correspondence with foreigners.

Overseas, the spread of Dutch was, of course, mainly the work of colonisers. Some of their settlements (notably in North-East Brazil and in North America, where until 1667 New York was known as New Amsterdam) were short-lived. Among those which survived and expanded, the Cape played a very special role from a linguistic point of view, since from Dutch there emerged there a new language, Afrikaans.

Outside the colonial sphere, the odd case of Japan should be mentioned. The Dutch had succeeded in obtaining, under very strict conditions, permission to trade there. As a result some Japanese diligently applied themselves to learning the language, the more so since, as the trading privilege had not been accorded to any other nation, they took Dutch to be **the** language of Europeans.

5. THE 18TH CENTURY: *The Periwig Period*

The Low Countries were not really outstanding in any field in the 18th century. One might say that after the magnificent endeavours of two or three generations, the Netherlands were content to rest on their laurels. In literature the colourful diversity of the Golden Age gave way from about 1680 to a soulless post-Classicism. The tone is set by a literary society with the revealing motto *Nil volentibus arduum*: art is the result of patient application and expertise.

Perfection of technique goes hand in hand with elegance of style. The comic dramatist Pieter Langendijk (1683–1756), whose work is far from worthless, severely condemns the 'coarse' and 'scandalous' language of farce, and in the later editions of his own *Wederzijds Huwelijksbedrog* (The Mutual Marriage Deceit) (1712) he amends forms which he considers too familiar, as though he were taking his cue from Boileau's dictum: 'Cent fois sur le métier remettez votre ouvrage...'. French influence is not, unfortunately, limited to the stylistic precepts of Boileau and other Neoclassicists, but takes increasingly outlandish forms. In his *Hollandsche Spectator* (so called after its English model), Justus van Effen delights in poking fun at the young generation, who pride themselves on not reading any Dutch, and the pedant who exclaims: ''t Is zoo glissant, dat had ik Mejuffer niet gesouteneert, zy zekerlyk zoude getombeerd hebben' (It is so slippery, that had I not supported the young lady, she would surely have fallen). He might also have quoted, among many examples, the following authentic gem: 'Een mysterieuse brief inquieteert mij terribel'. However, one needs to keep things in perspective; taking a random article from the *Rotterdamsche Courant* of 9th May 1767, one finds it contains 32 foreign words out of a total 340, in other words some 9%. Not an inordinate number — and a present-day journalist would be likely to use more or less as many. Except that, apart from half a dozen or so, they would not be the same ones.[31] On the other hand, French was still spoken fluently by only a very small proportion of the population. And in the end the malady produces its own cure; as a French word, following the process noted previously, becomes common coin, the higher echelons of society tend to rehabilitate the corresponding indigenous word. This explains why, to this day, *feliciteren* (to congratulate) and *visite* are a shade less refined than *gelukwensen* and *bezoek*.

The rational, formalistic climate of the time was bound to foster regimentation, indeed despotism, in linguistic matters. Balthasar Huydecoper, in his *Proeve van Taal- en Dicht-kunde* (Essay on Language and Literature, 1730) examines Vondel with a fine-tooth-comb and exposes countless formal imperfections. Huydecoper's work caused a great stir and gained him many emulators.

But if, as a champion of 'rational grammar', Huydecoper was very much a man of his age, as a philologist he was a considerable innovator. He made a study of Middle Dutch and his annotated edition (1772) of Melis Stoke's *Rijmkroniek* (from the end of the 14th century) was epoch-making. Huydecoper was convinced that Dutch had become debased in the course of the centuries. If, therefore, one wished to reform morphology and syntax, the wisest course would be to go back to the Middle Ages: 'Our ancestors, and they alone, will be able to teach us to speak and write properly.' Another, even more important name, is that of Lambert ten Kate, who, having steeped himself in Gothic,[32] published in 1723 his *Aanleiding tot de kennisse van het verhevene deel der Nederduytsche Sprake* (Introduction to the Study of Educated Dutch), in which he set up rules governing *Ablaut*[33] in Germanic and laid the foundations of serious etymology. His comments on the modern language are equally apposite. Rules must be derived from usage, more attention must be paid to the spoken than the written language, and also different stylistic levels distinguished. Of course, Ten Kate's historical cast of mind was bound to lead him like Huydecoper to look to archaic forms as an antidote to arbitrariness. In doubtful cases he too is inclined to 'consult the ancients'. Accordingly, he maintains a firm distinction between masculine and feminine, not, certainly, because of Latin usage, but because the distinction originally existed in *diets*.

In the last quarter of the century, English and German literature came into fashion. Sentiment was the order of the day, and it did not fit very well into the corseted language of Classicism. In the work of Bellamy, Van Alphen, Bilderdijk and others, new words, new meanings and new metaphors appear. All this is in danger of degenerating into a new rhetoric, but meanwhile Rhijnvis Feith, in the preface to his *Brieven over verscheide onderwerpen* (Letters on Miscellaneous Subjects, 1784—1793), declares that he aims to write 'as one would write to one's close friends' or 'as one speaks to a woman of sensibility'. The first great novel in Dutch, the *Historie van mejuffouw Sara Burgerhart* (1782) by Elizabeth Wolff and Agatha Deken, presents us with a host of characters: merchants, students, clergymen, bourgeois and maidservants, each one talking according to his station, and evokes a vivid panorama of Dutch society.

The taste for the epistolary novel derived partly from Rousseau and partly from Richardson. England also supplied certain political notions, while Germany had an influence in the natural sciences, educational theory and aesthetics. German philosophers and moralists were, moreover, much more popular in the Netherlands than German literary writers. Many innovations derive from them: *zwermerij* (< Schwärmerei) never really caught on, but *tijdschrift* (magazine), *voorlopig* (for the time being), *zelfzucht* (selfishness), *bijval* (applause), etc., have all survived. On the other hand, surprisingly few English terms were adopted during this period; one may mention *koffiehuis* and the now obsolete *nieuwspapier*, along with a few literary terms which are nonetheless significant, such as *ballade*, *bard* and *humor*.

*   *   *   *   *

In 1713, the Southern Netherlands passed from Spanish into Austrian hands. For the inhabitants the change was minimal: they remained the subjects of a foreign and distant monarch, represented by governors with French backgrounds, like Charles of Lorraine, who managed affairs for forty years. Certainly the Austrians did not set out to promote the use of French systematically, and in the Dutch-speaking areas government and the administration of justice were carried on in the local language. But to succeed one had to speak French. In addition, the War of the Austrian Succession led to a temporary French occupation of the country, during which officers and actors turned Brussels into a miniature version of Paris. From 1772 the Théatre de la Monnaie refused to put on any more Flemish plays, on the grounds that they were too vulgar. With the exception of religious books, all publishing was in French. The spread of French culture was a general feature of the age, but in the Southern Netherlands there was neither a national spirit to absorb outside influences nor a unified language to resist them, and French was not even felt as particularly foreign, since it was the native language of the Walloons, who made up half the population. A contemporary English visitor observed that 'the French language has become generally used, not only in conversation, but in epistolary style', and even confidently predicted that 'in a hundred years, French will be the only language spoken in these provinces'.[34]

In spite of all this, intellectual life was not totally Gallicised: the Imperial Academy in Brussels, founded in 1769, was of course French-speaking, but it accepted papers in Dutch, and a few were in fact presented. Around 1775, it is even possible to discern a reaction among the middle classes, merchants, low-ranking officials and estate managers. This explains the relative success of two (very dissimilar) works: *Nieuwe Nederduytsche Spraekkonst* (New Dutch Grammar) by Jan des Roches (1761) and the *Verhandeling op d'onacht der moederlyke tael in de Nederlanden* (Essay on the Neglect of the Mother Tongue in the Netherlands, 1788), by the lawyer J. Verlooy.

Des Roches came originally from The Hague. Having set himself up as a schoolmaster in Antwerp, he became secretary to the Brussels Academy and advisor on educational matters to the Austrian authorities. He, like the author of his preface, is convinced that Dutch is not inferior to any other language in force and clarity. His grammar is that of a practising teacher. Following his Northern compatriots, whom he has read, he retains the declension (with six cases!) of nouns and adjectives, but his teaching concerns prevent him from entirely losing sight of reality. Hence, in accordance with Brabant usage, he denies any formal distinction, with the articles, between nominative and accusative: 'One recognises the masculine by the article *den*, and the feminine by the article *de*.' Such words were enough to make the wigs of the theoreticians in Holland stand on end.

Verlooy's title speaks for itself. It is first and foremost an indictment: the Dutch language, that of 'the most numerous and best part' of the population, is being not only neglected, but held in contempt, whether it be in science, literature or in the theatre. An end must be put to this absurd Gallomania, and the same language should be spoken by the élite, the middle classes, tradesmen, peasants and, of course, women. Besides, Dutch has a host of qualities, for where else can one find such an abundance of vigorous expressions and striking onomatopoeic words, such a wealth of diminutives and derivatives? In more than one respect, Verlooy's case is a contradictory one. Although an apologist of Dutch, he himself, for all his eloquence, writes in somewhat stilted and derivative language, and though a supporter of the idea of the Greater Netherlands, he is basically ignorant about developments in the North. While fiercely opposed to French influence, he had been brought up on Rousseau. What is more, when the French Revolution spilled over into Belgium, Verlooy was one of the first to call for French annexation of Belgium and died in 1797, having served for a short while as French-appointed Mayor of Brussels. But such contradictions were part and parcel of the times, and posterity has not judged Verlooy too harshly. In 1829 his essay was deemed worthy of a second edition.

6. 1795—1830: *From One Revolution to Another*

As is known, the Revolution of 1789 soon brought about war with Austria and this war led to the annexation by France (confirmed at Campo-Formio in 1797) of the Austrian Netherlands and the principality of Liège, a state of affairs which was to last until 1814. In the North, the United Provinces formed themselves, in 1795, into a Batavian Republic, which gave way eleven years later to the Kingdom of Holland, first entrusted by Napoleon to his brother Louis, and finally abolished in 1810 and integrated into the French Empire. After the fall of Napoleon, the Northern and Southern Netherlands were reunited under Willem I, but in 1830 Belgium rebelled and its independence was recognised by the Great Powers in 1839.

The creation of the Batavian Republic, one and indivisible, could not help but further the process of linguistic unification. From the heart of Gelderland, the poet A. C. W. Staring wrote in 1800 that '*Hollands* is for us the language of Paris, used by those writers who wish to be read and understood throughout the Republic'.[35] Certainly this was still more of an ideal than a reality. The deputies from Holland in the Constituent Assembly smiled at the language of their colleagues from other regions, and in Holland itself much remained to be done.

The publicist Fokke Simonsz, in his *Ironisch Komisch Woordenboek* (Ironic and Comic Dictionary, 1797), makes a distinction between exalted language, administrative language and the language of the street, with the language of the average citizen being a combination of the three. 'Nothing is more shameful than to see a people despising its own mother tongue and preferring a foreign language' will be expressed in the first case as: *Niets is schandelijker, dan dat een volk deszelfs eigene moedertaal veracht, en eene vreemde boven dezelve stelt*, in the second as: *Niets is abominabeler, dan dat eene natie derzelver moedertaal meprissert, en eene aliene daarvoor praediligeert en anteponeert*, and in the third as: *Der is gien leelijker ding, als dat ien volk zen eige moers taal veracht, en ien vreemde veurtrekt.*

An entirely new development was that the authorities decided to intervene in the standardising of the language and more especially in spelling. The preliminary research was entrusted to Professor Matthijs Siegenbeek and was concluded in 1804. With divided loyalties between his Classical training and his interest in the first discoveries of German scholarship, Siegenbeek set about his task in an empirical fashion: he stressed the need for historical continuity and gave considerable weight to etymology, but also wanted spelling to be as close as possible a representation of what was pronounced by educated speakers. The following are examples of his results: *kagchel* (now 'kachel', 'stove'),[36] *jufvrouw* (juffrouw, 'lady'), *regt* (recht, 'justice') and *zettede* as the past tense of *zetten* (to put). In closed syllables *aa* was to be used in all cases instead of the older *ae*. In open syllables a single letter would suffice for long vowels (in principle at least, as Siegenbeek allowed some latitude with *e* and *o*, in order to take account of local peculiarities in pronunciation).

In view of its official nature, the Siegenbeek system was very widely adopted. However, it provoked heated protests, notably from the poet Willem Bilderdijk (1756–1831), an arch-enemy of Siegenbeek's, in his *Nederlandsche Spraakleer* (Dutch Grammar) of 1826. Bilderdijk makes an impassioned plea for language as sound and rhythm above all, with its written form taking only a secondary place. The philosopher Johannes Kinker, for his part, commented: 'The less current usage departs from that of prose-writers and poets, the more regularly it will develop, but the more too will written style, in conforming to current usage, gain in naturalness and spontaneity.'[37] Nevertheless, the majority of the prose-writers of the period are characterised by cold clarity, a horror of all familiarity and extravagance and a weakness for the solemn and unusual. The following generation, reared on Romanticism, was able to indulge its appetite for parody to its heart's content.

Although after the Liberation, the purists continued to raise their voices, the period of French rule does not seem to have left lasting traces on the language, except as regards institutions unknown under the old order: *Ministerie van Financiën, Ministerie van Buitenlandse Zaken, Ministerie van Onderwijs* are clear importations. Similarly, *werk in uitvoering* is too much like 'travaux en cours' not to be a loan-translation. German continued to make advances, to such an extent that in 1847 Siegenbeek felt obliged to publish a list of proscribed 'Germanisms', many of which, it is true, have since disappeared, but among which the modern reader is astonished to find such common words as *indelen* (to divide, classify), *overigens* (moreover) and *vrijgevig* (generous). English still counts for little.

*   *   *   *   *

'When the Austrian Netherlands were annexed by France in 1795, the ground was prepared for a thoroughgoing Gallicisation. In fact, the authorities and the upper classes had for centuries used French in their official dealings and in conversation. One of the goals of the French Revolution had always been the expansion of French language and culture: one of its leaders, Grégoire, had written a brochure *Sur la nécessité et les moyens d'anéantir les patois et d'universaliser la langue française* (1794). Belgium was an obvious testing ground for eliminating *patois* once and for all.'[38] Only the French text of acts and decrees was henceforward to have the force of law, and the same went for legal contracts. Justice was to be administered exclusively in French. Napoleon went even further: Flemish newspapers were either banned or obliged to publish a French translation of all 'political' articles. The old Chambers of Rhetoric, the traditional refuge of the national language, had to perform at least half their repertoire in French. Secondary education, entirely in French, had great care lavished on it as a seedbed for the Empire.

Still, the common people did not as yet take to speaking French. Moreover, a few intellectuals held firm, like Karel van Hulthem of Gent, an ambivalent character but a great bibliophile, who possessed among other things a priceless manuscript of the Medieval *abele spelen*.[39] Contacts with the North, which had revived at the end of the 18th century, were maintained: of twenty-seven entrants in the Gent literary competition of 1812, twenty had adopted Siegenbeek's spelling. The rest, on the other hand, sought their salvation in an attitude which heralds the later 'particularism' of the poet Gezelle and others. Among these was the doctor F. D. van Daele from Ieper, whose periodical *Tyd-Verdryf* (Pastime, 1805—1806) remains a curious document.

It is very likely, nonetheless, that the policy of systematic Gallicisation would have succeeded, if the political situation had not been reversed in 1814. As early as 1st October, Willem I announced his intention of making Dutch the official language of northern Belgium. Little by little Dutch was introduced into politics, justice and education. The process was completed by 1823, or in theory at least, since in practice many civil-servants were incapable of expressing themselves correctly in Dutch. The king realised that training was required and appointed Dutchmen like J. Thorbecke and the Rev. J. Schrant to posts at the University of Gent, which had been founded in 1817. Unlike Napoleon, he concerned himself with primary schooling, brought teachers from Holland and opened a teachers' training college at Lier. He also enjoyed the support of the literary societies, which were very active in Brugge, Gent, Ieper and Brussels.

It goes without saying that all this met with the passionate opposition of the French-speaking Liberal bourgeoisie. But on the other side, many of the teachers recently arrived from Holland did not hide their disdain for the local dialects, and took it upon themselves to impose a bookish language which exasperated the Flemings. Finally and most importantly, the monarch's anti-clerical policy alienated the whole Catholic population, which tended to see *Hollands* as the vehicle of Calvinism. The coalition of these disparate elements proved too strong, and various royal decrees of 1829 and 1830 (the last of them dating from 4th June, very shortly before the revolution) re-established 'freedom of language', which meant in effect the predominance of French in public and cultural life.

This does not mean that as far as the linguistic situation in Belgium was concerned the period 1814–1830 was nothing more than an interlude. The measures taken by Willem I had some profound effects. It was in colleges reorganised by him that the future leaders of the Flemish Movement, like J. B. David, born in 1801, Prudens van Duyse (1804), K. L. Ledeganck (1805) and C. P. Serrure (1805) were schooled. Of relatively humble origins, they took up and disseminated the ideas of Verlooy, under the leadership of Jan Frans Willems.

Willems (1793–1846) was brought up in Lier in an Orangist environment. He only ever occupied lowly official posts (solicitor's clerk, assistant librarian, registrar), but he was a man of talent and a born leader. He was to become the 'father of the Flemish Movement'. In his essay *Verhandeling over de Nederduytsche Tael- en letterkunde opzigtelijk de Zuidelyke provintien der Nederlanden* (Essay on Dutch Language and Literature in respect of the Southern Provinces of the Netherlands, 1819–1824) he proudly demonstrates the role played by the South in Dutch culture over the centuries. Another work of Willems, *Over de Hollandsche en Vlaemsche schrijfwijzen van het Nederlandsch* (On the Hollandish and Flemish Systems of Writing Dutch, 1824), goes further than the title leads one to believe. He is interested in more than spelling: his ideal is the linguistic unity of North and South, and to achieve this it is necessary to admit the predominance of Holland. It is in effect only the North which has an authoritative pronunciation and a generally accepted grammar. Therefore the Flemings ought to abandon among other things, *den* in the nominative, and conform to Siegenbeek in matters of spelling. Moreover, he is not asking for the impossible: he sees no problem in Flemings continuing to write *ae* for *aa*. Above all, aware of the difficulties of trying to reform everyday speech, his efforts are limited to the language of 'public speaking'.

Despite his relative moderation, Willems was far from preaching to the converted. Ideas diametrically opposed to his own had been expressed a little earlier by a certain Behaegel (*Nederduytsche Spraekkunst*, Dutch Grammar, 1817), whom we shall encounter again when we come to discuss the 'spelling war'.

7. 1830–1885 — I. THE NETHERLANDS: *Top Hats, Humour and Pince-Nez*

A Dutch text from the middle of the 19th century often strikes us as very old-fashioned. This is due to the use of the genitive (*des*, 'of the', *mijns*, 'of my', *eener*, 'of a') and of the pronoun *welke* (who, which), to

the fact that even in intimate letters the *gij* had not yet been abandoned. Most striking perhaps is the frequency of the pronoun *dezelve*
(the latter). Bilderdijk had already poked fun at this word, which
seemed to have no other purpose 'than to differentiate the written
from the spoken language, of which it has never formed part'.

To what extent did the attempt at literary renewal which manifested
itself from about 1835, particularly through the efforts of E. J. Potgieter
(1808–1875) and his magazine *De Gids*, influence the character of the
language? A number of tendencies must be distinguished. The
Romantics cultivated the historical novel: J. van Lennep, J. F. Oltmans
and Mrs. A. L. G. Bosboom-Toussaint were fond of stuffing their
narratives full of archaic forms, but their grasp of philology was
unsure, and the genre soon went out of fashion. Potgieter himself
writes brilliantly, but convinced as he is that the renaissance of Dutch
culture can only come from contemplation of the 17th century, he is all
too prone to archaism and complexity. Here, by way of example, is a
fragment from the opening chapter of *Het Rijks-museum te Amsterdam*
(1844):

> 'Er was een tijd, waarin het door zijn beleid geëerbiedigde, om zijn
> goud benijde, en voor zijne kennis gevierde Holland door deze drie-
> dubbele kroon de rozen der kunst vlechten mogt; waarin het gehoor
> voor muzijk, waarin het zin voor poëzij had, en zich in beider liefelijke
> bloesems verlustigde; maar Europa's bewondering wegdroeg door zijne
> schilderschool, de oorspronkelijke, met zijnen strijd voor de vrijheid
> geboren, en die de helden van deze heeft veraanschouwelijkt en
> vereeuwigd; eene eerzuil, door dat geslacht zich zelf gesticht; — eene
> eerzuil, welker meesterstukken we ten minste niet alle voor het goud des
> vreemdelings veil hadden, — hoe onverschillig onze achtiende eeuw de
> nalatenschap bewaarde, die in welsprekend zwijgen, het vonnis der
> erfgenamen wees; tot welk eene hoogte, in den aanvang der negentiende
> eeuw, de druk des geteisterden volks stijgen mogt; — eene eerzuil, voor
> welker luister het ons past het hoofd neder te buigen van schaamte, als
> zij al de gaven, al de krachten, al de deugden van het voorgeslacht, als
> een spiegel weerkaatst, tot we, voelende wat we eens geweest zijn, en
> wat we werden, ons aangorden...'[40]

Splendid prose, but it requires all one's attention not to lose the
thread.

Bringing the spoken and the written language closer together was in
the first instance the achievement of Jacob Geel (1789–1862), who
showed that drawing on familiar vocabulary did not necessarily
exclude either striking originality or artistic sense. He was much
admired by young students around 1840, all the more so since the
'mania for copying everyday life', as Potgieter had disapprovingly
dubbed it, and a taste for humour, led writers to a close observation of
the language of various social groups. This tendency, whose most
celebrated monument is Nicolaas Beets' *Camera Obscura* (1839), can be
accounted for in terms of foreign, and especially English influences

(Sterne, Dickens), but also links up with an indigenous tradition leading from Bredero to Wolff and Deken via Justus van Effen.

Twenty years later, in an entirely different spirit and context, and in a much more systematic fashion, Multatuli (the pseudonym of Eduard Douwes Dekker, 1820—1887) proclaimed in his turn the primacy of the spoken language. His work abounds in striking, even paradoxical formulations. 'If I were deaf, I could not write'; 'I strive to write living Dutch, but I have been to school'; 'There are few books from which one cannot learn how not to write'. One finds him, in the later editions of his *Max Havelaar* (1860), replacing *gij* by *je, zeide* and *weder* by *zei* and *weer*, and *eener* by *van een*. *Gehuwd* (married) gives way to the more familiar *getrouwd* and *wijl* becomes *omdat*. In his *Ideën* Multatuli goes a step further, proposing, for example, the dropping of the *ch* in *mensch* and *tusschen*, since it is never pronounced, and the abandoning of any doubling of the vowels *e* and *o* in open syllables. These suggestions were later to be adopted.

Multatuli, however, was no linguist and his etymologies, especially, are often fanciful. The scholarly study of Dutch was in fact inaugurated by Mattijs de Vries (1820—1892). Brought up on the rigorous methods of Classical philology, he applied them to the editing of various Middle Dutch texts. Then, having been appointed to a professorship at Leiden, he was able to gather enthusiastic pupils around him. Commissioned with compiling a standard dictionary, he considered it necessary to begin by putting spelling on a firm footing. The result was his *Grondbeginselen der Nederlandsche spelling*, 'basic principles' set out in collaboration with L. A. te Winkel, which appeared in 1863. It was less a matter of replacing Siegenbeek than of improving on him in the light of new scholarship.

The four main criteria of De Vries and Te Winkel (the first three of which remain in force to this day) are as follows:

1) **pronunciation** of the educated classes. One will therefore write *koninKlijk*, but *koninG, kouDe* and never the familiar *kouWe*. Nevertheless, final *n* will be retained, even though the vast majority of Dutch-speakers pronounce *hebbe* not *hebbeN* and *brode* not *brodeN*;
2) **uniformity**. One will write *riB*, not *riP*, because of the plural *ribben, hanDdoek*, not *handoek*, because the word is made up of *hand + doek*;
3) **analogy**. Although only one *t* is heard in *grootTe*, two will be written, by analogy with *dikte* and *hoogte*; this rule applies particularly in conjugation: *hij wordT*, because of *hij loopT, praatTe* because of *bakTe, laadDe* because of *leefDe*;
4) **etymology**.

This last guideline is of particular importance, as it takes us to the heart of the historical approach. Certainly the predecessors of De Vries and Te Winkel did not in any way neglect the past, so that they carefully distinguished *ei* and *ij*, since the latter derives from a diphthongisation of long *i* (cf. p. 17). But 'whereas up till then the past had been principally used to account for **existing** distinctions, it is now to serve as a motivation for **desirable** distinctions' [41] If one writes *hopen* with a single *o*, but *loopen* with two, this is because in the latter case *o* derives from a diphthong (cf. Germ. *hoffen* as opposed to *laufen*). By the same token, the *e* will be single in *weten* (Germ. *wissen*), double in *heeten* (Germ. *heissen*).

Although adopted by royal decree in Belgium the year after its publication, the De Vries/Te Winkel spelling did not make its official appearance in the Netherlands until the royal speech at the Opening of Parliament in 1883. Meanwhile, though, it had firmly established itself in education.

De Vries, however, found an opponent of stature in the shape of the orientalist T. Roorda, who in 1855 delivered to the Royal Academy a resounding address in which he stressed that living Dutch had only two genders and no longer had declensions. The latter only survived by appeal to Latin and German, and the most sensible thing would be to abandon them. De Vries was indignant at these 'revolutionary' views. Is not inflection the mark of a civilised language, and its loss a sign of decadence? The Academy took the side of De Vries, refusing even to print Roorda's text. The matter was for the time being forgotten, but later generations were to see Roorda as a pioneer.

The first instalment of the *Nederlandsch Woordenboek* (Dutch Dictionary) (which was later to become the *Woordenboek der Nederlandsche Taal*, abbreviated as *WNT*) appeared in 1864. De Vries considered himself entrusted with a national mission. He aimed to compile a true 'museum of the everyday spoken language', which is 'the revitalising source of true language'. Having said this, only the written language reaches the level of culture. The philologist is a gardener who must know how to use both secateurs and watering-can. De Vries's choice of texts is revealing. He takes as his starting point 1637, i.e. the *Statenbijbel* (cf. p. 21). He admits neither the 'vulgarity' of Bredero nor the 'daring innovations' of Hooft or the young Vondel. His successors were to depart increasingly from this critical and normative attitude and to aim at a description pure and simple of the facts of language. Besides this, they were to go back as far as possible into the 16th century, so as to ensure continuity with the *Middelnederlandsch Woordenboek*, published from 1885 onwards by J. Verdam, one of De Vries's pupils. They were to reduce the number of quotations, as De Vries had been too ambitious. Despite this, this colossal work has not been completely finished even now, and already incorporates a supplement.

While the scholars were at work in the silence of their studies, language went on changing along with society. More slowly than their powerful neighbours, and yet irreversibly, the Netherlands became modernised. This leads to a quite perceptible obsolescence in vocabulary: in 1887, for example, Beets felt obliged to publish an explanatory booklet for the use of later readers of his *Camera Obscura* — and above all the emergence of a host of new terms, sometimes with strange variations. In the early days of the railways, usage hesitated between *railwegen* and *ijzerbaan*, before becoming officially fixed as *spoorwegen*. *Locomotief* did not immediately supplant *stoomsleper*, and first-class carriages were at first called *diligences*, those of the second class *chars à bancs*, with the term *wagon* reserved for the third class.

From the last example, the importance of foreign words is apparent. French retains its place in literature, art and fashion, but the competition of English and German becomes more and more intense. Doctors, physicists, linguists and theologians read many works in German, and this is reflected in their specialised vocabulary. English invades the domain of industry, but also parliamentary life, sport and fashion. Thanks notably to the setting up of modern secondary schools (*HBS*, 'Hogere Burger school') in 1863, the knowledge of English made considerable strides between 1840 and 1880. In the Netherlands as elsewhere, one took the air full of *spleen* in one's *brik* (< break) or in a *victoria*. The well-to-do had a *nurse* and a *boy*, and wore a *cloak* and a *waterproof*. The man who looks after the books becomes an *accountant*, and so he has remained. Loan-translations appear, and their origin is soon forgotten: *geld maken* (< to make money) or *dat spreekt boekdelen* (< that speaks volumes).

It is at this time too, it seems, that certain Jewish words penetrate general usage: *sjofel* (shabby), *heibel* (hullabaloo), *lef* (nerve, cheek). The same applies to various Malay terms, and to those known since the 17th century are added: *kapok, rotting* (cane), *sago* and *gladakker* (rascal).

The inevitable purist reaction was inspired, as is usually the case, by political-economic motives. When neighbouring Germany became a threat, it was German influence particularly which had to be guarded against. Attention has already been drawn to the list of Germanisms compiled by Siegenbeek in 1847. The periodical *De Gids* and Beets are equally strict. De Vries tries to set up criteria. All these warnings were certainly not without effect, but they were unable to prevent the definite adoption of *gehalte* (content), *rustkuur* (rest cure), *gezant* (envoy), etc.

8. 1830–1885 — II. BELGIUM: 'Language is the Whole Nation'

In the wake of the revolution of 1830, the future of Dutch in Belgium may have seemed very bleak. True, the 1830 constitution did not impose a monopoly of French, but nevertheless again it became, as it had been under Napoleon, the exclusive language of the whole of public life and of the whole of education beyond primary school. What counterweight to French could be provided by these Flemish 'dialects' which, as the provisional government sarcastically observed, 'vary from province to province'? The Flemish (the name given henceforth to all Dutch-speaking Belgians) were forced to show great perseverance in asserting their claims, modest though these were at the outset. Not until 1873 and 1877 respectively were judges and civil-servants in Flanders bound in principle by law to use Dutch, and not until 1883 did Dutch become, still only in principle, the language of instruction in state secondary schools.

As true Romantics, the pioneers of the Flemish Movement regarded language as the expression par excellence of the national spirit. This is the thesis expounded as early as 1832 by P. Blommaert in his *Aenmerkingen over de verwaerlozing der Nederduitse tael* (Observations on the Neglect of Dutch), whose opening is characteristic:

> 'Nothing is so closely linked to the foundations of a nation as the language of its people. It is the language which spreads the same attitudes throughout all levels of society, which allows us to distinguish differences between peoples and which consequently is the basis of nationality. So that a national government has a duty to uphold with special care the language of the people.'

This manifesto won the support of Willems, who in the preface to his modern version of *Reinaert de Vos* (1834) referred to the efforts which he had long been making to reinstate Dutch and to defend it 'both against the pedantry of written Northern Dutch and against the bastardising influence of dialect in the schools of Flanders'.

But what kind of 'Dutch' was meant? Since the break with the North, Siegenbeek no longer had any authority. Should one nevertheless continue to take one's cue from the Netherlands, or rather create in Flanders, on the basis of living dialects and the grammarians of the previous century, an autonomous form of Dutch? Willems took the first view, tirelessly harping on the fact that Dutch as it existed was the common heritage of North and South, to which the Flemings had made the earliest contribution.

The discussion was at first centred on the 'spelling war'. In 1839, on the initiative of Willems and Canon J. B. David of Leuven, the government appointed a commission which came up with proposals very close to those of Siegenbeek. There ensued a great hue and cry, in which Behaegel was prominent. Des Roches was exhumed, the banner of Orangism was brandished. In fact, the struggle was a protracted one. The new rules were officially adopted in 1841 for the Flemish version of the *Bulletin des Lois et Arrêtés*, and in 1864 for teaching, administration and all public documents.

Relations between North and South were also reinforced by the establishment in 1849 of the *Taal- en letterkundige Congressen* (Linguistic and Literary Conferences). Representatives from Holland and Flanders met regularly, once every two years, up to 1914. In fact, hardly any concrete resolutions emerged. Nevertheless, it was at the first conference that the idea of the *Nederlandsch Woordenboek* was first launched.

But the 'particularists' would not concede defeat. In about 1860 they re-emerged. They were supported with great vigour by the poet Guido

Gezelle (1830–1890), who in the preface to his *Dichtoefeningen* (Exercises in Poetry) of 1858, and afterwards in his magazine *Rond den Heerd* (Round the Fireside), proclaimed with passionate conviction the superiority of West Flemish as a spontaneous, pithy and vigorous language over the 'hybrid language of Holland'. Gezelle and his followers did not, however, advocate a purely dialectal Flemish, but a Flemish at once close to its sources and 'purified'. He practised what he preached, and the magnificence of his language won him admirers even in Holland.

Notwithstanding this, in general, the written language of Flanders was impoverished and clumsy. Hendrik Conscience (1812–1883), the man who 'taught his people to read' is a striking example. His *Leeuw van Vlaenderen* (Lion of Flanders, 1838) teems with Gallicisms, arbitrary constructions and, indeed, with crude mistakes. The language of his rural novellas is undoubtedly an improvement, but when quite recently, in conjunction with a film, it was planned to issue a new, readable edition of *De Loteling* (The Conscript, 1850), the editor, Karel Jonckheere, had almost entirely to rewrite the book. And what is one to say of the official documents of the period, translated from French with often deliberate carelessness!

To redress the situation, one was forced to rely, more or less in the long term, on scholars and schoolteachers. Here again, we encounter Willems. His *Belgisch Museum* (1837–1847) contains many beautiful Middle Dutch texts. Serrure continued the work in his *Vaderlandsch Museum* (1855–1863). The foundation of the *Koninklijke Vlaamsche Academie* in 1886 marked at once the crowning of these efforts and a broadening of scope, for the Academy was obviously not solely concerned with the past. As for the pedagogues, C. L. Ternest carries off the palm with his *Beknopte Uitspraakleer der Nederduische Taal* (Concise Guide to Dutch Pronunciation), which went through three editions in 1860, 1872 and 1882. Ternest is decidedly an advocate of following the Northern line, apart from deviations permitted by the majority of people of discrimination. At the 1867 Congress, the poet Jan van Beers assured his audience that Ternest's ideas were being applied in almost all schools in the five Flemish provinces. But W. Pée, referring to his own experience is very sceptical: 'As for the beginning of this century,' he writes, 'I attended primary school in rural West Flanders, and no one spoke correctly, even in the classroom.'[42] Perhaps things were different in other provinces, but whatever the case, the Flemish militants still had plenty of work to do.

9. 1885–1945 — I. THE NETHERLANDS: *A New Lease of Life*

Compulsory education, which became law in 1900, the extension of secondary education, the creation of numerous adult courses, the development of the communications media, were all factors which combined to force the dialects to retreat, to the advantage of the standard language. On the one hand, the closing of the gap between the written and the spoken language, sketched for the preceding period, continues and accelerates. On the other hand, pronunciation sometimes tends to follow written usage. It sometimes happens that the articles *een* and *het* are pronounced as they appear on paper, and not, as is normal, as *'n* and *'t*. On the other hand, and most importantly, novelists and journalists tend more and more to avoid forms and turns of phrase alien to the spoken language. There still exists, of course, a degree of stylisation, but this affects construction more than morphology or vocabulary. One can discern a general dissemination of terms previously limited to slang: *foefje* (gimmick), *pietluttig* (petty) and *ratjetoe* (hotchpotch) no longer raise eyebrows. It should be added nevertheless that Dutch civil-servants tend towards conservatism. The average Dutch person weighs each word very carefully before composing a letter to the authorities. An additional complicating factor is that one has, both in the address and in the body of the letter, to use the precise form of address befitting the titles and function of the addresses. Is a particular mayor to be addressed as *hoogedelachtbaar*, *edelachtbaar* or *weledelgestreng*? This depends on the size of his constituency. Fortunately, a number of manuals or *'briefstellers'* are available in which all possible cases are covered.

1885 marks a watershed in the Netherlands. In that year in fact the first issue of *De Nieuwe Gids* appeared as the mouthpiece of a new school of writers (the *Tachtigers* or 'the men of 1880') which was to give a decisive new impetus to modern Dutch literature. Its merit consisted especially in disputing the existence of a language reserved for poetry. 'Form and content, in poetry, are one', proclaimed Willem Kloos. 'The man of true inspiration,' wrote Albert Verwey, 'looks for the language of nature, not to be eccentric or different from the masses, but only in this way can he express himself as he ought.' In Herman Gorter's ambitious lyrical poem *Mei* (1889) the modern reader is still captivated by the freshness and clarity of the language. Kloos and his friends, however, also saw poetry as 'the most individual expression of the most individual emotion'. This led in many cases to a rapid descent into anarchy and unintelligibility. In the same way, prose-writers originally drew their inspiration from French realism; Couperus's characters speak the language of The Hague aristocracy, those of Querido and Heijermans that of working-class Amsterdam. But when they are in search of picturesque effects, Van Looy and Van Deyssel resort to neologisms, while Ary Prins contorts syntax.

These excesses were short-lived, and a reaction soon set in. 'Broadly speaking, after the *Nieuwe Gids*-period, both younger and older writers, can be seen to show restraint and sobriety, in poetry and in prose: the ferment of the preceding period, which had been so liberating and enriching, continued to make its salutary effects felt.'[43]

During this time science and technology continued to develop by leaps and bounds. Many new terms were international: *photo[graphie]*, *auto[mobiel], radio*...Bold spirits begin taking of *televisie. Bioscoop* derives from 'bioscope', the instrument invented by the Frenchman G. Demenu in 1891. The most original word is undoubtedly *fiets* (bicycle), which had no difficulty in replacing the very formal *rijwiel*, but whose origin remains uncertain despite research.

The two World Wars (even that of 1914−1918, in which the Netherlands were not directly involved) also had their repercussions on vocabulary. An already-existing term like *distributie* makes tremendous gains after 1940. New words appear, some adapted from German (*spergebied*, 'no-go area', *tankval*, 'tank-trap'), others as authentic as can be, for example *bukshag* (tobacco obtained from cigarette-ends) and *moffenzeef* (anti-jamming device). The majority have now naturally fallen into disuse. Nevertheless, everyone knows that *hongertocht* meant a food-finding expedition during the terrible winter of 1944−1945 and that *onderduiken* can mean 'to go underground'. Already quite strong before 1914, the linguistic pressure from the Anglo-Saxon world was reinforced in the inter-war period. Usually it was a question of designating hitherto unknown concepts, but sometimes a foreign word competed with a perfectly current Dutch term, like, for example, *reporter* = verslaggever, or *shopping* = winkelen. In addition to these loan-words there are pseudo-English words (some possibly derived via Franglais), like *dancing, smoking* (evening-jacket), and more recently *camping, parking, babybox* (playpen), *babysit* (babysitter) and many more. Foreign influences, from Russian to American, may also explain the vogue currently enjoyed, in the Netherlands as elsewhere, by acronyms. Of course abbreviations like *PS* (postscript) and *HBS* (see p. 35) had long been used, but henceforth such abbreviations proliferate: radio-listeners can choose between the programmes put out by the *KRO* (*Katholieke Radio Omroep*), and *VARA* (*Vereniging Algemene Radio Amateurs*) and various other broadcasting associations, while the whole world knows the *KLM* (*Koninklijke Luchtvaart Maatschappij*).

That this situation once again provoked a great wave of purism need surprise no one. As in preceding generations the struggle was carried on with varying degrees of competence and success. One may mention the setting up in 1931 of the society *Onze Taal* (Our Language), which still exists and publishes a monthly newsletter which is an excellent source of information on the state of the language and the reaction of the public.

However, all this counts for little compared to the storm unleashed by spelling reform. In 1891, the philologist R. A. Kollewijn published what was to be an epoch-making article called *Onze lastige spelling* (Our Awkward Spelling). Two years later a very active organisation was set up to disseminate his ideas. These were not in any way radical, and boiled down to the following proposals:

1) In open syllables *e* and *o* should no longer ever be doubled. *Lopen* was henceforward to be treated in exactly the same way as *hopen* (cf. p. 34). Another consequence will be that *bOOm* will have the

plural *bOmen*, and one will write: *de vaas is brEEd*, but: *een brEde vaas*.

2) *sch* will become *s* (*mensch* > *mens*, *visch* > *vis*) except, of course, when the *ch* is pronounced, as in *schip*.

3) the suffix *-lijk*, where *ij* does not have diphthongised pronunciation, will be spelt *-lik*.

4) foreign loan-words should, as far as possible, be spelt in the Dutch way. Specifically, the suffix *-isch* should become *-ies* (*harmonisch* > *harmonies*).

5) the final *n* should be dropped from the masculine article and adjective in the accusative, since it belongs exclusively to the written language. Hence: *ik neem DE sleutel* (I take the key), and no longer *DEN sleutel*; *ze praat met DE buurman* (she talks to the neighbour), and no longer *met DEN buurman*.

This gave rise to heated discussions which were to continue for more than half a century. While most linguists and several younger writers adopted Kollewijn's views, the latter met with uncompromising opposition in conservative circles. In 1934 the Minister of Education, Marchant, introduced the proposals into his sector, though somewhat watered down. The *n* was to be retained solely for words designating animate subjects of the male sex, whether they be human (*soldaat, dokter*) or animal (*haan, stier*): hence one has *ik zie DE boom* (I see the tree), but *ik lees DEN dichter* (I read the poet). The suffix *-lijk* remained unchanged, and the question of loan-words was put off until later, so that one would continue to write *harmonisch*.

A new step, taken just after the Second World War, may be mentioned at this point. The official reform, made in 1946 in Belgium and 1947 in the Netherlands, adopted the Marchant system in broad outline, with the exception that final *n* (sexual or otherwise) was to be optional (in the event it very soon disappeared). As for foreign words and the delicate question of gender (to which we shall return at length, pp. 66—73), these were referred to a Belgo-Dutch committee under the chairmanship of Professor C. B. van Haeringen, whose labours resulted in the publication in 1954 of the word list (*Woordenlijst van de Nederlandse taal*), popularly known as *Het groene boekje* or 'Little Green Book'.

10. 1885–1945 — II. BELGIUM: *From Legal to Real*

The year 1898 was in principle very gratifying for Flemings. Laws and decrees had always been issued in both languages, but henceforward the Dutch text was to have the same force in law as the French. However, the Flemish Movement was not content with principles. In 1930 the definitive 'Flemification' of the University of Gent was finally re-started after a false beginning during the First World War. In 1932—1934 a series of laws established the primacy of Dutch in government, education and the administration of justice in Flanders. Monolingualism had triumphed. But the horizons of the Flemish

Movement had long since broadened. Lodewijk de Raet (1870–1914) had helped to give it a socio-economic dimension and in 1900 August Vermeylen had declared, in two formulas which have since become proverbial: 'In order to be anything we must be Flemings. We want to be Flemings in order to become Europeans.' Openness to the outside world is the keynote, and also the conviction that language does not exist in isolation but that its destiny is bound up with that of the community that speaks it.

The perfecting of linguistic legislation, considerable achievement as it was, was therefore not sufficient in itself. This was all the more true because of the fact that it was still a long way from the legal to the actual. A large part of the establishment resisted passively, but these rearguard actions were of secondary importance. The most difficult problem was that one could not just by waving a magic wand reverse a state of affairs which had existed for centuries. Even when they did not keep systematically to French, the governing classes faced many obstacles: 'Despite themselves, educated Flemings, mostly of middle-class origin, who were very keen to speak and write their mother tongue, transposed into Flemish the French constructions and phrases which came spontaneously into their minds, without being aware that with the best of intentions they were contributing to its bastardisation.'[44] As for the common people, they quite simply went on using their local dialects. More than that: daily life was constantly subject to invasion from French, as all technical innovation was derived from France or Wallonia. Even today, when a survivor of that generation thinks, for example, of bicycling, he calls brakes, rims, pedals and forks by their French names. Surveys have shown that this case is by no means an isolated one.[45]

It was obviously the task of the schools to remedy the situation. But here another difficulty arose. 'The first Flemish teachers who were obliged by the new language laws to give all their lessons in "Dutch" were faced with a very delicate problem. They themselves had studied entirely in French, and all the Dutch they knew was their dialect and at most some elements of a forced and bookish language.'[46] These remarks apply to secondary teaching and they may by virtue of this be a little exaggerated, but they are certainly true of primary schooling.

The diffusion of correct Dutch in Belgium, then, was a long-term operation, which was tackled with great resolution, with efforts directed principally towards pronunciation. In 1913 a *Vereeniging voor beschaafde Nederlandsche uitspraak* (Association for Correct Dutch Pronunciation) was set up at Antwerp, but its intensive efforts were cut short a year later by the war. It was realised that both in the struggle against dialects and from a scholarly point of view, a simplification of spelling would be welcome. Not everyone shared this opinion, however, and stormy debates rocked the Flemish Academy. W. de Vreese responded to the last fling of 'particularism' as follows: 'Adopting the correct language of the Northern Netherlands in everyday life is clearly in the interest of the South.'

The first scholarly study in Flanders devoted to pronunciation, which superseded Ternest's outdated book, was the *Nederlandsche Uitspraakleer* (System of Dutch Pronunciation, 1912) by the Leuven professor L. Scharpé, which, however, was never reprinted. On the other hand, E. Blancquaert's *Praktische Uitspraakleer van de Nederlandsche Taal* (Practical System of Dutch Pronunciation) of 1934 went through numerous editions, and forms the basis of virtually everything (and that is a considerable amount) that has appeared since. 'Blancquaert also bases himself, in most cases, on Northern usage. He wishes to promote linguistic unity between North and South, without wishing to "Hollandise" the language, and often recommends Northern usage even when his personal ideas would tend to make him prefer something else.'[47] It was therefore Blancquaert who was taken as a norm in the thoroughgoing reform of secondary education in 1946.

As far as vocabulary was concerned, the most noteworthy contribution was that of De Vreese in his *Gallicismen in het Zuidnederlandsch* (Gallicisms in Southern Dutch, 1899). He had had predecessors, but none of them was as well-equipped. The seven hundred pages of his book represented a huge work of analysis: sixty-eight writers and twenty-five magazines. De Vreese achieved his goal of 'demonstrating irrefutably the existence of a particular fault, and of opening many people's eyes'. Moreover, his findings were widely drawn on without acknowledgement.

These practical preoccupations did not exhaust the activity of Flemish philologists. Besides those already quoted, one must mention, at least in passing, Lecoutere and Grootaers in Leuven, and Verdeyen and Mansion in Liège. From etymology to historical grammar, from toponymy to dialectology, they produced work which is in no way inferior to that of their colleagues in the Netherlands such as De Vooys, Schönfeld and Kloeke (to mention only those who are no longer alive).

The public at large was, of course, more aware of literature. 1893 sees the emergence of the school associated with the magazine *Van Nu en Straks*. It is reminiscent, *mutatis mutandis*, of the *Tachtigers*, by whom it was to a certain extent inspired. 'Here as elsewhere,' wrote Vermeylen, 'the younger generation realise that they must rid themselves of all bookish language, that there should be no gulf between the written and spoken language, and that starting from a living language is the first prerequisite of a healthy and truly national literature.'[48] They also pay great tribute to Gezelle, who, moreover, at this period, shortly before his death, was composing some of his greatest masterpieces. The poetry of Karel van de Woestijne (1878—1929) evokes with equal felicity the elegance of the Quattrocento, the dynamism of the Baroque and the subtlety of Impressionism. Paul van Ostaijen (1896—1928), despite his premature death, left a lasting mark on Flemish literature by introducing various forms of Expressionism. But obviously, from our point or view, it is the prose-writers who are most important, and we shall return to them below (p. 86).

11. SINCE 1945: *Nuclear Energy, Blue Jeans and Old Problems*[49]

The Second World War represented a major turning-point for the Netherlands. 'In the social, economic and cultural fields, the country underwent a sudden acceleration, which has not yet finished.'[50] In addition, the expansion of telephone communication, the mass media and the tape recorder gave the spoken language a dominant position which is felt even in politics, education and literature. To these factors must be added the emergence of 'Randstad Holland',[51] which has entailed the voluntary movement of enormous masses of people from east to west.

The language reflects the development of social relationships. *Arbeider* (worker), which itself had been something of a step up compared to *werkman* is gradually giving way to *werknemer* (employee), which is free of any emotive connotations. In the same way, *dienstmeisje* (maid) has been replaced by *hulp in de huishouding* (domestic help). A phenomenon more specific to the Netherlands is that whereas it used to be quite normal to use the familiar *jij* and *je* in addressing porters, tradesmen, etc., the polite form *U* is now becoming the norm, even with the most menial staff.[52]

Another feature, due particularly to the mingling of population groups, is the dramatic rise of *ABN*.[53] 'For the majority of Dutch people this has become, much more than a century ago, a social reality.'[54] The dialectologists will have to hurry if they are not to run out of material.

This common language seems to be less and less rigid. Maybe in part because of television, which interviews all kinds of people, a mistake in stress like *catalógus* (instead of *catálogus*) is no longer felt as shocking. There is even an evolution in the phonological system, with many people no longer distinguishing between *vel* and *fel*, or seeing in the *s* of *suiker* and the *z* of *zoet* anything but a spelling difference.

Syntax has scarcely shifted. It is vocabulary which has shown the greatest change, in the first place, of course, because of the adoption of foreign words. The influence of German is fairly negligible (*pace* such doubtful cases as *gastarbeider*). French has provided, among other things, *fondue, polemologie* (a term coined by G. Bouthol), *permanente educatie, milieu* (in the sense of environment), *derde wereld* (a loan-translation of the term 'tiers monde', coined in 1956 by G. Balandier). It is, of course, from English that most has been borrowed. The Netherlands have perhaps been even more exposed than France or Germany to this invasion. In any case, the adoption of English words is made both easier and less problematic by the ability of Dutch to form verbs from foreign roots. This has produced, for example, *starten, droppen, checken* and *relaxen*. Sometimes also English terms have been neatly adapted: 'ball point' has become *balpen*, and 'feedback' *terugkoppeling*.[55] Indonesian independence in 1949 brought with it a progressive decline in the use of words of Malay origin. The 1974 edition of the Koenen-Endepols dictionary (ed. J. B. Drewes) contains fewer such words than previous editions, although it is slightly larger overall than its predecessors.

However frequent recourse to English may be, many technological and social innovations have been given indigenous designations: *aardgas* (natural gas), *kneedbom* (plastic bomb), *stiptheidsactie* (work-to-rule), etc. Those Dutch people who first 'opted' for Indonesian nationality and afterwards regretted it are consequently *spijtoptanten*. Certain recent coinages are real finds: someone who enjoys picknicking at the side of the road is a *bermtoerist* (lit. 'verge tourist'), a motorway telephone is a *praatpaal* (lit. 'talking post'), the schoolchild who, armed with a 'lollipop' sign, helps others across the road is a *klaarover(tje)* (lit. 'safe-across helper').

Certain words which had always been in use have suddenly taken on new meanings. Formerly *inspraak* meant only inspiration, in the religious sense; it now means 'consultation' or participation of all the relevant parties in an organisation. *Óverkomen*, 'to cross', has taken on the meaning of 'to be understood, gets one's message across'. *Ergens*, 'somewhere', may now mean 'in some way'. *Ludiek* (playful), brought into fashion by Johan Huizinga's famous book *Homo Ludens* (1938), now refers to a non-violent, festive political demonstration.

But 'the main tendency of post-war vocabulary is the clear desire for ease and spontaneity, the rejection of everything which may appear stiff or solemn'. Literature bears witness to this: 'the *Vijftigers* (poets of the 1950s) gave themselves over to experiments not only with the form of their poetry but also with the language.'[56] And so does conversation. Certain expressions previously banned from polite usage, like *belazeren* (to cheat) and *ouwehoeren* (to talk rubbish), are heard almost universally. But there is quite often confusion between the natural, the familiar and the vulgar. In certain self-styled artistic circles, people take pride in using deliberately coarse language. It is hard to know whether this represents a levelling process, a decline in values, or quite simply snobbery.

It is not surprising, given these conditions, that slang, which had begun its breakthrough in the preceding period, should be becoming increasingly widespread. Someone may be *maf* (daft, wet), someone else *link* (dodgy). On the other hand, T.V., powerful influence as it is in the renewal of language, is also responsible for a host of clichés and stop-gaps. *Ik dacht dat* means no more than 'I think', and *dus* is used at every turn, often without the slightest suggestion of a causal relationship.

It should not be forgotten that since the 1960s, one section of young people has developed 'its own culture, often also called a **sub-culture**, when one thinks of pop music, the drug scene, sexual permissiveness, the Provos, the hippies on the Dam Square and other such things'.[57] This microcosm has its own language in Holland as elsewhere, more so perhaps in view of the pull exerted by Amsterdam. But it remains to be seen whether the strange argot which developed around the Vondelpark in the 1970s will bequeath anything lasting to the Dutch language.

Whatever the case, the importance, both quantitative and qualitative, of the recent shifts in Dutch vocabulary is clear from the publication of R. Reinsma's checklist *Signalement van nieuwe woorden* (Amsterdam/Brussels 1975), containing no less than 2,000 words or usages unattested before 1945.

*   *   *   *   *

Amid all these upheavals, the question of spelling continues to be hotly debated, as it has been for more than 150 years. The 'Little Green Book'[58] left the user the choice, with words of foreign origin, between an 'authorised' and a 'preferred' spelling. Although the latter very soon became compulsory in the administration, and in education (at least in Belgium), and although the vast majority of the press has adopted it, the system turned out to be less than satisfactory, and a new committee was set up under the chairmanship of W. Pée and H. Wesseling, which reported in 1967. Exceeding its original terms of reference, the committee also made a number of suggestions relating to indigenous words. Consequently it was asked to continue its work and study the question of the homophones *ei/ij* and *au/ou*, the suffix *-lijk*, and the verb forms. The result of this were the committee's 'final proposals' of 1969.

The committee, regarding the rest as secondary, suggested modifications only to foreign words and verb forms. In the present tense of verbs with a stem ending in *d*, the *t* should disappear in the second- and third-person: *hij antwoord* instead of *antwoordt, ze wend zich om* instead of *wendt*. In the preterite of verbs with infinitives ending in *-den* and *-ten*, there should no longer be doubling of the consonant: *hij antwoorde*, and no longer *antwoordde, ze prate*, and no longer *praatte*.

Meanwhile, on the initiative of P. C. Paardekooper, the *Vereneging voor Wetenschappeleke Spelling* (Association for Scientific Spelling) had been set up in 1963, with the object of going as far as possible in the direction of phonology.[59] In 1970, the VWS contacted various teachers' associations with a view to establishing a 'minimum programme', relatively modest, yet bolder than Pée/Wesseling. The following year, an 'action group' came into being, aiming to propagate the minimum programme among the public at large.

This, by way of example, is how the sentence *Deze jongen wijdt al zijn vrije tijd aan zijn hobby* (This boy devotes all his free time to his hobby) would be written according to (a) P. Wesseling, (b) the 'minimum programme', (c) the views of the *VWS*:

a) Deze jongen *wijd* al zijn vrije *tijd* aan zijn *hobbie*
b) Deze jongen *wijt* al zijn vrije *tijt* aan zijn *hobbie*
c) Deze jongen *weit* al *z'n vreie teit* aan z'n *hobbi*

As for words of foreign origin:

At present	P/W	Min.Prog.	VWS
cape	*keep*	*keep*	*keep*
sociaal	*sosiaal*	*sosiaal*	*sosjaal*
mobilisatie	*mobilizatie*	*mobilizatie*	*mobilizasi*
mobilizatie			*mobilizaatsi*

But in the opposing camp, people were not just twiddling their thumbs. Not only linguists and teachers, but journalists, writers and politicans entered the lists on both sides. At the beginning of 1972, the mayor of Antwerp, L. Craeybeckx, rallied the conservatives around him and founded in his turn an 'action group', which also won much sympathy in the Netherlands. The polemics mounted, and although the innovators have on various occasions had the ear of The Hague and Brussels, it has not been possible to take any decision. Some years ago an armistice of sorts was concluded, but the fire is still smouldering beneath the ashes.

There is no way of analysing here the arguments, scientific, sentimental, didactic and social, which have been and continue to be bandied about in this debate at cross-purposes. For that matter, they do not differ that much from those with which we are familiar abroad. We shall limit ourselves to three remarks. The first is that the discussion cuts across party-political lines: members of all parties are found in both camps. 'Cuba and simplified spelling are not by definition each other's logical extensions.'[60] Nor is it a quarrel between the Netherlands and Belgium. The Flemings, for reasons which we shall see below, generally take a more radical line and in 1963 a Belgian minister stated in public that the Pée-Wesseling committee had been set up to get rid once and for all of Dutch 'conservatism'. Yet it was from Antwerp that the revolt against the 'final proposals' originated, and from 1967 the Flemish Academy had registered its concern.

Finally, one is bound to say that the virulence of this 'orthographitis' has one surprising aspect. Certainly no one would dream of saying that it is much ado about nothing, and a particular schools inspector was probably not wrong to speak of a 'tragedy' with regard to the teaching of verb forms in primary schools.[61] But one can after all 'note with justified satisfaction that despite the tiresome distinction between *ei* and *ij*, and the less tiresome one between *ou* and *au*, Dutch spelling does meet reasonable requirements'.[62] This opinion of a particularly well-qualified Dutchman is echoed in that of an experienced foreigner. Apart from some minor exceptions and irregularities, writes the American William Shetter, 'Dutch spelling can be said to be **almost entirely consistent'**.[63] This is surely not to be sniffed at.

---

1 German has a further method of dating at its disposal. In the dialects from which *Hochdeutsch* was later to emerge, a consonantal mutation occurred (see p. 111) which was virtually complete by the 7th century. Consequently, when a Latin word has undergone the mutation, this means that it was borrowed before that date. This is the

case with *Pfeil* (< pilum = arrow) and *Ziegel* (< tegula = tile). Dutch does not have this criterion, but it is highly probable that the corresponding terms in Dutch (*pijl, tegel*) are equally old.

2 'Certain' plurals, since Inguaeonic obviously has nothing to do with the recent proliferation of *-s* plurals in Modern Dutch (cf. p. 54).

3 M. Valkhoff, *L'expansion du néerlandais* (Bruxelles, n. d.), p. 43.

4 C. Verlinden, *Les origines de la frontière linguistique en Belgique et la colonisation franque* (Bruxelles, 1955), p. 130. This work contains a full bibliography. It scarcely needs adding that while Verlinden's book represents a milestone, it is certainly not the last word on the subject.

5 Ibid., p. 102.

6 Ibid., p. 132.

7 Cf. T. Frings/G. Lechner, *Niederländisch und Niederdeutsch* (*Sitzungsberichte der sächsischen Akademie der Wissenschaften zu Leipzig, Philologie — historische Klasse*) 110/6 (Berlin, 1966), p. 21. One must not, however, forget that the Limburg dialect also derives from East Lower Franconian.

8 A. van Loey, 'Altniederländisch u. Mittelniederländisch' in *Kurzer Grundriss der germanischen Philologie bis 1500*, I, hgg. von L. E. Schmitt (Berlin, 1970), p. 254.

9 M. Gysseling, 'Op verkenning doorheen het Oudnederlands', *Meded. van de Vereniging voor Naamkunde*, 37 (1961), p. 77. This quotation, as well as that from Frings and Van Loey, is taken from W. Sanders, 'Oudnederlands', *Tijdschrift voor Ned. Taal- en Letterkunde, XXXVIII (1972)*, pp. 161 ff.

10 Cf. W. J. H. Caron, *Klank en Teken* (Groningen, 1972), pp. 187—206, which also gives a full bibliography. See also G. Kettenis/J. Meijer, 'Veel trammelant om een klein zinnetje', in *De letter doet de geest leven*. Bundel opstellen aangeboden aan Max de Haan… (Leiden, 1980), pp. 9—25.

11 Cf. p. 127, n. 19.

12 A. van Loey, *Introduction à l'étude du moyen-néerlandais* (Paris, 1951), p. 48.

13 C. G. N. de Vooys, *Geschiedenis van de Nederlandse taal* (Groningen, 1970), pp. 43—44. There were also, on a much more modest scale, borrowings by French from Germanic, as for example *mannequin* (< mannekijn) and *étape* (< O. Fr. étaple < stapel, 'store'). Interestingly, both words were subsequently taken back into Dutch from French with changed meanings.

14 De Vooys, op. cit., p. 59.

15 J. Huizinga, 'Duitschland's invloed op de Nederlandsche beschaving', in *Verzameld Werk* (Haarlem, 1948—1953), II, p. 311.

16 This is at any rate the thesis defended by G. G. Kloeke in *De Hollandsche expansie in de 16de en 17de eeuw…*(1927). For a detailed account of the discussions to which the theory has given rise, one may refer to A. van Loey, *Schönfeld's historische grammatica van het Nederlands* (Zutphen, 6th ed., n. d.), paras. 72—77 and M. C. van den Toorn, 'Kloekes expansietheorie na vijftig jaar', *De Nieuwe Taalgids* (1977), 1, pp. 1—14. It is interesting to note that at the same time both English and High German also underwent the double diphthongisation: *house, Haus; to bite, beissen*. In view of the distances involved, any influence of one language on the other can be ruled out. The same mutation must have had the same causes in all cases, but these are very obscure.

17 G. G. Kloeke, *Gezag en norm bij het gebruik van verzorgd Nederlands* (Amsterdam, 1951), p. 21.

18 *De Werken van Vondel* (Wereldbibliotheek) (Amsterdam, n. d.), V, p. 485.

19 The influx of Huguenots after 1685 scarcely counts. They were very quickly assimilated and brought with them only a few technical terms. *Fabrikant, industrie, personeel* and *compagnon* (in the sense of business partner) are attributed to them.

20 Cf. De Vooys, op. cit., p. 112.

21 Quoted in De Vooys, op. cit., p. 98.

22 De Vooys, op. cit., p. 104.

23 Ibid., p. 107.

24 This comment of Bréal's (*Sémantique*. 6e éd., p. 172), referring to French grammarians from Ménage to d'Olivet, is applied to their Dutch counterparts by W. J. H. Caron in his edition of C. van Heule, *De Nederduytsche Grammatica ofte Spraeckonst* (Groningen, 1953), p. VIII.

25 Cf. J. Heinsius, 'De taal van den Statenbijbel', in *De Statenvertaling 1637—1937* (Haarlem, 1937), pp. 145—180.

26 There is no connection between this ancient negative *en* or *ne* (which was finally ousted by *niet* though often used in combination with it) and the present-day coordinating conjunction *en*, which originally had the form *ende* ('*Karel ende Elegast*').

27 Cf. De Vooys, op. cit., p. 247, n. 105.

28 L. L. Hammerich, in Hammerich/Fabricius/Lorentsen, *Holland-Danmark* (København, 1945), II, p. 486.

29 E. Wrangel, *De betrekkingen tusschen Zweden en de Nederlanden op het gebied van letteren en wetenschap voornamelijk gedurende de zeventiende eeuw* (Leiden, 1901).

30 J. de Rooij, op. cit., p. 16.

31 Cf. J. Veering, *Onze Taal*, 36 (1967), quoted in G. Geerts, *Taal of taaltje?* (Leuven, 1972), p. 271.

32 The Bible of Ulfilas (see above, p. 3) had been available since 1665 in the edition of Franciscus Junius.

33 Vowel mutation in conjugation, declension or derivation, e.g. in Eng. **sIng, sAng, sUng**.

34 J. Shaw, *Essai sur les Pays-Bas autrichiennes* (London, 1788), p. 9.

35 In De Vooys, op. cit., p. 153.

36 Siegenbeek justified his preference for the *gch* spelling in this and similar cases, on the grounds that in the spelling *ka-chel*, syllable division would yield a long instead of short *a* sound. Cf. J. A. Meijers, *Het Nederlandse spellingdrama* (Amsterdam, 1967), p. 56.

37 De Vooys, op. cit., p. 157.

38 Ibid., p. 163.

39 The four *abele spelen* (*abel* < Fr. *habile*, in the sense of 'artistic') are the oldest known secular dramas in Dutch. Dating from the middle of the 14th century, they seem to have no equivalent in other countries.

40 'There was a time, in which Holland, respected for its policies, envied for its gold and celebrated for its learning, was able to weave an artistic rose-garland through this triple crown; in which it had an ear for music, in which it had a feeling for poetry, and delighted in the sweet blossoms of both; but won Europe's admiration with its school of painters, its original one, born with its own struggle for freedom, whose heroes the school depicted and immortalised; a monument erected by that generation to itself; — a monument, not all of whose masterpieces we were prepared to sell for foreign gold, however indifferently our 18th century may have preserved the legacy, which in eloquent silence pronounced sentence on the inheritors, to whatever intensity the pressure upon the ravaged nation may have risen at the beginning of the 19th century; — a monument, before whose brilliance it behoves us to bow our heads in shame, reflecting as it does all the gifts, all the energies, all the virtues of our ancestors like a mirror, until the moment when we, sensing what we once were, and what we have since become, gird ourselves up...'

41 G. Stuiveling, 'Het spel met de spelling', *De Gids* (1972), III, p. 175.

42 W. Pée, 'Het Algemeen Beschaafd in Vlaanderen'; in *Bijdragen en Meded. der dialectencommissie van de Koninklijke Nederlandse Akademie van Wetenschappen te Amsterdam*, 39 (1970), p. 15.

43 De Vooys, op. cit., p. 204.

44 W. Pée, op. cit., p. 19.

45 Ibid., pp. 22—23.

46 P. C. Paardekooper, *ABN en dialekt* ('s-Hertogenbosch, 1969[3]), p. 38.

47 W. Pée, op. cit., pp. 16—17. De Vreese's unequivocal statement had been made in a paper presented to the Flemish Academy in 1909 (*Verslagener Mededelingen van de Koninklijke Vlaanische Academie*, 1909, p. 47).

48 In De Vooys, op. cit., p. 215.

49 As the situation in Flanders will have to be dealt with in Chapter III, it will be mentioned only incidentally here.

50 M. C. van den Toorn, 'Het Nederlands na de tweede wereldoorlog', *Tijdschrift voor Nederlandse Taal- en Letterkunde*, xc (1974), 3/4, p. 273.

51 The name given to the huge concentration of population in the area bounded by Amsterdam, Utrecht, Rotterdam and The Hague.

52 On the historical development of the second-person pronouns and recent developments in their use, see M. C. van den Toorn, 'De problematiek van de Nederlandse aanspreekvormen', *Nieuwe Taalgids*, 70 (1977), 6, pp. 520–521.

53 For the meaning of this abbreviation, see above p. 5, n. 3.

54 Van den Toorn, op. cit., p. 275.

55 The Dutch do their best to preserve the original pronunciation of English words. Many older Flemings on the other hand pronounce, for example, *tram, plastic, nylon, service* and *recital* in the French manner. Nevertheless, there is a tendency in the younger generation to follow Dutch usage. It is characteristic also that *back* and *match* (sporting and consequently popular terms adopted before 1940) generally retain their French pronunciation, while *fan*, more recent and belonging to a different register, is more often pronounced as in English (cf. F. van Coetsem, 'De rijksgrens tussen Nederland en België', in G. Geerts, *Aspekten van het Nederlands in Vlaanderen* (Leuven, 1974), pp. 169 and 174 ff.). Ironically, such is the influence of English in the North, that even a borrowing from French like *occasion* (bargain) may sometimes be given an 'English' pronunciation.

56 Van den Toorn, op. cit., p. 282.

57 Ibid., pp. 287 ff.

58 See above, p. 40.

59 The ideal of the phonological school can be summed up in the formula 'one sign per phoneme, one phoneme per sign'. A phoneme is a unit of sound with a distinctive feature. So that *paal* is made up of three phonemes *p,aa* and *l*, since *Vaal, pOOl* and *paaR* also exist, each with their own meaning.

60 A remark made by Rudolf Geel in *De Gids* (1972), III, p. 210. This special issue of *De Gids* gives an excellent insight into the whole debate on spelling.

61 I. van der Velde, *De tragedie der werkwoordsvormen. Een taalhistorische en taaldidactische studie* (Groningen/Djakarta, 1956).

62 C. B. van Haeringen, 'Wankele normen', in *Taalkunde—'n Lewe, feestbundel voor W. Kempen* (Kaapstad/Johannesburg, 1974), p. 135.

63 W. Z. Shetter, *Introduction to Dutch* (The Hague, 1958), p. 15.

CHAPTER II

Elements of a Portrait

The following comments are hopefully weaned of romanticism and of any aspirations to collective psychology. No attempt will be made to define the 'genius of the language', so as to be able to draw conclusions about the national character or the 'soul of the country'. Preference has been given to more down-to-earth, less contentious observations.

Nor does this chapter purport to give sophisticated analyses or explanations perfect in every detail. It simply tries to illustrate, with precise examples, certain typical aspects and tendencies found in Dutch: not that these are always confined exclusively to Dutch, but they are at least particularly clearly defined or well-developed.

1. FLEXIBILITY AND SUBTLETY

At the end of the last chapter, the relative regularity of Dutch spelling was touched on. Indeed, while it is not always possible for a foreigner, or a Dutch-speaking child, to know the correct way of writing down a word they hear, they will at any rate very quickly learn the correct pronunciation of a word presented to them in black and white, which is something one could certainly not claim for either English or French. The simplicity of Dutch manifests itself in many other ways too. While there are in principle three genders, Dutch has only two definite articles (*de* and *het*) and a single indefinite article (*een*). Except in a number of set expressions, declension is limited to the ending *-e*. With the same qualifications, the subjunctive has disappeared, and there are a mere seven verbs (*zijn, hebben, komen* and four modal auxiliaries) whose present tense is not entirely regular.

This simplicity, however, goes hand in hand with a degree of imprecision, in that one and the same basic grammatical notion may be expressed by various forms or constructions. In some cases the choice is entirely free, in others it is governed by meaning, while in yet others it allows one to introduce nuances into expression. By virtue of this fact, Dutch is a very flexible and subtle language.

First morphology and then syntax will be examined in the light of this assertion.

A. Morphology

Let us look for a start at **personal pronouns**. In the third-person feminine singular, dative and accusative, it is permissible to replace *haar* by *ze*: *ik heb HAAR or ZE gezien* (I have seen her). The same applies to the plural (where the dative and accusative feminine form *haar* is now archaic): *ik heb HEN or ZE gezien* (I have seen them), *ik heb HUN or ZE een boek gegeven* (I have given them a book). The meaning is exactly the same; the most that one can say is that *ze* tends to be avoided when the stress falls on the pronoun.

This is also the principle underlying the difference between the following pairs:

	Nomin.	Dat./Acc.
first-person sing.		*mij/me*
second-person sing.	*jij/je*	*jou/je*
third-person sing.	*zij/ze*	
first-person pl.	*wij/we*	
third-person pl.	*zij/ze*	

The forms on the left (the pair *gij/ge* should be added for those who use that pronoun) are used to give emphasis. 'Have you come?' will be expressed as: *Ben JE gekomen*, whereas *Ben JIJ gekomen?* means 'Have **you** come?'. With the exception of *jij*, which is of its nature familiar, the left-hand forms are also obligatory in formal style: *WIJ, Boudewijn, Koning der Belgen...* (We, Baudouin, King of the Belgians), and frequent in administrative and business correspondence: *WIJ gaan akkoord met Uw brief van 3 mei* (We accept the terms of your letter of 3rd May).

The above table covers only the written language. There are, in addition, syncopated forms belonging to spoken usage. *Hem* (third-person masc. sing., dat./acc.) is commonly reduced to *'m*, and *haar* (the corresponding fem. form) to *d'r* or *'r*. On the other hand, it is possible to place a stress mark on any word, including pronouns. Hence the gradations: *ze, zij, zíj; 'm, hem, hém*, etc.

The third-person masc. sing. nominative, *hij/-ie*, is a rather special case. Here the distinction is above all one of position: *-ie* is in fact only used after the verb, or after subordinating conjunctions and interrogatives. Within these limits, the same distinction applies as above. *Waar sliep-IE?* (Where did he sleep?), *Als-IE er niet was...* (If he were not there), and *Begrijp je wat-IE bedoelt?* (Do you understand what he means?) are neutral, whereas *Waar sliep HIJ?*, *Als HIJ er niet was...*, and *Begijp je wat HIJ bedoelt?* highlight the pronoun. However, usage requires that the pronoun should always be written as *hij*. The efforts of Multatuli and other writers to introduce the form *-ie* into the written language were to no avail. In consequence, many people, especially when speaking into a microphone, are led to pronounce *hij* in cases where *-ie* would be more appropriate.

Verb forms also contain a number of duplications. *Jullie loopt* and *jullie lopen* are in principle interchangeable (though the former is felt increasingly to be either dialectal or antiquated), and the same goes for the two infinitives *zijn* and *wezen*, except that *wezen* cannot be used as a normal auxiliary and, conversely, *zijn* cannot be substituted for it in a construction like: *Ze is kolen wezen halen* (She has been to fetch coal).

The polite pronoun *U* can be used with either the second-person or third-person form: *U bent* or *U is, U hebt* or *U heeft*. Basing themselves on the origin of the pronoun (which is a contraction of *Uwe Edelheid*, 'Your Honour'), some believe that 'if one wishes to be very correct, one should use the third-person'.[1] However, this view, which would in any case only apply to *zijn* and *hebben*, is very controversial.

On the other hand, there is general agreement on the nuance implied in using *jij* or *U* with the second or third person respectively of modal auxiliaries. It is as permissible to say *jij kan* as *jij kunt*, or to say *U kan* instead of *U kunt*; the same is true of *wil/wilt, zal/zult* and *mag/moogt*, and in the preterite *wou/wilde* and *zou/zoudt*. But the first form in each case is more familiar, so that an increasing degree of formality can be expressed in:

KAN je ME helpen?
KUN je ME helpen?
KAN U ME helpen?
KUNT U MIJ helpen?
ZOU U MIJ Kunnen helpen?
ZOUDT U MIJ Kunnen helpen?

Inflection of adjectives never poses a problem when an adjective qualifying a neuter noun is used alone or with the indefinite article. In this case it is uninflected: *mooi weer, een klein huis*. There are no exceptions to this rule. In other cases the adjective in principle takes the ending *-e: de mooiE boom, het kleinE huis*. 'In principle', because although it is, for example, obligatory in the last two examples, this is by no means always the case — which brings us to one of the most fascinating and unusual aspects of Dutch grammar.

Sometimes there is no difference between an inflected and an uninflected form. One may prefer *zijn rustig optreden* (his calm action) to *zijn rustigE optreden*, or *het smartelijk verlies* (the painful loss) to *het smartelijkE verlies*, but the meaning remains the same.

Take on the other hand the case of an adjective preceded by the indefinite article qualifying a male subject. Why does one find: *hij is een NederlandsE makelaar* (he is a Dutch broker), but *ik heb een Nederlands makelaar gesproken* (I have spoken to a Dutch broker)? In the former case one is highlighting the nationality of the broker. If this example does not suffice, here is a clearer one: *Picasso is een Spaans schilder* (Picasso is a Spanish painter), but *Picasso is geen FransE, maar wel een SpaansE schilder*.

Often the absence of inflection may be explained by a close link between adjective and noun. *Een groot man* is a great man, *een grotE, sterke man* a big, strong man. The abstract expression *een groot man* forms, as it were, one unit. The same goes for *een vreedzaam mens* (a peaceful person). An admirer may exclaim: *Dat is een Frans edelman!* (That is a French nobleman!), whereas in making introductions one would say: *Hier is een FransE edelman*. In the second case the nobleman happens to be French, in the first he embodies all the qualities of French aristocracy. The link may be of a quite different nature when the adjective relates to an action expressed or suggested by the noun, and more or less fulfils the role of an adverb: *een geniaal schrijver* (a brilliant writer) (= iemand, die geniaal schrijft). By analogy, one will say *een bekwaam dokter* (a competent doctor), because the doctor in question is competent in the exercise of his duties,[2] but *een vriende-lijkE dokter* (a kind doctor), because in the second instance it is his qualities as a man and not as a practitioner which are being referred to. *Een oud-minister* (note the obligatory hyphen) is an ex-minister, *een oudE minister* an old one; *een jongE dichter* is a young poet, *een jong dichter* one making his debut. More subtle, but no less real, is the distinction between *een slim advokaat* (who argues astutely in court) and *een slimmE advokaat* (who is astute in all circumstances). As has been quite wittily remarked, *een goedE echtgenoot* is a reasonable match, but *een goed echtgenoot* is an ideal partner.[3]

What has been said above is also true to a certain extent of the masc. adjective preceded by a definite article. In *de rechtskundig adviseur* (legal advisor) the adjective is uninflected because the expression con-stitutes a single unit. Hence also the difference between *de cultureel attaché* (the cultural attaché) and *de bejaardE attaché* (the elderly attaché). The more usual a particular combination of adjective and noun, the greater the likelihood that the adjective will be uninflected. The same applies with neuter nouns: *het centraal station, het gemeen-telijk gymnasium* (municipal high-school). *Het koninklijk belsuit* is the royal decree, an official term, whereas *het koninklijkE besluit* would be the decision taken personally by the monarch. One finds *het dagelijks bestuur* (executive committee), but *het nieuwE dagelijks bestuur*. An insurer with only one office might speak of his *Haags kantoor*, while if he also had offices in Amsterdam and Utrecht he could differentiate by referring to his *HaagsE kantoor*.

The case of the feminine is more complicated, though here too there are some constants. A female social worker is *een maatschappelijk* (or *sociaal) werkster*. Conversely, over and against *het stedelijk(e) gymnasium* one has *de stedelijkE school*, the only possible form. Between these two extremes, however, is a large blurred area. Thirty years ago a well-known school grammar noted the 'occasional' use of *een goed pianiste* or *een vlot spreekster* (a fluent (female) speaker).[4] Today these forms are perfectly normal. The doyen of Dutch linguists, now in his nineties, accepts *een groot dichteres*, and, if pushed, *een groot actrice*, and while doubting whether anyone would dare write *een beroemd actrice* 'would not raise his eyebrows' at *een bekwaam gitariste*.[5] It is hard to know whether to attribute this development to the fact that the uninflected form is gaining ground generally, to the increasing fre-quency with which women perform the same professional tasks as men, or to a combination of factors.

The relationship between adjective and noun, as expressed by the presence or absence of inflection, has even more nuances than emerges from the examples quoted. The four expressions *een bekwaam dokter, een cultureel attaché, een maatschappelijk werkster* and *een beroemd schrijfster* are only apparently completely parallel. If we replace *een* by *de*, we shall be left with: *de bekwamE dokter, de cultureel attaché, de maatschappelijk werkster,* and *de beroemdE schrijfster*. In the plural we shall have: *bekwamE doktoren, culturelE attachés, beroemdE schrijfsters* and *maatschappelijk werksters*. This shows the closest unit to be *maatschappelijk werkster* (*werkster* used by itself meaning 'cleaning lady'!). Next comes *cultureel attaché*, less homogeneous, since there exist other kinds of attaché, financial, agricultural, etc., but more cohesive than *bekwaam dokter* and *beroemd schrijfster* because it is a title.

Two remarks in conclusion. The writer Jan Greshoff, no mean stylist, once wrote: *Hij ontmoet in een grote Spaanse stad een FransE handelsreiziger en een Spaans koopman die zich een hartelijk vriend van Frankrijk noemt* (In a large Spanish town he meets a French commercial-traveller and a Spanish businessman who calls himself a great lover of France).[6] Why is it that the Frenchman merits an *-e*, while his Spanish friend does not? Given that there is no basic difference in meaning,[7] it is in all probability a matter of euphony or rhythm. This is by no means an isolated case. The *e* is only rarely added to comparatives of three syllables (*een anderE, ruimerE, ietwat deftiger woning*, 'another, more spacious, somewhat smarter house'), and is virtually excluded for four or more syllables. So that a critic may write for the same reason: *Nijhoffs dunnE, maar adembenemend boekje* (Nijhoff's slim, but breathtaking little volume). This may also explain why a certain encyclopaedia, where one finds systematically *X, Duits wijsgeer* (German philosopher), *Y, Zweeds schrijfster, Z, Italiaans musicus,* on one occasion talks of: *N, ZuidnederlandsE schilder*. And how is one, unless it be for reasons of euphony, to account for the fact that *een orthodox predikant* (an orthodox minister) is possible, whereas **een orthodox dominee* (an orthodox clergyman) is not?

The second observation concerns (widely-used) expressions such as: *een flinkE eter, een hardE werker, een goedE speler*. Why is it that inflection is here not just permissible but compulsory, when the first expression obviously means 'someone who eats heartily', the second 'someone who works hard', etc.? This is a problem which has attracted hardly any attention from specialists.[8]

With a few exceptions, Dutch nouns form their **plural** either in *-[e]n* or in *-s*, and in the majority of cases the choice is clear-cut. The only conceivable plural for *moeder* is *moeders*, and for *soort, soortEN*. Some nouns, however, may have alternative plurals. Sometimes there is no difference in meaning (*hersenS/hersenEN*, 'brains', *aardappelS/aardappelEN*, 'potatoes'). In other cases the difference is obvious: four *stuks* are four copies, etc. of an item, as opposed to *de stukkEN*, the pieces (or documents). In still other cases usage shifts, which is what interests us here.

Let it be clear at the outset that it is impossible to give convenient rules for the choice between -s and -n, and we shall have to limit ourselves to observing certain tendencies.[9] What strikes one first and foremost is the advance of -s, especially for words ending in -e. This is understandable, as the final -n is often mute, so that its addition does not allow the ear to distinguish between singular and plural. An -s, therefore, brings clarity. *Groentes* (vegetables) and *leemtes* (gaps) have established themselves alongside the traditional forms *groenten* and *leemten*, though it is difficult to understand why other nouns, both concrete like *bediende* (servant, attendant), and abstract like *ziekte* (illness), *periode* or *gave* (gift) are more resistant (though that resistance is on the wane).[10] The phenomenon is, however, not limited to nouns ending in -e. In daily usage, *wapenS* is increasingly winning out over *wapenEN*, and *dokterS* over *doktorEN*. In Professor Pauwels' words: '-s is the living, democratic form, the form of the future.'[11]

At the same time, however, the very democratic nature of -s plurals is a hindrance to their diffusion. The -n ending is often unconsciously felt to have more *cachet*. In administrative texts one finds *provinciËN*, and in school geography books *provincieS*. One is likely to say *directeurEN*, but will always say *ingenieurS*, because the latter are subordinate to the former. *TralieS* is everyday, *traliËN* poetic. *Eigenaar* usually takes an -s, but property-owners form themselves into a *Bond van EigenarEn*. The form *leraars* has a long and respectable pedigree; nevertheless, no secondary school teacher in the Netherlands will accept any other plural but *lerarEN*. Though the 19th-century politician Groen van Prinsterer regularly used the form *beginselS*, this has given way entirely to the 'nobler'-sounding *beginselEN*.

This difference in affective value between the two endings, though it is now assuming growing importance, is not a recent development. To demonstrate this, it suffices to juxtapose *letterS* (of the alphabet) and *letterEN* (literature), *vaderS* (in the usual sense) and *vaderEN* (ancestors), or *tekenS* (concrete signs) and *tekenEN* (signs of the times). The first series is more literal, more physical and more down-to-earth than the second.

The distinction between *letterS* and *letterEN*, etc., exists throughout the whole language-area. But for the rest the nuances mentioned above 'may be used no doubt by those Flemings who wish to speak and write cultivated Dutch, that is inspired by a Northern norm, but they remain a little artificial because they are entirely without supraregional support'. The same goes for the form *lerarEN*, which 'is sometimes used in writing or speech: it seems forced, maybe a little pretentious, but it will not occur to a Fleming to see it as a symbol of social status' (J. L. Pauwels).[12] In fact, as far as Pauwels is concerned, all words ending in -aar take their plural in -s, with the exception of *ambtenaar* (official), *dienaar* (servant) and *exemplaar* (copy). He does not even entirely reject *ambtenaarS* and *dienaarS*.[13] If *beginselEN* has finally won the day in Flanders too, it is because the word does not belong to everyday language. A counter-example is provided by *artikel*. Anyone wanting to write 'correct Dutch' will swear by *artikelEN*, even in

Flanders. This is the form found in all the authorities, but if one opens a trade paper in Leuven or Gent, one will find nothing but *artikelS*. Certainly the Fleming will always use *hooglerarEN*, a learned word, but in conversation he prefers *professorS* (by analogy with words in *-er*) at the risk of startling his Dutch interlocutor.

We shall return to such more or less marked divergencies between North and South and the reasons for them in Chapter III.

B. Syntax

For the record, a few Gallicisms may be mentioned in passing, which, by avoiding the use of a relative or qualifier allow greater concision. *De ervaringen, bij vorige gelegenheden opgedaan* (The experiences gained on previous occasions) is a neat alternative to *de ervaringen, die...opgedaan waren* or *de...opgedane ervaringen*. The examples are legion: *dit was maar een naam, haar in scherts gegeven* (it was a name given to her in jest); *de stille binnenpret, landmensen vaak eigen* (the quiet inward pleasure, so often found in country people), etc. They belong almost without exception to the written language.

Let us briefly point to a phenomenon which is very striking at first glance, but is without much practical importance. In compound verb forms in a subordinate clause the auxiliary may be placed either before or after the past participle or infinitive. One can say: *dat moet vorig jaar gebeurd zijn* (that must have happened last year), or...*zijn gebeurd, ik weet niet of ik hem ooit terugzien zal* (I don't know if I will ever see him again), or...*zal terugzien*. Back in the 17th century Vondel considered the two forms equally correct and present-day grammars are unanimously in agreement with him.[14] But is one of the two constructions more common, or better usage? What one can say for certain is that, despite a very widespread opinion among the public, putting the auxiliary in final position is in no way a Germanism. The whole question has been admirably illuminated in A. Pauwels's study *De plaats van hulpwerkwoord, verleden deelwoord en infinitief in de Nederlandse bijzin* (Leuven, 1953).[15] What emerges is that as far as the spoken language is concerned, the choice between the two constructions is a matter of region. On the other hand, in written style there is no perceptible link between regional habits and the usage of authors (even those with strong local allegiances like Claes, Timmermans or Coolen). Moreover, in individual authors, usage is far from consistent, so that one fails to see why in a particular case the author has preferred the 'green' construction (auxiliary in second position) and in another the 'red' (auxiliary in first position).[16] What one in fact finds, then, is completely free variation.

Of the three great underlying principles of Dutch sentence construction, the first, relating to the position of the verb in the main clause, need not concern us here. The other two requirements are, (1) that the past participle and the infinitive be preceded by their complements, and (2) that in subordination the verb takes last position. The application of these rules is, however (fortunately, one might feel, from the point of view of stylistic variation), far from being mechanical. Only the position of the direct object (or, in the case of intransitive verbs, the complement) is fixed. For the rest, 'it is not going too far to say that word-order is just as much determined by the **context** and by the **type of information** conveyed by the words in question'.[17]

Sometimes, it is true, the difference in construction does not presuppose any special intention. *Ik heb een pakket gestuurd aan mijn zuster* (I have sent a package to my sister) is entirely equivalent to . . . *aan mijn zuster gestuurd*, as is *ze heeft moeten afzien van het leraarsambt* (she has had to give up teaching) to . . . *van het leraarsambt moeten afzien*. And it would be a clever man indeed who could make a clear distinction between *een boer die onder een boom viool speelde* (a farmer who was playing the violin under a tree) and . . . *die een viool speelde onder een boom.*

Mostly, the departure from the rules is perfectly easily explainable. There may be reasons of form or content. Dutch likes to keep antecedent and relative clause as close together as possible. One naturally says: *Heb je nog altijd niet op de brief van je oom geantwoord?* (Have you still not replied to your uncle's letter?), but *Heb je nog altijd niet geantwoord op de brief die je toen van je oom had ontvangen?* (. . . to that letter that you received from your uncle?) flows better than . . . *nog altijd niet op de brief geantwoord die . . . .*[18] In other cases rhythm is decisive. If to the sentence *Hun blik verraadt dat ze aan hun geboorteland denken* (The look in their eyes shows that they are thinking of their native land) we add a qualifying adverbial phrase, it will (preferably) become: . . . *dat ze met weemoed denken aan hun geboorteland* (. . . that they are thinking wistfully of their native land). Alongside *Een vent die ons met zijn impertinente vragen verveelde* (A chap who pestered us with his impertinent questions), one has (again preferably) *een vent die ons steeds weer verveelde met zijn impertinente vragen.* For the same reason, namely that one should not be kept waiting too long for the verb, particularly if it is a simple one and the complements are in danger of piling up, one will have *De commissie heeft het niet gemakkelijk gehad, omdat ze STOND voor een warwinkel van verklaringen, echte en valse* (The Committee did not have an easy task, because it was faced with a tangle of statements, true and false). One might also have: . . . *omdat ze voor een warwinkel STOND van verklaringen*, etc., but the putting of *stond* in final position would be difficult to accept.

Take for example Van Schendel's sentence: *Tamal ervoer dezelfde onverschilligheid weder, die hij gevoeld had, toen hij in het blok had gelegen verleden zomer* (Tamal felt the same indifference he had felt when he had been in the stocks last summer). Why not: . . . *toen hij verleden zomer in het blok had gelegen?* Probably because of a concern with formal balance, but maybe also to some extent because of stress. Writers and speakers do, in fact, often detach an element of the sentence in this way in order to highlight it. *Geweerschoten kondigden het naderen van de jagers aan* (Rifle shots heralded the approach of the hunters) is neutral, but if one says... *kondigden het naderen aan van de jagers*, one tends (especially if I support it with stress and intonation) to focus special attention on the hunters. *Ik heb hem gezien en ook gesproken* means 'I saw him and also spoke to him', while... *en gesproken ook* adds a suggestion of insistence, indicating malice, exasperation, etc., on the fact that I addressed the person in question. *Hij zegt dat hij binnenkort naar Amerika vertrekt* (He says that he is leaving for America shortly) calls attention to the departure,... *dat hij binnenkort vertrekt naar Amerika* to the fact that America is his destination. *Ze spieden of er niemand uit de rij valt dit keer* (They peep to see if anyone will get out of line this time) implies that on previous occasions in the same circumstances there was something of a scene. The impatience of the lonely lover could scarcely be better expressed than by Multatuli's construction, so odd as to be considered ungrammatical: *ze had moeten daar zijn*.[19]

There are limits to this flexibility, but they may be very difficult to define. Why does one rarely hear: *Ik heb gezeten in de tuin* (I sat in the garden), whereas *Ik heb geluierd in de tuin* (I lazed in the garden) is perfectly natural? The reason is that in the former case the link between verb and predicate is much closer. Let us consider a one-word adverbial like *thuis*, like *in de tuin*, an adverbial of place, which behaves like a verb prefix. One would never say: *Ik heb gezeten thuis*. The form *Ik heb gezeten in de tuin* will only be admissible if one wants to define precisely the attitude I was in in the garden (i.e. sitting, and not lying or standing). The second construction on the other hand, may be paraphrased as *Ik heb geluierd toen ik in de tuin was* (I lazed when I was in the garden).[20] Following the same line of thought, it would be a little unnatural to say: *Ik hoop dat ik morgen met mijn broer mag rijden naar Antwerpen* (I hope that I can drive to Antwerp with my brother tomorrow), but it is sufficient to replace *rijden* by *meerijden* (get a lift) for the objective to lapse: the link between verb and predicate has been broken, with the former having been in a sense 'liberated' by the prefix.[21]

One may draw a lesson and a practical conclusion from all this. The lesson is that once again in a general sense 'when it comes to syntax, variants are not simply the product of imagination, and have a stylistic, affective and even semantic value'.[22] The conclusion is borrowed from a specialist in the comparative stylistics of French and Dutch who is in addition a teacher of English. Thanks to the flexibility of Dutch syntax, he says, 'the translation of German, English or French texts into Dutch may be done more or less literally, and when completed these versions will exhibit precise differences of structure depending on the source-language, while remaining perfectly correct grammatically, at least as far as the written language is concerned. This, to my knowledge, is a degree of adaptability not found in any other Germanic language at this time'.[23]

2. A LITTLE PHONETICS

Three things will be concentrated on: assimilation, word-stress, and the development of intervocalic *d*. The last topic could just as well have been raised in the preceding section, as it contains that margin of uncertainly which allows the use of subtle nuances.

Assimilation is a change brought about in the articulation of a speech-sound by neighbouring sounds which impart to it some of their articulatory characteristics. This phenomenon is found in many languages: Latin *an(i)ma* has become French *âme* through assimilation of *n* to *m* in Vulgar Latin. But in Dutch, assimilation occupies such a prominent place that it may be regarded as one of the essential features of the language.

It affects consonants above all. These are divided, as we know, into voiced and unvoiced, according to whether there is or is not vibration of the vocal chords. The unvoiced consonants of Dutch are: *f*, *s*, *ch* (hard guttural, cf. Eng. 'loch'), *p*, *t* and *k*, and their unvoiced equivalents *v*, *z*, *g* (velar, as in *gij*, cf. Eng. Hugh), *b*, *d* and *g* (as in Eng. *good*). The rules of assimilation may be summarised as follows:

1) When a voiced fricative follows an unvoiced consonant, it becomes unvoiced: the *z* of *opzij* becomes an *s*, the *v* of *uitvaren* becomes an *f*, the *g* of *geven* is (often) a velar sound, that of *afgeven* a hard guttural.

2) Before *b*, *d* and *w* an unvoiced consonant becomes voiced. In *hefboom* one hears a *v* instead of an *f*, in *pakdrager* an English *g* instead of a *k*, and in *huiswerk* a *z* instead of an *s*.

3) Nasals adapt to the articulatory base of the following consonant, so that *n* tends to be pronounced as *m* in *inmaken* and in *onbepaald*.

4) Before *m*, *n*, *l* and *r*, or before a vowel, unvoiced fricatives become voiced. In *lees maar* (at least for many speakers) and *lees eens* one hears a *z* at the end of *lees*, and in *half en half* the first *f* becomes a *v*.

It will be noticed that in rule 1 assimilation works, as it were, both forwards and backwards.

In all the cases quoted so far the assimilation is partial: one of the two sounds is modified, but not suppressed entirely. It is, however, possible for assimilation to be total. When two identical consonants are juxtaposed, only one sound is heard: the ear detects only one *d* in *hoofddoek*. The same happens when two adjacent consonants have the same articulatory base: in *vriendschap* and *zandpad* the *d* tends to disappear, as does the *t* in *nichtje*. In a few rare instances the assimilation is rendered in the spelling. *Pollepel*, for example, has replaced the original *potlepel* and *lommer* successfully disguises its French origin, *l'ombre*.

As has already been seen from the examples given under 4) above, assimilation operates not only within a word, but also between words. This is called external assimilation. Further examples are: *ik zie*, where one hears *s* rather than *z*, in *het bed* with *d* instead of *t* in *het*, and *is dat waar?*, where *s* becomes *z*.[24] It is virtually impossible to use the

smallest phrase without external assimilation playing a part, and this
has far-reaching consequences. The importance of assimilation is comparable, though on an entirely different scale, to that of *liaison* in
French. The fact that a word reacts phonetically to the words preceding
and following it, gives the language a fluency which strikes the
foreigner, though Dutch-speakers are scarcely aware of it:

> 'Assimilation in spoken language results naturally from successive ar-
> ticulatory positions, but this variability does not endanger word-
> recognition. We recognise words as we recognise our friends, even if
> they are dressed differently. And by changing our tie or waistcoat we do
> not really change. This is the reason why some people, in all innocence,
> refuse to admit that they assimilate; they believe that they do what they
> think they are doing; they quite simple refuse to believe that in
> *onbekwaam* they pronounce the letter *n* as *m*, that in *vaststaan* they
> pronounce only one *s* and one *t*, and in *postzegel* only a lengthened *s*,
> that the first *k* in *zakdoek* is not a *k*-sound at all but a hard *g* (like in
> French *garçon*), a frequently occurring sound in Dutch, though not
> represented by a character of its own.'[25]

As in all Germanic languages (and in many others) **word-stress** is of
crucial importance in Dutch, but in certain cases obeys rules which do
not, or scarcely, apply elsewhere.

In compound nouns, it is the first constituent which in principle
carries the stress. Nevertheless, one says: *hogeschóol, plattelánd,
boerenzóon* and *burgermán*.[26] These are only apparent exceptions, as the
first element in these cases functions as an adjective. This is clear in
hogeschool and *platteland*, and one senses that *boeren* does not have the
same sense in *boerenzoon* (young man of peasant origin) as in
boerenoorlog (war waged by peasants), nor *burger* in *burgerman*
(member of the bourgeoisie) and *burgerplicht* (civic duty). But what
about *stadhúis* and its associated *burgeméester*? Why does one find
vléesetend alongside *onrustbárend* and *nietszéggend*? One may find an
explanation for each individual case, but it is not the intention to
dwell on individual cases here.[27]

It is more important to observe those displacements of stress, which
occur regularly, either purely mechanically, or to mark differences
in meaning, or again because required by the rhythm of the sentence.

Adjectives formed by the addition of one of the suffixes *-ig, -(e)lijk,
-isch, -baar*, and *-zaam*, are stressed on the syllable preceding the suffix
(unless of course it includes an unstressed *e*). The accent jumps from
áandacht to *aandáchtig*, from *vriendschap* to *vriendscháppelijk*, from
áfgod to *afgódisch*, from *ómkopen* to *omkóopbaar*, and from *árbeid* to
arbéidzaam. The suffixes *-isch, -baar* and *-zaam* may not be very productive, but words ending in *-ig* and *-(e)lijk* are numbered in thou-
sands. Apart from *kóninklijk*, there are no exceptions to the rule.

The difference in meaning between *úitstekend* applied to a pro-
truding rock and the same word describing a piece of work (*uitstékend*),

is obvious. That between *een dóorlopende voorstelling* (a continuous performance) and *ze is doorlópend ziek* (she is continually ill) may be harder to grasp, as may that between *de áanhoudende regen* (the continuous rain) and *de aanhóudende druk van de opinie* (the continuous pressure of public opinion), but it becomes transparent again when juxtaposed *een íngewikkelde mummie* (a wrapped mummy) and *een ingewíkkelde zaak* (a complicated matter). What then is the deciding factor? One might quite simply explain this by saying that when the accent falls on the separable prefix, the participle is felt to be a true verb form, whereas in the other case it becomes an adjective. In reality, the phenomenon extends much further. It is found where there is no adjective present. Alongside *óverleggen* (hand over (document), save (money)) and *óverwegen* (re-weigh), one finds *overléggen* and *overwégen* both of which mean, with slightly different nuances, 'consider'. Conversely, there is the adjective *krampachtig*, which though it contains no participle element, may be stressed in two different ways: *de stervende maakte krámpachtige bewegingen* (the dying person made convulsive movements), as opposed to *de verdachte deed krampáchtige pogingen om zijn positie te redden* (the accused made desperate efforts to save his position). It appears, therefore, that the distinction is not a grammatical one. The stress falls on one syllable or another according to whether the word has a concrete or an abstract sense, or is interpreted literally or figuratively.

In his now classic manual of pronunciation, Blancquaert discusses the case of compound adjectives whose first element gives the compound the value of a superlative. If such an adjective is used attributively, it does not carry the main accent: *het is pikdónker vanavond* (it is pitch dark this evening); *ik was nog piepjóng toen dat gebeurde* (I was only tiny when that happened); *die man is stokóud* (that man is ancient). The opposite applies if they are used before the noun: *het was een píkdonkere nacht; ik was nog een píepjong ventje; hij was toen al een stókoude man.* 'The same distinction is sometimes made with other adjectives: *haar japon was lichtgéel* (her dress was light yellow), but *zij droeg een líchtgele japon.*'[28]

The examples quoted by Blancquaert are suggestive, but his interpretation is open to question. Does it enable us to distinguish between *áanstaande zondag* (next Sunday) and *zondag aanstáande, hélemaal niet* (not at all) and *niet helemáal*, or *júffrouw Maartens* and *dag, juffróuw*? It would appear rather that if the epithet takes the stress on the first element and the attribute on the second, it is not properly speaking because of their grammatical function, but because of their position in the sentence, with the attribute of necessity placed after the verb and the epithet before the noun. In other words, it is entirely a matter of rhythm and sentence-balance. Here are three more examples:

een ónplezierige dág	'an unpleasant day'
die dág is onplezíerig	'that day is unpleasant'

het álgemeen beláng   'the general interest'
deze méning is algeméen   'this opinion is general'

hij is víjf en tachtig jaar óud 'he is 85 years old'
hij is júist vijf en táchtig   'he has just turned 85'

These are cited by W. Pée, who concludes: 'Wherever the clash of two elements of a similar nature are in danger of disturbing the rhythmic flow, our sense of rhythm, through a subconscious shift, subordinates one of the elements to the other.'[29]

The fate of **intervocalic** *d* in Dutch has given rise and continues to give rise to a great deal of controversy. Leaving the phoneticians to determine the exact nature of the phenomenon, we shall content ourselves with showing its extent and its semantic and affective implications.

In some cases *d* disappears, taking with it the following neutral *e*. Sometimes this *e* is word-terminal: *lade > la* (drawer), *vrede > vree* (peace), *salade > sla* (salad), and sometimes it is followed by a consonant: *weder > weer* (weather, again), *bladeren > blaren* (leaves). Both cases are combined in the name *Brederode*, which becomes *Breero*. Elsewhere the *d* becomes an *i/(j)*, or, after the diphtong *ou*, a bilabial *w: rode > rooie* (red), *kwade > kwaaie* (angry, evil), *oude > ouwe* (old).

The *d* is retained either in archaic set-phrases like *iets ten kwade duiden* (give something an unfavourable interpretation), or when it fulfils a grammatical function, particularly in weak preterites. Nevertheless it has disappeared in *zei* and *zou*, and one finds *wou* alongside *wilde*.[30]

In many cases, the original form and the form without *d* exist side by side, which is the most interesting thing.

It may be that there is a perfectly clear distinction of meaning. There is no way of interchanging *ijl* (rarefied) and *ijdel* (vain), *boel* (lot) and *boedel* (belongings), of confusing *vergaren* (gather (dust)) and *vergaderen* (have a meeting), *teer* (delicate) and *teder* (tender), or even *preken* (preach, fig.) and *prediken* (preach, lit.). But far more often the two forms are separated by only a nuance. The general principle is that the syncope of *d* or its replacement by *i/(j)* or *w* are increasingly frequent as the language becomes more spontaneous. The same speaker will say *goeie vriende* (good friends) in private, and *goede vrienden* in a speech. One almost always hears *een rooie doek* (a red cloth) and *rooie Willem* (red-haired Willem), but always *het Rode Kruis* (the Red Cross): there is a difference of register. *Een dode mus* (a dead sparrow) is slightly odd (one would expect *dooie*), and *dooienherdenking* (commemoration of the war dead) (instead of *doden*) is quite unacceptable. In conversation, *verkouden* (having a cold), instead of *verkouwe* would be likely to raise a smile, but *ophouden* (stop doing something) is already more acceptable, and *onophoudelijk* (constantly) is the only possible form: the first usage is in fact familiar, the second fairly colloquial (though less so than *uitschei[d]en*), the third quite 'literary'. For the same reason, *verraje* (= *verraden*) and *verrajer* (in the sense of 'informer') are quite common in popular speech, whereas *verraderlijk*, an abstract word, never becomes *verrajerlijk*.

Of course, it is not always easy to make distinctions according to stylistic levels. *Geleje, snije* and *rije* are used in everyday speech instead of *geleden* (ago), *snijden* (to cut) and *rijden* (to ride), even by upper-class speakers. On the other hand, *laaien* (= *laden* 'to load'), *bloeien* (= *bloeden* 'to bleed'), *bieje* (= *bieden* 'to offer') are felt to be vulgar. *Beneje* (= *beneden* 'below') and *tevreje* (= *tevreden* 'pleased') are on the borderline of acceptability, while *hoeie* for *hoeden* (hats) would fall below it, though it is difficult to give hard and fast rules.

The same principle enables us to understand why the *d* does not disappear in such words as *gade* (spouse), *nederig* (humble) and *redenen* (pl. of *reden* 'reasons'): these words are not part of conversation style. *Vaar* and *moer* exist, but, since their use may appear disrespectful, have not crossed the boundary of dialect, except in a few set expressions; cultivated Dutch uses exclusively *vader* and *moeder*.

The written language is strangely opposed to the extension of forms without *d*. This can quite easily accommodate syncopated forms: *meelij* vies with *medelijden* (sympathy), *moe* is displacing *moede* (tired) (at least in attributive use), *voederen* is being ousted by *voeren* (to feed) and *klederen* by *kleren* (clothes), while *breien* (knit) and *gedwee* (meek) have triumphed once and for all. On the other hand, it resists the substitution of *i/(j)* or *w* for *d*. *Geleje* is never found in black and white, and the *de goeie ouwe tijd* (the good old days) looks rather strange on paper. This results in the natural evolution of the language being hampered and distortions multiply. Excluded from the written language, certain perfectly legitimate forms are relegated to a level of familiarity, which in a certain atmosphere and in a certain context, may descend to the sloppy and coarse. In this way stylistic differences are introduced to which any Dutch-speaker who knows his language is extremely sensitive.[31]

3. FONDNESS FOR THE DIMINUTIVE

With the possible exception of Italian and Portuguese, no European language is as fond as Dutch of the diminutive. A foreigner's reaction is often that of Wilhelm Busch, who considered 'droll, these -*je*'s which dangle from the ends of words like the shirt-tails of an urchin'.[32]

Droll or not, both the formation and use of diminutives need studying.

'There is so much and so many diverse things to say on the form of the diminutives, that we cannot hope to deal exhaustively with them here.' This prudent prefatory warning of Kruisinga's[33] will be adopted here too.

The basic suffix is -*tje: strootje, natietje, staaltje.*[34] Depending on the final consonant of the root word and the preceding vowel, one may have not -*tje* but either -*etje* (*kannetje, bolletje, zonnetje* as opposed to *zoontje*), *-pje* (*bloempje, Duimpje*), *-kje* (*woninkje, koninkje*, with *k* replacing *g*), or simply *-je*, as in *lapje, oogje*, etc.[35] Sometimes there is vowel mutation: *glas > glaasje, vat > vaatje, schip > scheepje* — in general, the same applies to the plural of these words (the *a* of *glas* is short, that of *glazen* long). There are also double forms: *poppetje* or *popje, weggetje* or *wegje, kindjes* or *kindertjes*. In some cases the double form corresponds to a difference in meaning: *bloempje* is a small flower, *bloemetje*, a bouquet.

Apart from words ending in *-te* (*behoefte* = 'need', *anekdote* = 'ancedote'), which for reasons of euphony tend to resist diminution, one may say that all Dutch nouns may be put in the diminutive, even collective nouns (*vergaderinkje* = small meeting) or abstracts (*aardigheidje* = joke, nice gesture, *gevalletje*, as in *een metalen gevalletje* = 'a little metal affair, device'). Some diminutives are obtained by particularly radical contraction: *grootje < grootmoedertje* (grandmother), *strijkje < strijkorkestje* (string orchestra), *bedankje < bedankbriefje* (letter of thanks). Moreover, there are some 'false' diminutives, for which one will look in vain for a root word: *dubbeltje* (10 cent coin), *kwartje* (25 cent coin), *tientje* (10 guilder note).[36]

This last observation leads us on to note that many diminutives are not formed from nouns. The root word may be an adjective: *een blauwtje lopen* (be jilted), *zuurtje* (acid drop), *koeltje* (a cool breeze); depending on context, *'n bruintje* may mean (most commonly) a bay horse, a kind of loaf, a brunette or a beer. It may be a numeral: *in z'n eentje* (on one's own), *'n zesje* (in the language of schoolchildren, a mark of six) or it may even be a separable prefix: *toetje* (dessert), *uitje* (excursion). Strangest of all are the diminutives formed from adverbs and attributive adjectives. These are marked by the addition of *-s*: *stilletjes* (quietly), *netjes* (nicely), *ik ga (het) kalmpjes aan doen* (I am going to take it easy), *ik vond zijn lezing maar magertjes* (I thought his lecture was a bit thin).

On some little 18-century prints (*prentjes*) described by the writer Albert Verwey, we see little figures (*mannetjes*) busy fishing: 'Achter hen staan de bomen van het grindpad, stil in een helder *zonnetje*, en in de verte prijkt een *dorpstorentje* boven het hout uit...Ter linkerzijde is een vergezicht van weilanden, gestoffeerd met *koetjes* en *schaapjes*.'[37] The intention is plain: by piling up diminutives in this way, Verwey is trying to convey the mannered and conventional nature of Rococo art. But there is no need of such pronounced examples to make us aware that diminutives do not always refer to the **dimensions** of the person or object in question. Having been offered a broken-down table by a secondhand-furniture salesman, the customer will retort: '*Zo'n tafeltje? Wat heb ik eraan?*' (A table like that? What good is it to me?) Conversely, *ons tafeltje*, in the right context, might have sentimental and nostalgic overtones.

The diminutive may serve to excuse or soften: *Het duurt maar 'n jaartje* (It will only be a year). It may express modesty: *Het is maar een klein cadeautje* (It is only a small gift). Or friendliness: *Een kopje koffie?* enquires the lady of the house with a charming smile. Or sympathy: Gezelle's *Boerke Naas* wins over the reader with his cunning and his decisiveness. In other cases, the diminutive may express endearment: *'t is 'n schatje* (He/she is a poppet), or on the contrary, contempt: *'t is maar 'n leraartje* (He is just a schoolmaster). Despite this last example, one may say that the diminutive generally contains a positive, favourable element: *meevallertje* (stroke of luck) is normal, *tegenvallertje* (from *tegenvaller* = 'setback') virtually impossible. Let us leave this enumeration of the various shades of meaning which may be contained in the diminutive, but not before quoting the famous motto of Thomas à Kempis: *Met een boekske in een hoekske* (with a good book in a quiet nook), which conveys all that appetite for study and need for contemplation so characteristic of the *Devotio moderna* (cf. p. 11).

Nevertheless, Wilhelm Busch, and many others before and after him, would have less cause for complaint if Dutch-speakers did not make glaring overuse of diminutives. The case of *spoorboekje* may be excusable: compared with railway timetables elsewhere, the Dutch version takes up little space. But how can one justify *spoorkaartje* (rail ticket), *retourtje* (return ticket), etc.? These objects are neither particularly big nor particularly small and the diminutives quite clearly do not have the slightest affective value. German does not talk of *Fahrkärtchen*, or even Italian of *bigliettino*.

It seems that diminutives are more popular with women than with men. At least, so the latter are convinced. 'When in the course of our reading we come across the expression *'n snoezig lampje* (a gorgeous lamp), we may be sure that the judgement is that of a woman, both because of the use of the word *snoezig* and because of the diminutive.' Kruisinga, to whom we owe this observation, adds that the abundance of diminutives in cooking recipes published in the weekly press 'is often proof that the writer delights in his job, quite apart from the fee involved'.[38] It is also to women's names that diminutives are most easily applied. *Arendje* and *Geertje* can only denote either children (of either sex) or women. In the same way *de Bakkertjes* are either the (small) Bakker children, or the young daughters of the Bakker family.[39]

Do diminutives enjoy the same popularity in Flanders as in the Netherlands? In the absence of systematic studies of the question, one is reduced to impressions. Much indicates that they do not. If this is the case, it may be connected with the fact that, however cordial Flemings may be in their own way, *gezelligheid* (cosiness) is a specifically Dutch phenomenon.

In conclusion it should be pointed out that according to recent surveys diminutives are somewhat on the retreat, even in the Netherlands themselves. *Baantje*, which used to be the normal word for profession or career, has taken on, since about 1960, either a slightly pejorative or restrictive tinge, meaning in the first case a dead-end (poorly paid) job or in the second a part-time or vacation job. It may even happen that a 'false diminutive' loses its suffix and a new word comes into being. A normal-sized snapshot is no longer *'n kiekje* but *'n kiek*. If one says *klusje* instead of *klus*, this is because it really is a **small** chore that is meant. *Flikje* (a kind of chocolate drop) has become a children's word, on the same level as *jasje* and *bedje*: grown-ups prefer *flik*.[40] If this tendency does establish itself, it will give future students of Dutch food for thought.

4. THE ISSUE OF THE FEMININE

Before considering this point, which has caused so much ink to flow in the past, we shall say something about another aspect of the gender problem: **incongruence**, or lack of agreement. This means the use of a masculine or feminine pronoun to refer to a neuter noun and vice versa. Incongruence may be explained in some cases by an appeal to logic, in others by psychological factors.

'Logic' in this case means the predominance of nature over grammar, and of sex over gender.[41] *Het hoofd* means not only 'head' but 'headmaster' or 'headmistress'. Using it in the latter sense, one will say: *Waar is het hoofd? HIJ/ZIJ komt zo terug* (Where is the head? He/she will be back in a moment). *Meisje* is also neuter, but nevertheless one says: *Ieder meisje moet zelf zorgen voor HAAR kleren* (Every girl is responsible for her own clothes).

'Logical' agreement exists in other languages, for example, both in English ('What a blue stocking! I can't stand *her*') and in German (*'Das Fräulein kommt mit ihrem Bruder'*). Nor is 'psychological' incongruence in principle unique to Dutch. Neither a German nor a Frenchman would be surprised at the pejorative implications of the neuter pronoun applied to either a man or a woman, in: *DAT praat maar van uitgaan, of 't niets is* (Listen to him/her talking about going out, as though it were the simplest thing in the world). But the special characteristic of Dutch resides in the reverse process: the substitution for psychological reasons of masculine for neuter, when one is referring to a clearly-defined individual object. A bookseller will say to a customer about a particular book *(HET boek): Ik geloof wel dat ik HEM heb* (I think I've got it); *misschien light-IE in de etalage* (Perhaps it's in the window). There is also a tendency to use the masculine for an inanimate object of neuter gender: *Het is met dit horloge zo gek; als ik HEM neerleg, staat-IE stil* (The odd thing about this watch is that whenever I put it down, it stops). It has also been observed that the masculine pronoun, used for an animal of neuter gender, can be an indicator of the interest one has in the animal: *Wat heb je daar een mooi paard! Hoe oud is-IE?* — *HIJ is zes jaar.* (What a beautiful horse. How old is he? — He is six). But: *Heb je dat bruine paard niet meer?* — *Neen, ik heb HET verkocht* (Haven't you got that bay any more? — No, I've sold it).[42]

Though sometimes difficult to detect and even more so to analyse,

these subtle distinctions are nonetheless a perfectly legitimate use of
the language. The same cannot be said of a particularly arbitrary use of
the feminine pronoun, which Father Royen once christened with the
picturesque name of '"haar"-cultuur'.[43] Witness the following strange
sentences: *Het rythme dwong de klanken in HAAR sterke greep* (The
rhythm forced the sounds into its (lit. her) strong pulse). *Het schip is uit
HAAR koers geraakt* (The ship has gone off (her) course). *Het verdrag,
door Japan gesloten, zal HAAR sterk maken* (The treaty concluded by
Japan will make her strong). Oddly enough, the latter two examples do
not necessarily shock an English-speaking reader or listener, sug-
gesting as they do the frequent personification in English of both
ships and countries, but there is universal agreement that they are
anomalies in Dutch. They may be found less frequently nowadays
(opinions on this are divided), but their very possibility is symptomatic. There is another side to every coin: flexibility can lead to
carelessness with those who have neither the inclination nor the time
to cultivate a careful style.

*   *   *   *   *

This brings us to the main problem.

Agreement and lack of agreement have never led to very heated
arguments. Equally, the distinction between neuter and non-neuter is
more or less self-evident for everyone. But as soon as the discussion
turns to 'masculine' and 'feminine', there is only a general consensus
on a limited number of words. If an attempt is made to find a criterion
for the rest, the debate becomes rancorous and each side entrenches
itself. At least such was the position twenty years or so ago.

The boundary between the two 'camps' is formed by the Rhine and
the Meuse. In general terms, the opposition boils down to the fact that
'north of the great rivers' there is scarcely any question of anything
but two categories, namely neuter and masculine, whereas 'south of
the line' the three genders are still very much alive and kicking. At
almost every turn the Northerner seems to say *hij* when the Southerner
says *ze*.

This state of affairs has not come about overnight.[44] Confusion of
gender begins in Middle Dutch, and in his *Twe-spraak*, published in
Leiden in 1584, Spiegel noted, with regret, the parallelism in the
declension of the article in the masculine and in the feminine. In the
Statenbijbel of fifty years later, it is common for one and the same noun
to be used first in the masculine and then in the feminine or vice
versa, within the space of a few pages. A 17th-century navigator writes
perfectly naturally: *(Wij) settede de tonne op ZIJN bodem, en dronckenSE
eerst leech* (We stood the barrel on its (lit. his) end, and first drank it
(lit. her) dry). The grammarians did try to establish rules, but these
were 'either so summary that they offered little help to the reader, or
so theoretical that they were impossible to observe in practice'.[45]
Hooft and Vondel have in the last analysis only their own instinct to

guide them, and they often hesitate. It was on their usage that Hoog-straten (and with him the whole of the 18th century) was to take as his guide. At the turn of the 19th century it is still the usage of 'cultured people', i.e. great writers, that is to be invoked by Siegenbeek. In this way De Vries' and Te Winkel's famous list was arrived at. When there was disagreement among their predecessors, or for words which the latter had omitted or overlooked, De Vries and Te Winkel appealed either to analogy or to very dubious reasoning. (The names of musical instruments, for example, are to be feminine, as the said instruments are passive!)

Ultimately all these efforts were equally doomed to failure. There was an obstinate reluctance to face up to reality, or even to take it into account. The very fact that the list had to be compiled, or rather the fact that in order to write correctly people were obliged to consult it constantly, sufficed to demonstrate the artificiality of the enterprise. Protests like that of Roorda found no echo, or at least had no effect. In 1892, however, the Kollewijn bomb exploded. As far as the use of pronouns was concerned, Kollewijn proposed a very liberal solution: one was to trust, in both South and North, in popular educated usage. The battle was long and fierce. Finally came the decision of 1946–1947. The question of the choice of pronouns was, however, shelved, and it was to be in 1954, thanks to the Van Haeringen Committee and its 'Little Green Book',[46] that this was finally settled. But the greatest stumbling-block at least had been removed, namely that of the *n*.

This unfortunate *n* had in fact up till then complicated everything, by creating a link between two problems which were in other respects quite distinct: spelling reform and the gender of nouns. What was the issue? According to the grammar operating at the time one should say: *Zie je deN mooieN boom, dieN ik geplant heb?* (Do you see the lovely tree I planted?) but *Zie je de mooie tafel, die ik gekocht heb?* (Do you see the lovely table I bought?) because *boom* was 'masculine' and *tafel* 'feminine', and masculine nouns 'must' take an *n* in the object case. And if some people were so determined to preserve the distinction between masculine and feminine, it is above all because they clung to the principle of inflection as the mark of a civilised language. In practice, even the most educated, though advocates of the *n*, often went astray. Resistance gained some support also among Flemings, who were afraid that the legal suppression of the *n* would assimilate their language to that of the North. This ignored the fact that the Flemish spoken *n* in the definite article has nothing to do with case: it is found in both the nominative and the object cases, and its presence or absence is simply a question of euphony. Moreover, as soon as the law sanctioned, from 1946, the dropping of *n* in writing, it disappeared as quickly in the South as in the North, which would seem to indicate that the battle had been so much tilting at windmills.

The gender of nouns denoting **persons** should not, one would have thought, call for any comment. However, even in this area Dutch has some surprises in store. There are regions, in fact, where the masculine pronoun is used to refer to women and girls. The east of the Netherlands, the Achterhoek and Twente on the German border, is well-known for this idiosyncrasy. But it is found only in dialect and no one would dream, in standard Dutch, of referring to their mother as *hij*.

On the other hand, even the most polished stylist may hesitate over the gender of nouns which may designate either men or women, such terms as *deugniet* (good-for-nothing), *getuige* (witness), *wees* (orphan), *concierge* (caretaker), *dokter* (doctor), not to mention adjectives and participles used as nouns. These are more numerous in Dutch, partly because of the atrophy of inflection (*de heilige* may be a saint of either sex). In most cases the choice of pronoun is determined by the context. If it is not, in the North the masculine always prevails, while in the South certain words, *elf* for instance, are felt to be feminine. In the latter case, the Van Haeringen Committee decided to mark such words 'v[rouwelijk], m[annelijk]', indicating that the feminine was preferable but not obligatory. For the quite separate *wees*-group they used the sign 'm.-v.' giving both genders equal validity. In so doing the Committee was following in the footsteps of De Vries and Te Winkel, who had for once shown themselves magnanimous.

Next, **animals**. With male animals there is no problem. *Hengst* (stallion), *bok* (billy-goat), *haan* (cockerel) and *stier* (bull) are beyond all doubt masculine. Terms denoting a species irrespective of sex, such as *poes* (cat), *bij* (bee), *vlieg* (fly), *mus* (sparrow) and *muis* (mouse), are masculine to the north of the great rivers and feminine to the south. De Vries and Te Winkel had adopted the latter usage, and the Committee also came out in favour, without however making it compulsory. In such cases we find 'v(m.)'.

The gender which has aroused most passions is that of nouns denoting female animals: *koe* (cow), *merrie* (mare), *geit* (nanny-goat), etc. The split has never been so marked as on this point, and nowhere is the preference of Northerners for the masculine more pronounced. *HIJ zit te spinnen* (He is purring), they will say of a female cat, and of a cow: *Ik zag HEM gaan, en HIJ was zo mooi, ik heb 'M nog over Z'N neus geaaid* (I saw it (lit. him) walking along and it (lit. he) was so beautiful I stroked its (lit. his) nose). There is no getting away from these facts, and one can imagine the indignation and sarcasm which this usage engendered, not only in the South, but also among Northern purists. However, Kollewijn and his successors have insisted that one should not over-emphasise the link between sex and gender. The division of nouns into different genders was based in primitive Indo-European (and for all we know in even earlier systems) on psychological considerations of which we do not have much inkling, though undoubtedly sex must have played some part. In the meantime in any case, assimilation and many other factors have been at work, so that present divisions are as often as not arbitrary. Why, for example, is *wijf* neuter and not feminine like *vrouw*? Consequently, instead of trying to impose alien principles on the language, it would be better to look, in the context of the problem with which we are concerned, at Dutch in relation to the other Germanic languages.

Leaving aside German, which has preserved the three 'classical' genders of Indo-European, we are left with the Scandinavian languages and English. Since the latter has only one article, gender distinction can only apply to pronouns. This is very clear cut with a few easily listed exceptions (like the personification of ships and countries mentioned above, as well as that of animals, and the use of the plural 'they' with grammatically singular collectives like 'police' etc.): *he* for man, *she* for women, and *it* for animals and things. Scandinavian, like Dutch, has retained the division into neuter and non-neuter. In Danish the masculine is reserved for men, the feminine for women, and non-neuter animals are grouped with inanimate objects in the 'common' gender. The same applies to Swedish, although the boundaries are more blurred here: some animals are either masculine or feminine. One can therefore discern, in Germanic languages other than German, a tendency to attribute different genders to persons, animals and things. Does Dutch share in this tendency? One might claim that in the absence of a common gender it has been led, in order to distinguish human beings from animals, to use rather haphazard methods: in the South the subtle difference between *zij* and *ze* (for *zij* and *haar* are reserved for people only), and in the North the use of *hij* for female animals. Seen in this perspective, the latter phenomenon would appear much less shocking. The hypothesis, however, is a weak one. Even discounting the use of *hij* for women in the North-east (it is not certain whether this represents a purely local aberration, or rather the conclusion of a logical development), the sum total of the observations which it remains for us to make leads one to the conclusion that Dutch, or at least Northern Dutch, is tending to eliminate the feminine, and that it is here that its distinctiveness, especially in relation to German, resides.

Be that as it may, Southern protests have triumphed. The Committee forbade the use of *hij* or *hem* when referring to a female animal. *Koe, merrie*, etc., could only be replaced by a feminine pronoun.[47] It follows that a word like *geit* will be either 'v.' or 'v.(m.)', depending on whether one is referring to a nanny-goat or to an unspecified goat.

Less surprisingly than with regard to female animals, the attitude of the North is scarcely less firm on the subject of nouns denoting **abstract notions** (*taal, gedachte, ziekte, grootheid*) or **collectives** (*club, regering, partij*). All these words are feminine in Southern usage, but in the North one says: *De taal en de mensen die HEM spreken...*(The language and the people speaking it) *De commissie heeft ZIJN plan doorgezet* (The committee went ahead with its plan). As far as the possessive in particular is concerned, there is no hesitation. With the personal pronouns, matters are a little more complicated. *Ze* retains (for Northerners at least) something strange, but neither is *hij* entirely satisfactory. So that for preference one is likely to say: *Die vervelende* *kwestie? DIE hebben ze bijgelegd* (That troublesome issue? They've settled that) (instead of: *ze hebben HEM* or: *ze hebben ZE*).

The Committee, adopting a formal criterion, decided that the feminine pronoun would be obligatory for all abstract nouns containing the Germanic suffixes *-heid, -ing, -nis, schap, -st, -ij, -de* or *-te*, or with suffixes of foreign origin such as *-ee, -ie, -iek, -teit*, etc. For other nouns (*deugd* = 'virtue', *kracht* = 'strength', *leer* = 'doctrine', 'theory', *zorg* = 'care', it strongly recommended that they be considered feminine, though masculine would also be permitted at a pinch.

In its preliminary report the Committee observed that the Northern Dutch-speaker who, in a discussion on the government (*de regering*) hears *ZE heeft besloten*, immediately grasps the sense of the sentence, but if one says of a pen (*de pen*): *Geef ZE maar hier*, or of a briefcase (*de tas*): *Leg ZE op de stoel*, the *ze* will immediately suggest a plural. He would have naturally used *hem*. There are, then, a large number of **concrete objects** which even more than in the case of abstracts and collectives, are felt in the North to be masculine while the South, again, opts for feminine. In reply to the question: *Wat doe je met die tafel?* (What are you doing with that table?), the Northerner says: *IK schuif HEM weg* (I'm pushing it out of the way), where Flemish usage, which De Vries and Te Winkel had followed in their day, demands *ze*. Hearing the person next to him on a train say: *ZE ligt in het bagagenet*, a Dutchman from north of the great rivers would not dream that an article of clothing or a travelling-bag was being talked of, but would expect to find a little girl in the luggage rack. If in the North all non-neuter objects are masculine, in the South the division is entirely unpredictable: *eik* (oak) and *stroom* (river) are masculine, but *linde* (lime-tree) and *rivier* feminine.

It was difficult for the Committee to proceed with as much clarity of purpose as it had in the previous case. However, careful scrutiny of the list allows one to formulate the following principles:

1) Those nouns which were classed as masculine by De Vries and Te Winkel remain so. However, when despite De Vries and Te Winkel, feminine gender prevails in the South as a whole, as is the case with *burcht* (citadel), *dood* (death), *plicht* (duty) and some fifty other words, then masculine and feminine are considered equally admissible.

2) The vast majority of words classed as feminine by De Vries and Te Winkel are henceforward 'v.(m.)', i.e. the feminine is still preferred, but masculine has gained acceptance. This applies to parts of the body (*dij* = 'thigh', *knie*), plants, flowers and fruits (*linde, roos, peer* = 'pear'), general geographical terms (*beek* = 'stream', *golf* = 'wave', *stad* = 'town') and astronomical ones (*ster, zon*). It should be noted, however, that modern words always used in the masculine, but for some unknown reason classed as feminine by the successors of De Vries and Te Winkel, are henceforward to be masculine only: *auto, tram, tank*. For other words in the same situation an identical solution has been

adopted, except where a certain respect for Southern usage has induced the Committee to put the two genders on a par with each other (*boot, distel* = 'thistle').

There remains one paradoxical fact. While as we have so far seen, the North (except in the case of human females) systematically uses the masculine, it must be noted that **one** category is not always governed by this rule: the names of **substances**.

The latter, generally masculine in the South, are generally feminine in the North. 'Generally', however, does not mean the same thing in both cases. In Flanders, it means that the **majority** of names of substances are masculine, whereas in the North it means that one and the same word is **more often** used in the feminine than in the masculine. *Hoe smaakt de soep? ZE smaakt best* (though *hij* would not raise eyebrows). When a word can indicate at the same time a substance ('I am eating fish') and a specific object ('I bought a fish'), many older Northern speakers use a feminine pronoun in the first case and a masculine one in the second. It should be added that feminine is excluded for the possessive. One would never, for example, say of silk which is losing its sheen: *De zij verliest D'R glans*, but *Z'N glans*, or better still, *Dan gaat de glans D'R af* (where *d'r* is no longer a contraction of *haar*, but of *daar*, which is not specifically feminine). Within these limits this surprising use of the feminine in the North is a very persistent one. Half a century ago, Kollewijn even observed its regular development. Today, however, I am assured by Professor Van Haeringen that among younger speakers the feminine is becoming reduced to the status of a provincialism.

Eager to seize this opportunity of promoting the use of the feminine, De Vries and Te Winkel took, exceptionally, the side of the North, without, however, daring to remove *wijn* or *mosterd* from the class of masculine nouns. The Committee, though, once again followed Southern usage: *chocola* was to be masculine, *melk* by preference feminine, and there was no longer to be a distinction between *vis* the food and *vis* the animal. It is, though, expressly stated that for no common noun denoting a substance will a feminine be considered incorrect.

One can see how arduous the Committee's task was. If it had confined itself to a slight modification of the De Vries and Te Winkel list it would have satisfied the South, but left the North to muddle along as best it could. If it had sought to extend Southern usage, it would have had everyone north of the great rivers up in arms. Of course, the simple solution would have been to allow everyone to go their own way. But the Committee's brief was precisely to preserve unity.

A degree of compromise was therefore inevitable. That arrived at by the Committee is remarkable in two respects.

Firstly, in contrast to all previous 'lists', from the 17th century down to De Vries and Te Winkel, the list proper is less important than the accompanying commentary. That is to say, that for anyone who has thoroughly absorbed the considerations, it is possible to determine *a priori* the gender (either obligatory or at least permissible) of almost all words, with the list operating as a kind of check. Whether intrinsic, as with the names of females, or formal, as with certain abstract terms, the criteria adopted by the Committee, while they may not be entirely immune to scholarly objections,[48] do on the other hand have the enormous advantage of being simple, easy to remember and above all easy to teach. The linguists on the Committee were working not for other linguists, but for the public at large and for all concerned in education.

In other respects too, the Committee exhibited a considerable breadth of vision. In most cases it has taken the side of Southern usage, and has put a check on Northern initiatives. But in building dams it has not forgotten to include some sluice-gates. It recommends far more than it makes obligatory: apart from certain precise categories of noun, the Dutch of the North is free, without making 'mistakes', to indulge its predilection for the masculine. It is true that the Dutch and Belgian governments, in giving the Committee's views force of law from 1st September 1955, amended them so as to make them more restrictive. Nouns marked 'v.(m.)', in other words those for which the Committee **preferred** feminine gender, were to be **obligatorily** feminine in official usage. As for the schools, a distinction was made between abstracts (*deugd* = 'virtue', *drift* = 'urge, passion', *eer* = 'honour') for which the use of the masculine is forbidden, and concrete words (*naald* = 'needle', *roos* = 'rose', *aarde* = 'earth'), for which it continues to be tolerated. It is hard to explain these legislative inconsistencies, but, be that as it may, the question was to all intents and purposes settled, as it has not surfaced since. The Committee had done its work well in providing a common-sense solution to a thorny problem.

5. TWO WORDS IN CONCLUSION

Two words merit separate consideration: *OF* and *ER*, the first in a particular sense, the second across the whole range of its many uses.

OF may be a co-ordinating conjunction: *Hij OF ik* (He or I); *Een dame die lelijk OF niet bijzonder elegant was* (A lady who was plain or not particularly elegant).

It may also be a subordinating conjunction:

— *Ik weet niet, OF ik vanavond zal uitgaan* (I don't know if I'll go out this evening):[49] in indirect questions, or more generally in a dubitative function;

— *Hij stond te kijken, OF hij het in Keulen had horen donderen* (He stood as if thunderstruck). Here *of* stands for *alsof*. With or without *als*, this use of *of* dates back to the period when the word had a conditional sense (like that of *als* or *indien* today);

— *OF je zonder ophouden huilt en tiert, niemand zal je horen* (Even if you cry and scream, no one will hear you): in the sense of 'even if'.

All this is straightforward enough. There remains, however, one last case, so important that C. H. den Hertog, in his celebrated *Neder-landsche Spraakkunst* (1882—1896) refers to it no less than ten times. It is that in which a clause is introduced by *of*, which depends directly on a word in the preceding main clause.

This word may be *pas* (only just), *nauwelijks* (scarcely), *niet lang* (not long), *niet zodra* (no sooner) or *ternauwernood* (hardly). In this case *of* expresses a time relation:

1) *Nauwelijks was vader gestorven, OF de jongen werd ziek* (His father was scarcely dead, when the boy fell ill).

This may be a negation. In this case *of* may introduce a topic-clause:

2) *Het duurde niet lang, OF de jongen kwam verschrikt uit het bos gelopen* (It was not long before the boy, startled, came running out of the wood),

or a restrictive adjectival clause:

3) *Ik twijfel er niet aan, OF hij is al lang thuis* (I don't doubt that he has been home for ages),

or a restrictive adjectival clause:

4) *Er was geen mens, OF hij vernam het nieuws met verbazing* (There was no one who was not astonished by the news),

or lastly, an adverbial clause:

5) *Het vraagstuk is zo moeilijk niet, OF we kunnen het wel oplossen* (The problem is not so difficult that we cannot solve it).

Such sentences are a case apart, in that in the clauses governed by *of*, the verb is not in final position. In other words, the subordinate clause seems to be constructed like a main clause.

But is it actually a main clause? Grammarians are chary about giving an answer. 'The isolated position of this problematical *of*' leads Den Hertog to conclude that 'it should be grouped neither with co-ordinating nor with subordinating conjunctions.'[50] 'The clause introduced by *of* is usually regarded as a subordinate one, even though it often expresses the main idea of the sentence,' observed Rijpma and Schuringa.[51]

The first thing to note is that there is no essential difference between sentence 1) on the one hand and 2), 3), 4) and 5) on the other. The proof of this is that one can replace *nauwelijks* or *pas* by *niet zodra* without the sense being changed. The construction under discussion presupposes that the first part of the sentence contains a negative, or at least a restrictive word.

It is the result of a very long process, and history allows us to pin down the problem a little.[52] To express 'I saw no one who was not happy', M. Du. had:

ic ne sach niemen, hine was blide,

that is: 'ik zag niemand (van wie men zeggen kon): hij is niet blijde' (I saw no one (of whom one could say): he is not happy). This yields two juxtaposed main clauses. Later on, the sentence became:

ik (en) zag niemand, of hij en was blijde.

Since the medieval construction was no longer properly understood, *of* was introduced with a conditional sense: 'ik zag niemand *indien* hij niet blijde was', 'if someone was not happy, I did not see him'. However, (and this is the crux of the matter), the old construction was too rooted in habit to be changed. It persisted, paradoxically, despite the addition of *of*.

The third stage was when the old negative *en* fell into disuse,[53] and disappeared here too. The turning-point is the 17th century. Called on to choose between *'t Leed niet lang aen, oft zij EN quaemen* (It was not long before they came) and. . .*oft zij quaemen*, Hooft comes out in favour of the latter construction. So that one is left with *of*, which from then on was to be felt in this context to be a **coordinating** conjunction, introducing the second element in an alternative.

And all things considered, this way of viewing the matter is quite defensible. Sentence 4) can be interpreted correctly, if not elegantly, as: 'there was no one, **or else** no one was astonished by the news' and sentence 5) as: 'the question is not so difficult, **or else** we are capable of solving it'. As for the sentence beginning with *nauwelijks*, the alternative is perhaps more difficult to express, but is nonetheless real. One of two things: **either** the father was not yet dead, **or** the boy fell ill.

This explains, through a combination of modern intuition and historical displacement, a construction which at first sight may seem odd in the extreme.

*   *   *   *   *

After the articles and the auxiliaries *zijn* and *hebben*, ER is probably the most frequently occurring word in spoken and written Dutch.

Er has a double origin. This is of essential importance, even if people have long since ceased to be aware of it. *Er* is at once a weakened form of the adverbial of place *daar*, and of an old personal pronoun.

A. In the first case, *er* may have

1) a local meaning, of course: *Hij was naar de stad gegaan om ER met zijn zoon te praten* (He had gone into town to talk to his son (there)).

This is linked to the use of *er* as a pseudo-subject (although its function is felt to be purely syntactical): *ER gebeurt steeds weer iets* (Something new is always happening). *ER stond een man in de tuin* (plural: *ER stonden mannen*) (There was a man in the garden).

Hence the equivalent of 'there is': *ER is geen kans van succes* (There is no chance of success). *ER zijn toch goede vrienden* (There are still good friends).

2) *Er* may also be combined with a preposition to make a pronominal adverb: *Ik werk ERAAN* (I'm working on it). *Een fles met een etiket EROP* (A bottle with a label on it). Very often, *er* may be separated from the preposition by one or more words: *Hij is ER de eerste keer niet, maar de tweede keer wel IN geslaagd* (He succeeded, not the first time, but the second time in (doing) it).

3) Whether *er* is a place adverbial or a pronominal particle, it may in principle be replaced by *daar* or *hier*: '

Dit is een meesterwerk: U mag ER (or *DAAR*, or *HIER*) *trots op zijn* (This is a masterpiece: you can be proud of it).

However, these three words are not absolutely interchangeable. *Daar* is stronger than *er* and *hier* stronger still. This sometimes leads to a number of variants in the construction. Over and against: *Is je buurman ER al?* (Is your neighbour there already?), we have: *Is je buurman al DAAR?* (Is your neighbour already **there**?).

B. In its 'partitive' or, if one prefers, 'quantitative' sense, *er* derives from *der*, the genitive of the third-person plural personal pronoun (cf. Germ. *deren*):

Hoeveel boeken heb je? — Ik heb ER duizend (How many books have you? — I have a thousand).

Wat voor beelden? — Ik zie ER geen (What pictures? — I can't see any). This use of *er* is obligatory before a number and in most other cases. However, when precise objects are not being referred to, there is a certain degree of latitude: *Pluk [ER] dan maar. Ik heb [ER] al genoeg* (Go ahead and pick [some]. I have enough [of them] already).

C. Often, *er* may be found twice in the same sentence, a possible cause of confusion.

Initial *er* is compatible with partitive *er*:

Zoekt u de schriften? ER liggen ER drie op tafel. (Are you looking for the exercise-books? There are three (of them) on the table).

Hence the expression: '*ER zijn ER die...*', 'there are those who..., there are some people who...'

On the other hand, locative *er* is 'absorbed' by initial *er*:

Hij zei dat het huis goed was en dat ER drie families konden wonen (He said that the house was a good one and that three families could live there).

The same applies to *er* as an adverbial particle:

We moesten de deur openbreken, want ER zat een verroest slot OP. (We had to break the door open, because there was a rusty lock (on it)).

These are the main guidelines. They are relatively simple, but they do not enable one to solve all problems.

The first of these is that it turns out not always to be possible to put *er* at the beginning of a sentence. One can perfectly well say:

1) *ER is nooit aan gedacht* (No one ever thought of it. Lit.: There has never been thought of it),

but not:

2) **ER heeft men nooit aan gedacht* (Lit. There has one never thought of it). One must either replace *er* by *daar* (*DAAR heeft men nooit AAN gedacht*), or else change the construction (*Men heeft ER nooit AAN gedacht*).

The reason for this is that in sentence 1) *er* is both an adverbial particle and a 'support' to the impersonal verb. On the other hand, in 2) the verb has a subject (*men*) and the support is no longer necessary. And what applies to the adverbial particle is also true of the locative.

One cannot say: *Het was te heet, *ER konden we niet blijven* (It was too hot. Lit.: There we could not stay). If this distinction does not exist for *daar*, it is because *daar* is not a weak form and therefore can always be highlighted by being put in first position.

Another problem is posed by the use of 'expletive' *er*. Let us take two perfectly ordinary sentences:

Moeilijkheden zijn ER plotseling gerezen. (Difficulties have suddenly arisen).

Wat is ER van hem geworden? (What has become of him?)

Er clearly adds nothing to the sense here, and has no other grammatical function. Nevertheless, it is impossible to omit it. All well and good, but there are also cases in which the presence of *er* seems not just superfluous, but illogical. In the following sentences:

Wat is ER is Holland gebeurd? (What has happened in Holland?)

Ginder op de weg komt ER een reusachtige kerel aangestapt (From a long way down the road, a huge fellow approached).[54]

There is already an adverbial of place (*in Holland, ginder op de weg* = 'over there on the road'). What then is the point of adding *er* for good measure? The same goes for partitive *er*:

Ik heb drie vrienden, waarvan (or *van wie*) *ER twee in Den Haag wonen.* Does this *er* not duplicate the meaning of the relative *waarvan/(van wie)*? And yet the language demands that it be included.

One must accept things as they are. It should be said that for Dutch-speakers these questions hardly ever pose themselves. True, there are some sentences where *er* is optional. One can say:

Hij beweerde dat [ER] een groot leger in aantocht was (He claimed that a great army was approaching).

't Was meteen alsof [ER] een afstand tussen ons ontstond (It was suddenly as though a great gulf opened between us). But these are rarities. Nine times out of ten there is no hesitation, and when required, *er* comes spontaneously to the speaker's lips or the writer's pen. This is no doubt why the only general scholarly studies which have been made so far of this curious monosyllable are the work of foreigners.[55]

1 J. P. M. Tackx, *Nederlandse spraakkunst voor iedereen* (Utrecht/Antwerpen, 1972), p. 146.
2 *Een bekwamE dokter* is not impossible, but if one wishes to stress his professional qualities, *bekwaam* is required.
3 M. van Nierop, *De taal waarmee wij leven* (Antwerpen, 1962), p. 159. The following discussion (and that on pp. 75 f. below, concerning *er*) owes much to the comments of Dr. J. van der Stap, Université Paris-X.
4 E. Rijpma/F. G. Schuringa, *Nederlandse Spraakkunst* (Groningen/Batavia, 1949[12]), p. 150.
5 L. C. Michels, quoted in P. Brachin 'Nog eens de Spaanse koopman en de Franse handelsreiziger', *Onze Taal*, 43/3 (1974), p. 23.
6 *Latijnsche Lente* (1919), p. 200.
7 Or should one take into account the difference in social status between a businessman and a commercial traveller? This hypothesis was cautiously put forward by Van

Haeringen (cf. *Onze Taal*, 41/11−12 (1972), p. 55).

8 It is only incidentally touched on by Verdenius in *De Nieuwe Taalgids*, 33, pp. 361 ff. The article by T. van den Hoek, 'De ambiguïteit van woordgroepen als "een goede speler": een syntaktische homonymie?', in *Handelingen van het 33ste Nederlandse Filologencongres*, pp. 186−196, had an entirely different object. But at least, by highlighting the 'adverbial' function of adjectives used in this way, it contributes indirectly to focusing the problem more clearly.

9 C. B. van Haeringen, *Nederlands tussen Duits en Engels* (Den Haag, n. d.), p. 35. We are also greatly endebted to the same author's article 'De meervoudsvorming in het Nederlands', in *Neerlandica* ('s-Gravenhage, 1962), pp. 186−208.

10 According to Pauwels, the five forms in question may be put in the following order of diminishing frequency: *groentes, ziektes, periodes, leemtes, gaves.*

11 In a private letter.

12 Ibid.

13 G. Vannes, in his *Grammaire du néerlandais de base parlé et écrit* (Bruxelles, 1970[9]), p. 53, claims that '*de leraren* is less familiar and more commonly used than *de leraars*'. While it is undoubtedly less familiar, the assertion that it is less common, in Belgium, conflicts not only with Pauwels' experience, but with the impression left by a reading of Flemish teachers' periodicals.

14 Provided that in the case of a past participle it is not used as an adjective. *Het boek dat van een inleiding voorzien is* may mean 'the book which is provided with a preface'. The other construction would be incorrect in this sense. But if the meaning is 'the book which has been provided with a preface /by X or Y/, then one may choose either *voorzien is* or *is voorzien* (cf. L. C. Michels 'Op de grens van copula en werkwoord', repr. in J. Hoogteijling, *Taalkunde in artikelen* (Groningen, 1968), p. 230).

15 See also J. Stroop, 'Systeem in gesproken werkwoordsgroepen', *Taal en Tongval*, 22 (1970) 1, pp. 129−146.

16 Cf. A. Sassen, 'Endogeen en exogeen taalgebruik', repr. in J. Hoogteijling, *op. cit.*, pp. 343 ff.

17 J. G. Kooij, 'Jan vraagt Piet, als Jan Piet ziet, of: hoe leg ik woordvolgorde uit', in *Vijfde Colloquium van hoogleraren en docenten in de neerlandistiek aan buitenlandse universiteiten, Leiden/Noordwijkerhout 1973* ('s-Gravenhage/Gent, 1976), p. 66. (The emphases are mine, P. B.)

18 Tackx (op. cit., p. 80) even allows, although it is here the direct object which is involved, a sentence such as: *Ik moet toch ook betalen mijn huishuur en verdere kosten die zo hoog zijn dat er maar zeer weinig overblijft* (I have also got to pay my rent and other expenses which are so high that very little is left).

19 Such a construction would be much less surprising from the pen of a Flemish writer (cf. p. 93 ff.).

20 Cf. J. Kooij, op. cit., p. 68.

21 Cf. J. L. Pauwels, *Les difficultés de la syntaxe néerlandaise* (Liège/Paris, 1967[6]), p. 47.

22 C. B. van Haeringen, 'Wankele normen', in *Taalkunde, — 'n Lewe, feestbundel voor W. Kempen* (Kaapstad/Johannesburg, 1974), p. 140.

23 J. Zajicek, 'Caractéristiques essentielles du français et du néerlandaise', in *25 ans d'études néerlandaises à Lille*, Université de Lille III (n. d.), p. 57.

24 Some speakers say, instead of *iZ dat waar, is Tat waar*. The question is a controversial one, but in any case, assimilation is operating.

25 G. Stuiveling, 'Het spel van de spelling', *De Gids* (1972), 3, p. 170.

26 Although *búrgerman* is equally acceptable.

27 Cf. B. van den Berg, 'De accentuering van Nederlandse samenstellingen en afleidingen', *Nieuwe Taalgids* 46, (1953), 3, pp. 254−260, and the same author's *Foniek van het Nederlands* (Den Haag, 1972[6]), pp. 91 ff. Many geographical names also present problems: why *Rotterdám* and *Dórdrecht, Zuiderzée* and *Nóordzee?*

28 E. Blancquaert, *Praktische uitspraakleer van de Nederlandse taal* (Antwerpen, 1953[4]), p. 148.

29 W. Pée, 'Beitrag zum Studium der niederländischen Intonation', *Archives néerlandaises de phonétique expérimentale* VII−VIII (1932/1933), p. 4.

30 Similarly, *kon* has replaced *konde*, but this is no longer a case of intervocalic *d*.

31 C. B. van Haeringen, 'Weder en weer', in *Mededelingen der Koninklijke Akademie van Wetenschappen*, Afdeling Letterk, NR, deel 26 (1963), p. 262.

32 *Wilhelm Busch an Maria Anderson, 70 Briefe* (Rostock, 1908[5]), p. 52.

33 E. Kruisinga, *Het Nederlands van nu* (Amsterdam/Antwerpen, 1951[2]), p. 49. Moreover, many points are still moot ones (cf. Van den Berg, *Foniek*, p. 69).

34 In Belgium and even in the Netherlands below the great rivers, and in certain northerly areas, the popular suffix is *-ke(n)*, *-ske(n)*. As far as Flanders is concerned, W. Pée noted in 1936 that 'there is a shift from *ken* to *tjen*, and in certain areas the process is still in full swing' (*Dialectgeografie der Nederlandsche diminutieven*, p. 59 ff). Since then, the development has gathered even more momentum. In any case, *boekske* and *tafelke* are not part of *ABN*.

35 It is worth pointing out that *leerling* and *wandeling* have the diminutive forms *leeringetje* and *wandelingetje*, while *koning* and *vergissing* become *koninkje* and *vergissinkje* respectively. This is because the latter pair has a secondary stress on the final syllable. A further illustration, if any were necessary, of the importance of rhythm.

36 Cf. Van Haeringen, 'Concentratie door diminuering', in *Gramarie*, pp. 134–141.

37 A. Verwey, *Toen de Gids werd opgericht* (Amsterdam, 1897), pp. 51–52. 'Behind them is a tree-lined gravel path, silent in the bright sunshine, and in the distance a tiny village spire glistens above the woods...On the left is a view of meadows, dotted with little cows and sheep.'

38 E. Kruisinga, op. cit., p. 51.

39 Van Haeringen, *Gramarie*, p. 141.

40 Van Haeringen, 'Diminutiva op terugtocht', *Taal en Tongval*, XXVII/1–3 (1975) p. 104.

41 Cf. Van Haeringen, *Genus en geslacht* (Amsterdam, n. d.).

42 This phenomenon was focused on particularly by P. J. Simons in his studies in the *Nieuwe Taalgids* (VI, pp. 27–40, 65–76, 273–292; VII, pp. 81–89; XIII, pp. 120–129, 196–215).

43 G. Royen, *Pronominale problemen in het Nederlands* (Tilburg, 1935), pp. 38 ff.

44 For all the historical references in this paragraph, see Chapter I.

45 G. Geerts, *Genus en geslacht in de gouden eeuw* (Leuven, 1966), p. 114.

46 *Woordenlijst van de Nederlandse taal*, samengesteld in opdracht van de Ned. ende Belgische regering (Den Haag, 1954). Cf. above, p. 40.

47 It is interesting to note that this decision caused no great difficulty, as the Dutch members of the Committee were as reluctant as their Flemish colleagues to allow *koe* or *merrie* to be considered as masculine nouns.

48 Thus, strictly speaking, *-ij* should have been put in the category of foreign suffixes. But no Dutch-speaker, unless a professional linguist, is aware that *-ij* derives from French. The Committee was bound to take this into consideration in its classification.

49 This example, like those that follow down to (5) below, are taken from J. L. Pauwels, *Les difficultés de la syntaxe neérlandaise*, pp. 39 ff.

50 Op. cit., III, p. 246.

51 Op. cit., p. 75.

52 Cf. *WNT*, art *of*, col. 77.

53 Cf. p. 48, n. 26.

54 Some would argue that *er* is optional in this case, when the sentence begins with a place adverbial, at least in written Dutch.

55 G. Bech, *Über das niederländische Adverbialpronomen ER*, repr. in J. Hoogteijling, op. cit., pp. 147–174; R. S. Kirsner, *On Deixis and Degree of Differentiation in Modern Standard Dutch* (Diss. Columbia University, 1972), passim., and *The Problem of Presentative Sentences in Modern Dutch* (Amsterdam, 1979), passim. Perhaps the remarks in the last paragraph should be qualified a little; an astute observer of the situation writes: 'I notice increasing disagreement among people in the Netherlands about the use or non-use of *er*, and there are in addition differences between North and South' (J. de Rooij, in a private letter).

CHAPTER III

North and South
or
The Dynamics of Unity

On 29th March 1966 there appeared in the Frankfurt edition of the *Börsenblatt für den deutschen Buchhandel* an article entitled *Sprach-verwirrung*. Its author was Georg Hermanowski, the well-known German translator of numerous Flemish novels. 'It is true,' he wrote among other things, 'that people are fond of invoking the "18 million Dutch-speakers in the Netherlands and Belgium". But this notion is a very relative one, since the differences between North and South are considerable and are by no means "solely a matter of vocabulary". In the Netherlands today, besides a large number of dialects, an official language called *ABN (Algemeen Beschaafd Nederlands)* is spoken. Flemings, however, speak Flemish Dutch, and this is as far removed from ABN as, for example, Afrikaans, which is also a variety of Dutch.'

Reaction was very fierce, and led in particular to a 'clarifying statement',[1] signed by almost all (twenty-four out of twenty-five) university professors of Dutch Language and Literature in the Netherlands and Belgium, who 'utterly repudiated' Hermanowski's presentation of the state of affairs:

'From a scholarly point of view, it is preposterous and fallacious to assert that the language spoken in Flanders and the official Dutch spoken in the Netherlands are as different as, for example, the latter and Afrikaans. It is equally indefensible to claim that Afrikaans is, in the same way as Flemish, a variety of Dutch: this entirely overlooks the fact that Afrikaans has eventually become an autonomous Germanic language.

There is no such thing as a "Flemish" language or a "Hollandish" language; there is only the **Dutch language**, which is officially recognised and compulsory both in Flanders and in the Netherlands. With many nuances, of course, such as one finds in every language, including German. The differences in pronunciation, vocabulary and syntax between Dutch people and Flemings are certainly no greater than those between Viennese and Hamburgers. These nuances in no way entitle one to speak of an actual separation. For this reason we, the under-signed, feel obliged to reject Mr Hermanowski's remarks as untenable and vitiated by ignorance.'

The parallel drawn by Hermanowski between the case of Flemish and that of Afrikaans is so patently grotesque that such a solemn refutation was possibly not called for. But it was good that the fundamental linguistic unity of the Netherlands and Flanders should have been reaffirmed, and reaffirmed by such competent spokesmen.[2]

Notwithstanding this unity it is imperative and, moreover, fascinating, to look a little more closely at 'the differences in pronunciation, vocabulary and syntax', and more generally at the very complex and controversial problem of the relations between the language of the North and that of the South.

1. THE SPREAD OF ABN IN FLANDERS

The standard language in the Netherlands is to all intents and purposes fixed: there is today universal agreement on it.[3] The dialects are on the retreat, and as for everyday speech, there may (as we shall see below) be variation in pronunciation from one place to another, but 'the written language admits of such regional variants only by way of special effects, as a specifically literary device. One cannot tell when reading something written by the average Dutch person, whether they live in Amsterdam, Groningen or Maastricht'.[4] If one takes down in shorthand a conversation between Dutch people from different parts of the country, 'almost nothing any longer allows one to detect which sentences come from an Eastern speaker and which from a Westerner'.[5] The syntax and the vocabulary allow only very little room for manoeuvre. At most, a particular use of a feminine pronoun will give away someone hailing from 'south of the great rivers', and if someone speaks of *missie* instead of *zending* (mission) or (more oddly) *OP de eerste plaats* instead of *IN de eerste plaats* (in the first place), it marks him as a Catholic. Although, in this last case, the opposite proves nothing.

If the Netherlands have in this way reached the same degree of linguistic unity as Britain or France, this, as was seen in Chapter I, is due to the independence enjoyed from the 17th century on and to the regulating role played by the towns of Holland. There is nothing to parallel this in Flanders. For centuries, the Fleming lived in a country under foreign domination, governed in French, and in addition half French-speaking. Dutch in the South was even less able to resist the penetration of French, since none of the numerous dialects was able to impose itself on the others. The following little scene dates from as recently as 1890. A young woman, wanting to adopt an Amsterdam orphan, introduces him to her mother, a French-speaker from Brussels, who asks: 'Est-ce qu'il est intelligent? Il ne sait que le flamand.' (Is he intelligent? He only knows Flemish.) 'Non,' replies her daughter 'le hollandais. Le flamand est un patois et le hollandais une langue. (No...Dutch. Flemish is a *patois* and Dutch is a language...)'[6] This was very true, except that it would have been more accurate to speak of a whole collection of *patois*.

Admittedly, even then the efforts of the Flemish Movement were beginning to bear some fruit. But the following shows the situation as recently as 1930:

> 'A large number of teachers and young ecclesiastics are full of the best intentions, and in some schools they are already achieving considerable results, bearing in mind the pull of the street and the absence of a good example on the part of the leading circles. One has only to listen to the language of railway or tram employees, apprentice barbers or butchers, hotel bellboys and newspaper-sellers. A large number of younger speakers, assuming you yourself speak carefully, will answer you in a Dutch which is astonishingly superior to that spoken twenty or so years ago. Nevertheless, there is still much to be done. The teacher himself, once having left the classroom, speaks either dialect or at best an inter-mediate language between dialect and correct Dutch. I am quite aware that in an environment which has its own dialect, one is still subject to legpulling if one tries to speak correctly. But is it not a mistake and a sign of lack of character to base one's conduct on the judgement of ill-qualified people? Moreover, one is more likely to invite mockery if one only half-succeeds in speaking correctly, which gives one's speech something stiff and derivative. But why do not the teachers at the same school, the students in the same club or other groups of well-intentioned friends, encouraged by their headmasters, their theatre directors and others, begin and experiment among themselves? Little by little the circle of those speaking correctly will in this way extend to the remotest villages; with the help of habit it would seem less unnatural and finally the dialect-speaker would be more tempted to imitate than poke fun. And the children of these pioneers, brought up to speak correctly, would soon exercise a salutary influence on those around them.'[7]

This passage from Blancquaert is perhaps a little long but it was worth quoting at length. The year 1930 was in fact a turning-point. It was the year of the great language laws, which finally established the principle of monolingualism, when the process of making Gent a Dutch-speaking university was begun in earnest, and when radio made its first appearance.

The importance of these factors, favourable to the spread of ABN, only grew greater as time went on. 'The adoption of a norm by speakers coming from a dialect-speaking environment is a slow process, and is encouraged by more intensive communications and by public life, but above all by improvements in education.' These words of De Vooys'[8] refer to the situation in the Netherlands at the time of the Batavian Republic, but they are equally applicable to present-day Flanders. The 'Dutchification' of teaching is snowballing, in the sense that the quality of the language at secondary and university level is improving with the disappearance of those teachers who had them-selves been taught in French. As for primary education, the impove-ment of textbooks in the last thirty or so years is there for all to see.

Radio, which has now been joined in almost every home by tele-vision, exercises its influence daily. The Dutch-language news programme of Belgian radio is written and read, in the judgement of many in the Netherlands, in excellent Dutch. Lecturers, of course, use ABN both on the platform and on the air, where their audience is vastly greater. From the other side, Hilversum radio is much listened to in Flanders and if, before, Dutch TV could easily be picked up in border districts, the advent of cable television has brought both Dutch and Belgian TV within reach of most parts of the Low Countries. On the other hand, the press scarcely penetrates. *The N.R.C./Handelsblad* is no more read in Leuven than is the *Standaard* in Leiden. But the diffusion of books from the Netherlands is considerable. In 1970, 70% of the books read in Flanders came from the Netherlands and 200 Dutch publishers were more or less active in the Flemish market.

Systematic efforts to promote ABN should not be forgotten. These are sometimes carried out in cooperation with the Dutch, as in the case of the General Conference of Dutch Letters (*Algemene Conferentie der Nederlandse Letteren*), whose activity is not limited to literature.

In Belgium itself it has taken enormous effort, especially in the area of administrative language, where for a long time people had had to make do with very clumsy translations from French. Since 1945 a whole series of committees have been set up to this end.[9] There is even a specialist magazine called *Taalbeheersing in de administratie* (Correct Language use in the Administration). Elsewhere, individuals and organisations vie with one another in zeal. A *Vereeniging voor Beschaafde Uitspraak* (Society for Educated Pronunciation), founded in 1913, did not survive the First World War, but the torch was taken up by the *Vereeniging voor Beschaafde Omgangstaal* (V.B.O. = Society for Educated Informal Speech). The latter disappeared in its turn at the outbreak of the Second World War, but thanks to E. Blancquaert and his disciple W. Pée, it revived in 1947 and since 1951 has published the periodical *Nu Nog* (To this Day).[10] Newspapers, radio and T.V. have regular language features, sometimes with picturesque names like *Taaltuin* (Language Garden) or *Taalwacht* (Language Sentinel), which are very popular: collected in book form, the columns of Van Nierop, Florquin and Galle sell in large quantities. The culmination of many years of endeavour came on 9th September 1980, when the *Nederlandse Taalunie* (Dutch Language Union) was ratified in Brussels by the Dutch and Belgian governments. The Union incorporates in both constitutions the principle of linguistic and cultural unity, and provides for ongoing consultation at the highest level on the formulation and coordination of policy relating to the promotion of Dutch language and culture at home and abroad. Its main advisory body, the *Raad voor de Nederlandse Taal en Letteren* (Council for Dutch Language and Literature), is made up of experts from both countries, and its decisions are implemented by a General Secretariat. The battle for ABN is being fought on two fronts: against Gallicisms and against dialect.

The list of Gallicisms is endless. Leaving aside pronunciation (for example, French *j* in *adjudant* and *justitie*), let us proceed directly to the heart of the matter, vocabulary. There are borrowings pure and simple, some very old like *koer* (courtyard), others more recent like *soupape* (valve), *camionnette* (van), *dactylo* (typist), *syndikaat* (trade union) and *compteur* (meter). But Gallicisms are also often found in the form of loan-translations in the most diverse areas. In commerce: *reekseinde* (< fin de série), *te koop aan zoveel franken* (< en vente à...francs); in the administration: *bureelhoofd* (< chef de bureau), *die universiteit wordt ontdubbeld* (< dédoublée); in journalism and everyday language: *ik houd er aan* (< j'y tiens), *die auto kost duur* (< cette voiture coûte cher), *we gaan nu de parenthesis sluiten* (< fermons le parenthèse).

Gallicisms are of varying degrees of gravity. Twenty-five years ago, there was to be seen on Kortrijk station a poster put up by the *Unie der professoren van dans van België* (< Union des professeurs de danse de la Bélgique). No less frightful is *een kwestie op punt stellen* (< mettre une question au point). The culmination (if one can call it that) seems to have been reached with *hij komt van te vertrekken* (< il vient de partir). On the other hand, *de 50ste verjaardag van de bond* (le 50ème anniversaire...) or *hij was van hoge gestalte* (< de haute taille) are scarcely shocking, and it needs the nose of a specialist to detect the Gallicism in *telkens was zijn vrouw weer daar* (instead of *er weer*) = 'time and time again his wife was there' or in *de politieke richting van die krant is eerder* (< plutôt, instead of *tamelijk, nogal*) *links* = 'the political leanings of that paper are somewhat left-wing'.[11]

Of course, these loan-translations are more often than not unconscious and consequently difficult to eliminate. Three more examples, this time of a grammatical nature, have possibly not until now been given sufficient attention: 1) *indien* (Fr. 'si', denoting a contrast, Du. *ook al*): *INDIEN hij op 10 mei het woord voerde te Valence, op 16 te Parijs en op 17 mei in twee kleine dorpen, toch kon de kandidaat niet overal zijn* (Even though he addressed meetings at Valence on 10th May, in Paris on the 16th and in two small villages, on 17th May the candidate could not be everywhere at once); 2) *opdat* (Fr. 'pour que', Du. *dan dat*): *Hij dronk te veel OPDAT zijn gezondheid daar niet onder zou lijden* (He drank too heavily for his health not to suffer); 3) *dan wanneer* (Fr. 'alors que', Du. *terwijl*):

> '...het blijft toch een feit dat al wie gevormd werd tijdens het Franse regime ofwel niet meer in staat zal zijn in het Nederlands te schrijven ofwel er eenvoudig niet meer zal aan denken dit te doen, DAN WANNEER in de tweede helft van de 18de eeuw ook de hogere standen...de Nederlandse taal nog kenden en zich niet schaamden deze te gebruiken.'[12]

If such usage provokes Dutch indignation or mockery, Flemings are able to ask in turn why *reçu* or *impasse*, so current in the Netherlands (as in Flanders for that matter), should be less reprehensible than *chauffage*, and to observe that they do not use either *fatuiteit* or *succumberen*, and are loth to talk of *ravages op de etage* (havoc in the flat), while loan-translations are rife, even in the most polished language, from *rekening houden met* (< tenir compte de) to *ik maak me sterk dat...*(< je me fais fort...). Some people even go so far as to suggest that Northern Dutch 'consists entirely of foreign words'. In fact, limited but precise surveys have shown that both in the press and in broadcasting the percentage of borrowings is nevertheless higher in Flanders than in the Netherlands.[13] But this is not the issue. There is a twofold and crucial distinction between North and South. Firstly, the Gallicisms used in the Netherlands are understood throughout the whole language-area, which is not the case with the majority of those found in Flanders. On the other hand, Dutch as spoken in the North is stable enough to be able to 'digest' foreign words and expressions, which are often an enrichment, while in Flanders, where the language is still developing, they represent a permanent danger.

As regards dialectal influences, in matters of pronunciation these are reflected in the first place in mistakes in accentuation: *onderwíjs, omwénteling*. Most striking of all is the non-aspiration of *h* at the beginning of a word or syllable. In spontaneous speech the majority of Flemings have a tendency to pronounce *ond* instead of *hond, ier* instead of *hier*, or *onge-uwd* instead of *ongehuwd*. This carelessness is often confusing, since many words can only be distinguished by the presence or absence of initial aspirated *h: haar/aar, hoor/oor, huur/uur*. In other words, *h* is here a phonological distinctive feature. Many Flemings are aware of this, but occasionally go from one extreme to the other: anxious not to drop any *h*'s, they are over-zealous and add them where they do not belong.[14] This tendency to hypercorrection is by no means a recent phenomenon: it is already found in the oldest Dutch text we possess (cf. p. 9), with *hi[c]* instead of *i[c]*. It also forms the basis of the legendary etymology of *Antwerpen* (< *hand werpen*, 'to throw the hand', the reference being to the severed hand of the giant Antigoon, cut off by the city's founder, Brabo).

On the level of grammar, dialect often leads Flemings to drop the adjectival inflection with a preceding definite article before neuter nouns: *het wit huis, het groen kasteel, het klein ongemak*,[15] though this is not particularly serious. On the other hand, archaisms like the verb forms *kloeg* (for *klaagde*) and *miek* (for *maakte*) are generally recognised as such. However, archaisms proliferate in many other guises. It is quite common for *lijk* to be used instead of *gelijk* ('the same as'), *gasthuis* for *ziekenhuis* ('hospital'), or *spijzen* for *voeden* ('to feed'). The following is a sentence, admittedly a very 'literary' one, from a relatively recent novel *klaaglied om Agnes* (Lament for Agnes, 1951) by Marnix Gijsen: *in den beginne had ze zonder verpinken de bloemruikers besteld* (in the beginning he had ordered the bouquets without batting an eyelid). It contains no less than two archaisms (*in den beginne* instead of *in het begin* and *bloemruikers* instead of *boeketten*), not to mention *verpinken* (to blink), unknown in the Netherlands.

In these circumstances, although the fostering of dialects is a perfectly inoffensive, and in some respects even praiseworthy activity, in Flanders their influence on the standard language should be combatted at all costs. Dutch will never be able to achieve the status of a completely autonomous cultural language unless it rids itself of the influence of local speech, however great the affective value or folkloristic charm.

What then is the present state of ABN in Flanders? It is far easier to draw up a balance for the written than for the spoken language. As far as writers, and more especially novelists, are concerned, progress is obvious. Stijn Streuvels and Felix Timmermans (born in 1871 and 1886 respectively) both loved to draw on their dialects, West Flemish in the first case and Brabant in the second, both by natural inclination and for local colour. The recent edition of Streuvels' Collected Works contains many explanatory footnotes, and while it is true that Timmermans had his novels corrected by a teacher he knew, the latter does not appear to have been very rigorous. Herman Teirlinck (born 1879) from Brussels, shares the same tendency to a lesser extent. On the other side are Johan Daisne (1912), Jos Vandeloo (1925) and even more so the younger generation of writers, who use a language almost identical to that of their Northern colleagues. The transition is marked by a figure like Marnix Gijsen, born in 1899. Gijsen, widely regarded as an accomplished stylist, does his best to stick to Northern Dutch. His attempts, however, can scarcely be called successful: educated in French, he cannot on the other hand be said to distance himself sufficiently from his Antwerp dialect. Between four and six times per page on average, one finds something to make an attentive Dutch reader shake his head, however well disposed he may be.[16]

It goes without saying that the development does not proceed in straight lines. Cyriel Buysse (1859) wrote in Dutch which was remarkably pure for its time, and the same is even more true of Willem Elsschot (1882), though it must be remembered that both spent extended periods in the Netherlands. In addition the nature of the language used depends on the subjects being dealt with. Gerard Walschap (1895) and more recently Piet van Aken (1920) are, for very different reasons, rooted in their native regions and are also more affected by local speech than is a representative of the psychological novel like Maurice Roelants (1895). The style may vary in one and the same writer according to his inspiration. There is André Demedts (1906) the novelist and André Demedts the literary columnist for *De Standaard*. Hugo Claus (1929) uses very different language to evoke the life of migrant Flemish sugarbeet-workers in France and to adapt Seneca. As for extra-literary works, historical studies, art criticism and philosophical essays, their language is scarcely distinguishable any longer (with the occasional exception of minor syntactical details to which we shall return below) from that of similar works from the North.

It should be added that Flemish writers enjoy a large readership in the Netherlands. Some of them are regularly published there. In itself, this does not prove anything about their language: Streuvels and Timmermans in their day were precisely enjoyed for their exoticism, and were considered *leuk* (quaint). But it is a fact that nowadays modern Flemish writers are read without their little 'slips' causing offence and often without them being noticed.

Books have a profound influence, but only immediately affect a limited number of people. The case of the press is very different, and the language of the newspapers is not homogeneous. As a rule leading articles and editorials are written in excellent Dutch. On-the-spot reporting, on the other hand, often leaves much to be desired: for example when a Brussels journalist puts a specifically Flemish expression into the mouth of the Mayor of Amsterdam. This is even more true of the sports pages and local news items, but the worst offences are committed in the small ads, though even here there has been considerable progress.

The staff of daily newspapers of course work against time. Less frequently appearing publications are produced at a more leisurely pace, and accordingly the linguistic quality of weeklies and monthlies is mostly very high.

To sum up, one may reasonably predict that within a short space of time the situation in Flanders, as regards the written language, will be the same as anywhere else and that quality of style will no longer be determined by anything but personal factors: intellectual training, conscientiousness and alertness.

The spoken language is quite another matter. Two separate questions must be distinguished here: (1) to what extent are Flemings capable of speaking ABN? (2) to what extent do they actually do so in everyday life?

Some thirty years ago, Van Haeringen was able to write:

'Any conscientious observer is bound to notice that the linguistic difference between any Dutch town and a large Flemish city like Antwerp or Gent (to say nothing of provincial towns or the countryside) is not simply one of degree but a fundamental one. There is no better way of realising the authority of ABN in the Netherlands than noting the facility and ease with which the common language is used in every shop and railway station, how every policeman and school pupil, admittedly without always achieving perfection, approaches it very closely. The tendency is everywhere so recognisable and obvious that not for an instant does one doubt the existence of a norm. What a great step forward it would be if town councils and other "official bodies" in Flanders were to use a language like that which can be heard daily in the Netherlands at youth-club gatherings, trade union meetings or chambers of commerce, that of ordinary people, who may sometimes offend a little against phonetic and syntactical rules, but nonetheless speak a language which no one would hesitate to call supraregional.'[17]

To see to what extent things have changed since 1951, we can turn to another, no less famous linguist, but this time a Fleming, whose various pronouncements span a long period of time. Writing in 1963, W. Pée observed: 'It is pronunciation to which most attention has

been and still is being given in Flanders, and no one who knew
Flanders forty years ago could deny that much progress has been made
in this area... But this is not enough. Vocabulary and syntax often
leave much to be desired.' Certainly, he adds, the interest of the public
at large in linguistic matters is becoming much more lively: 'This
should fill us with hope, were it not that the ultimate goal is still far off
and the route strewn with traps and pitfalls.'[18] By 1970, his tone is
more optimistic: 'I believe I am correct in saying that in this field [i.e.
pronunciation] much progress has been made in the last forty years. I
have been able to register it at first hand. Undoubtedly much remains
to be done, but we are on the right road.'[19] Note the stress laid on
pronunciation. This point of view is shared by a much younger
observer, J. Goossens, who also believes that it is in this area that
normalisation has advanced furthest, since 'in lexical matters the conscious need for a norm has only been felt for the last twenty or so
years, and so far as morphology and syntax are concerned it is
virtually non-existent'.[20] Obviously, pronunciation is a matter of extreme importance. In the view of Pauwels it is even the most important. 'Compare a Fleming whose pronunciation is impeccable, but who
from time to time uses a provincialism or commits some slight pec-
cadillo, with someone whose language is 100% authentic Dutch, but
whose pronunciation is defective. The language of the former will,
despite its shortcomings, give an impression of cultured distinction,
which cannot be said of the latter.'[21] But let us return to Pée, who
quite recently laid stress on the social upheaval which the Second
World War entailed, in Flanders as elsewhere. There are now many
dialect-speakers to be found in leading circles, who while not knowing
French, have a poor knowledge of ABN, 'but their children do have a
good command of the language, and in this way, in the not too distant
future, the battle will be won'.[22]

However, the victory of ABN will not be assured unless one in-
sidious difficulty is overcome. For the last century, the Flemish Movement has been so keen on eliminating French from public life, that it
has neglected to define the language which it hoped to put in its place.
Certainly, in theory, particularism is a spent force. It is just that in
practice people were satisfied with a vague *vloms*, sometimes dubbed
schoon Vlaams. It is still to be found in kindergartens and primary
schools. It is 'a fictional language, generally even clumsy', an
amorphous mass. Consequently, for most Flemings there are three
stages to pass through: dialect, 'schoon Vlaams' and ABN. The average
Fleming is quite happy to stay at the second stage and this rough-and-
ready compromise may well prove to be more dangerous than dialect
itself.[23] The language of those who wish to express themselves correctly 'oscillates between a kind of purified dialect and in some cases
more or less pure Northern Dutch'.[24]

Thus far we have only quoted impressions and opinions. Is it possible to be more precise and put forward figures? They are to be
found in a number of surveys, the first of which was carried out by

B. Meeus in 1972.[25] Though based on too small a number of informants, Meeus' survey is nonetheless very telling. From it, it appears that a small section of the Flemish population (5.2%) knows only local dialect. This comprises mostly aged country folk. The remainder fall into the following categories in the following percentages:

	Country	Town
Purely passive knowledge of ABN	22.1	16.6
Mediocre active knowledge of ABN	53.2	43.3
Reasonable active knowledge of ABN	19.5	40

The age distribution is particularly interesting. Below 30, 27% of country people and 55.6% of town-dwellers reach reasonable level, while over 50 the figures are 4.2% and 30.8% respectively. The direction of the development is clear, and it is bound to accelerate.

But it is one thing to know a language and quite another to use it. As for the active use made by Flemings of ABN in speaking, opinions vary widely. 'The dialects,' wrote Van Coetsem in 1957, 'are still very much alive. Everyone, or almost everyone, speaks or can speak their local dialect. It would appear that ordinary people are in general content for the time being to add a little school Dutch and school French to their knowledge of dialect. For some, especially in the towns, French exists above dialect as a common language of culture and communication. The number of those who more or less regularly use the Dutch *koiné* is still far too small.'[26] Twelve years later, Mrs De Vriendt observed that in her area, East Flanders, ABN 'still has little or no place in the intimacy of family life'. People, she suggests, are reluctant to use it for fear of appearing 'pretentious'.[27] On the other side, Pée notes in 1975 that whereas some thirty years ago ABN was spoken by hardly anyone except the mayor, the priest, the solicitor, the schoolteacher and civil-servants from elsewhere, at present, due to economic prosperity, the development of Dutch teaching, successive language legislation, 'the time would not seem to be very far off when Dutch will achieve the position in Flanders that the common cultural language occupies in the surrounding countries'.[28] The old warhorse is once again supported by Goossens, according to whom 'on the one hand, there is a growing number of people who in their daily practice, use a language which is no longer dialect, and on the other, one can observe with a growing number of these that the distance separating them from the norm (generally still quite considerable) is increasingly being whittled away'.[29]

In other words, 'we can conclude that in the last thirty years the Southern variant of Dutch has lost its artificial character of occasional language and is tending to become a natural spoken means of expression'.[30]

It is, however, undoubtedly still somewhat risky to pronounce judgement on the situation in Flanders as a whole, as it varies from place to place. 'In Hasselt, a significant minority of speakers under the age of twenty-five use ABN in everyday conversation, and in Genk [another locality in Belgian Limburg] this probably applies to the majority. On the other hand, in the more important urban areas of West Flanders, such as Kortrijk or Brugge, the number of ABN-users is minimal. Its oral use is still almost exclusively restricted to school, church and public speaking.'[31] The privileged position of ABN in the east of the country seems confirmed by a survey carried out at Hoeselt: the proportion of *ABN-sprekers* there varies, at least on their own testimony, from 39.1% to 49.6%, depending on the amount of education enjoyed.[32]

This brings us to a second factor: profession and social status, though here one must be cautious. In 1963, while deploring the fact that 'young people in secondary, technical and higher education persist in considering Dutch as a separate language, solely for use at school or college,' Pée noted an improvement: 'One hears an increasing number of girls expressing themselves in ABN. The setting up by Gent students of a junior branch of the V.B.O. seems to me to presage a happy change in the situation.'[33] In fact, there exist *ABN-kernen* (ABN-cadres), groups of younger people (particularly secondary school pupils) who are committed to the use of correct Dutch in all circumstances. But their teachers do not always set the example they should. 'There are quite a few people with university degrees, especially in the teaching profession, who imagine that it is possible to speak dialect in the family circle, with their friends and in their lives in general, and yet that they will be able to use ABN with their pupils.'[34] The frame of mind denounced in this way by Grauls in 1951 has not died out to this day, as Professor Goossens was recently able to confirm from experience. In the course of a study tour with his students, all Germanists and as such prospective teachers of Dutch, he was horrified at the *patois* they used among themselves, from which he picked out the following sentence: *Hij zei dattem van niks en wist* (= hij zei dat hij van niets wist, 'He said he didn't know anything about it'). This contains one clear archaism (the negative particle *en*) and one glaring solecism ('*em* as subject). 'Our people,' concludes Goossens, '**know** how to speak more correctly, but they don't **dare** to.'[35] The same fear of standing out in a crowd that Blancquaert had deplored back in 1930 . . .

Nevertheless, the use of ABN is very widely regarded as a precondition of social advancement: according to Meeus in from 50% to 100% of cases. But many other factors are involved. In this way, the use of ABN attains its highest frequency on the telephone, and drops to its lowest in conversations between parents and children. 'One can say in conclusion that speakers whose level of education is lowest use the standard language only exceptionally and in the most formal situations, while speakers with a high level of education do so with ease, even in informal situations.'[36]

From all this it will be apparent that even in the most favourable interpretation — i.e. looking only at those people with a command of ABN who use it systematically — the latter has not yet become in

Flanders a true *omgangstaal* (everyday language). For 'a language is not truly complete unless it embraces the infinite number of registers which the members of the linguistic community need for the various spheres of life, unless one can use it to quarrel and preach, gossip and write poetry'.[37] This ideal has been achieved in the Netherlands, where there is no longer a rift between the official language, strictly codified, and the freer language of everyday life. But it has taken centuries to reach this point. Why should it surprise us then if, despite the changed times, a few decades have not been sufficient for the Flemings? A number of consequences ensue. Flemings often speak a purer Dutch, all other things being equal, than Northern Dutchmen, for the simple reason that they are more on their guard. Their Dutch, on the other hand, is less nuanced. They are unaware, partly at least, of the subtleties referred to in Chapter II, for example in regard to such pairs as *werpen/gooien*, the formation of the plural or diminutives, because these relate precisely to the multiplicity of registers, whereas the Fleming tends to speak 'like a book'. Hence the antiquated impression that his speech, even in the absence of unfamiliar words and expressions, makes on a Dutchman. It is, in fact, a general rule that the written language to some extent lags behind the everyday spoken language.

As for the future, one can think of the precedent of Dutch Limburg. As a result of the geographical position of Maastricht and also because of historical developments (in 1839, if the wishes of the people had been heeded, they would have become Belgian), ABN was scarcely favoured until about 1900. The common people used only their dialect, and the upper classes were divided between French and German. Today, on the other hand, 'ABN is dominant in educated circles, even if everyone knows Maastricht dialect. Working people usually use dialect, but also know ABN, albeit with a Maastricht tinge. This in my opinion is the state of affairs towards which we must strive in Flanders'. The words are Pée's.[38] Nor is it beyond the bounds of possibility that a position analogous to that in German-speaking Switzerland will develop. In practice, whatever their social status, Zurich or Basle people speak exclusively in their own dialects among themselves. But everyone is capable not only of writing correct German, but also, as soon as they are conversing with a 'foreigner', of switching to *Hochdeutsch*. For the time being there is at least a three-fold difference between Switzerland and Flanders. In the first place, many Flemings are obviously still incapable of conversing in correct Dutch when the need arises. But equally obviously this will come in time. In the second place, the situation in Switzerland is quite clearly-defined: people are quite well aware in what circumstances Standard German is appropriate and in what circumstances dialect can be re-tained. In Flanders the boundaries are blurred and fluctuating in this respect. Finally, for the Swiss, *Hochdeutsch* poses no problem, even if they cling to their guttural pronunciation and are bound to use terms relating to their own institutions. Flanders' linguistic alignment with the Netherlands has never been fully achieved, nor is it even universally considered desirable. It is this question which remains to be discussed.

2. DIVERSITY IN UNITY?

Once again our starting-point is an article by Van Haeringen. In 1957 the Utrecht philologist, in order to illustrate 'the strange relationship of the two cultural languages to the north and south of the political frontier', insisted on the difference separating, as far as ABN is concerned, two towns as close in dialectal terms as Turnhout (in Belgian Brabant) and Tilburg (in North Brabant, part of the Netherlands). It is of little importance in this context that the users of ABN are much less **numerous** in the former town than in the latter. The remarkable fact is that those few people in Turnhout who speak ABN do so **differently** from the inhabitants of Tilburg. And one would be wrong to imagine that the ABN of Turnhout is more strongly coloured by Brabant dialect than that of Tilburg. 'In Turnhout there begins something that might be called Belgian ABN, a Dutch which may even contain less residual local elements than that of Tilburg, and must in that sense be classed as superior, but which manifestly draws on a different source. There is no continuity between the standard language, where it is used in everyday life, as spoken on either side of the frontier.'[39]

Things are moving fast in Flanders and it may well be that the passage above no longer applies to today's situation. Whatever the case, there is no doubt that differences exist. Let us try to distinguish the main ones, in the areas of spelling, pronunciation, syntax and vocabulary.

Spelling does not call for lengthy discussion. Some would say that the originality of the Flemings lies in their concern, with loan-words, to move as far as possible from French spelling: *x* is replaced by *ks, ch* by *k* and *th* by *t*, so that one will write *eksamen* (exam), *kristelijk* (Christian) and *tema* (theme). Most often they stay within the bounds of what is at least permitted by the official ruling: for example, *princiep* (principle) instead of *principe*. But this is not the case with *machien* (machine), *kontrool* (check) and *tribuun* (rostrum), all forms for which one will look in vain in the 'Little Green Book'. Likewise, the very numerous words ending in *-atie* are increasingly spelt with a *z*: *mobiliZatie, sensibiliZatie*, etc. On this point Flemings are at one with the advocates of the minimum programme of the VWS, whose ideas in other respects raised a storm of protest in Belgium, as we have seen above.[40] The tendency is so pronounced that it occasionally leads to manifest excesses: neither *psyKologie* nor *kloor* (chlorine) correspond to correct pronunciation. It should not be forgotten that to a lesser extent the same tendency exists in the Netherlands: *vaKantie* (holiday) and *KontaKt*, rare thirty years ago, are now very common.

Pronunciation matters are still very complicated. We shall limit ourselves to one observation of a general nature and the discussion of three particularly striking phenomena:

— Flemish pronunciation is sometimes more strict and sometimes more lax than Dutch. In the Netherlands, *i(e)*, *u* and *oe* are longer before an *r* (*bier, muur, boer*) than elsewhere (*liet, minuut, toen*); Flemings do not always observe this distinction. On the other hand, for them *ee, oo, eu* and *oe* are pure long monophthongs rather than diphthongs as they tend to be in the North, and unlike the Dutch they do not identify the neutral *e* (*vadEr, bEstuur*) with the *u* of *put*: the latter is slightly less open.[41]

— for words ending in *-atie, -itie, -otie* and *-utie* the *ts* pronunciation is favoured in the Netherlands, or at least this pronunciation is considered more cultivated: Flemings, on the other hand, do not hesitate to pronounce an *s* in *motie, politie* and *revolutie*. The Dutch are no doubt following German (*Revolution*) and the Flemings French (*révolution*) in this respect.[42]

— in contradistinction to the vast majority of Northern Dutch-speakers some Flemings, particularly in West Flanders, tend to pronounce final *n* after neutral *e* (cf. p. 5, n. 10). It is thought that this is because the former attack the vowels more strongly than the latter. If the following vowel 'has a weak attack, as is almost always the case in Flemish dialects, the consonant *[n]* seems to be necessary as a transitional sound'.[43] Moreover, this phenomenon is fairly localised: final *n* remains mute in most of Brabant.

— in the Netherlands initial *w* (except in the combination *wr*, where *w* becomes semi-voiced *v*) is labiodental (cf. Engl. *vat*): 'The lower lip pushes against the upper teeth across its whole breadth.' In Flanders it is bilabial: 'Closure and sound are produced entirely by lip-movement.'[44] This brings it close to the English *w* in 'water'. A striking difference, one might think. However, it is of quite secondary importance, since it is not a distinctive phonological feature: whether bilabial or labiodental, the *w* remains a *w*. And what is more, the bilabial pronunciation is not restricted to Flemings: it can also be found even in the highest circles, in Zeeland, Dutch Limburg, in the east of North Brabant and also in other parts of the Netherlands.[45]

In **syntax**, Belgian Dutch differs from the Dutch of the Netherlands on two points:

1) In subordinate clauses introduced by a pronominal adverb or relative, Flemings put the preposition after the auxiliary:

Hoewel hij daar al lang heeft OP gewezen (Although he has pointed this out for a long time).

De redenen die er de schrijver hebben TOE gebracht (The reasons which led the writer to do it).

Iets waar ze nooit iets had VAN gehoord (Something she had never heard of). Similarly, where there are two or three or more infinitives, the preposition is inserted between the infinitives:

Ik zou daar nog heel wat kunnen OVER zeggen (I could say a lot more about that).

Een levenswandel waar niemand zou hebben willen AAN verzaken (A way of life which no one would have wished to abandon).

'This peculiarity is quite clearly deeply rooted,' writes a Dutch commentator: 'to the point where Flemish actors playing in our theatre companies cannot rid themselves of it, and prefers to amend their scripts!'[46] It is absolutely excluded in the Netherlands, and the moment one comes across such a construction, one may be sure that the author is a Fleming.

2) Conversely, a sentence such as: *ze wist dat het bestuur spoedig AF zou TREDEN* (she knew that the committee was soon going to resign), possible in the Netherlands, sounds very odd to Flemish ears. For his part, a Fleming would almost invariably say: *ze wist dat...zou aftreden*. Nor will he willingly accept:

Dat ik het licht UIT heb GEDAAN (That I have put the light off).

Het spijt me U dit MEE te moeten DELEN (I regret to have to inform you of this). It should be added that this specifically Northern construction is not in any sense obligatory in the Netherlands, and that it is not even the most frequent form. Flemings are perfectly within their rights in not using it. But their tendency to avoid separating the particle from the verb often leads them to treat in the same way words or groups of words which, in their eyes belong with the verb in the same way as particles. This results in constructions of the type:

De man, die de Vlamingen WILDE TER HULP KOMEN (The man who wanted to come to the aid of the Flemings).

Waar het woordenboek ons ZOU IN DE STEEK LATEN (Where the dictionary would desert us). Or even:

Een verklaring waarover men HAD KUNNEN VAN GEDACHTEN WISSELEN (A statement which we could have discussed).

Zou je DURVEN DE HAND AAN JE MOEDER SLAAN? (Would you dare to strike your mother?).

The last sentence, where the violation of usual syntactical rules is particularly flagrant, occurs in Cyriel Buysse's work. But one could find equally glaring ones in modern writers, although the purists are inclined to avoid them.[47] On the other hand, while the Flemish construction is generally excluded in the North, it is found in certain set expressions:

Omdat deze hem kaarten HAD TER BESCHIKKING GESTELD (Because the man had offered him tickets).

Ons land, dat een stricte neutraliteit HAD IN ACHT GENOMEN (This country, which had observed strict neutrality).[48]

Such constructions are the remnants of an old usage, so that their present use cannot be called arbitrary, but rather marks the persistence of a construction which was still widespread in 16th- and 17th-century Dutch.

The question of **vocabulary** will be dealt with a little further on. For now we shall go into only two aspects: purism and second-person pronouns.

Purism consists essentially in the proscription of terms of French origin used in the Netherlands, where they have been, in an amusing phrase, 'airlifted across Flanders'.[49] The reaction of Flemings to French words adopted by the Dutch is reminiscent of that of Canadian Québecois to English borrowings which the French use without turning a hair. The same Flemish newspaper which uses *sensibilizeren* and *sensibilizatie* (words unknown in the Netherlands) feels the need to replace *subsidie* by *toelage*. It should be added that Flemings take particular exception to pseudo-French terms with which Northern Dutch is prone to adorn itself: *geadresseerde* (cf. Fr. *destinataire*) becomes *bestemmeling*, *advertentie* (cf. Fr. *avertissement*) becomes *aankondiging*, and *centrifuge* ('spin-dryer', cf. Fr. *essoreuse*) becomes *droogzwierder*.

The procedures to which purism resorts are very diverse. Some of the substitutions are coined *ad hoc*, either through derivation (*drukking* for *pressie*, or *nijveraar* for *industrieel*), or by compounding (*ereloon* for *honorarium* or *bijhuis* for *filiaal*, 'branch (-office)'), or by a combination of the two (*opsteller* for *redacteur*). In other cases the foreign term makes way for one which is known in the Netherlands, but which may be either little used (*uitstalraam* for *etalage*, 'shop-window', or *gebeurlijk* for *eventueel*, 'possibly'), or in a more or less different sense: *bestuurder*, for example, means the driver of a vehicle throughout the whole linguistic area, but in Flanders is also used to mean *directeur*; *voetpad*, in the wider sense, means any footpath; in Flanders it is more specifically a pavement.

Perhaps the past tense would have been more appropriate in the last paragraph, since on the latest information, purism of this kind is losing momentum. Not only is *directeur* far more usual than *bestuurder*, but *subsidie*, *geadresseerde* and *advertentie* are also rapidly gaining ground.

The use of the **second-person pronouns** is an extremely delicate matter. It affects both individual sensibilities and social relationships in all their most subtle ramifications.

In the Netherlands, at least north of the great rivers, one is nowadays limited in one's choice to either *U* (both as subject and as object) for the polite form, and *jij/je* (dative and accusative *jou/je*, plural. *jullie*) for the familiar. *Gij/ge* (dat. and acc. *U*) has been totally eliminated from conversation and is becoming increasingly rare in formal occasions. Since Queen Juliana ascended the throne in 1948 it has been replaced in the monarch's speech on the State Opening of Parliament by *U*. If it persists on occasion in formal letters, it is to avoid embarrassment: lawyers who may use the familiar with each other in private may use *gij* in writing to each other in their official capacity, since *U* would be too distant and *je* unacceptably informal. *Je*, however, is full of subtle variations: the switch to the familiar form, among equals, is rapid, but one may use *je* without necessarily immediately going as far as *jij* and particularly *jou*.[50]

None of this applied to Flanders until very recently. The only form, for everyone and in all circumstances, was *gij/ge* in the nominative and *u* in the object case.[51]

The transition from the Flemish system so that of the North is beset with difficulties. The first is grammatical, since with the polite form in all cases and more often than not with the familiar it presupposes the abandonment of the distinction between subject and object case, and conversely introduces a distinction between singular and plural (*je was, jullie waren*). On the other hand *gij/ge* has the advantage of eliminating all the problems posed by the choice between polite and familiar form. Lastly and above all, there are psychological barriers. With *gij* the Fleming feels at ease, while *jij*, and even more so *jullie*, remains a foreign importation. Moreover, the host of nuances in the Northern pronoun escape him and it is often as difficult for him to use it correctly as it is for someone to master the relation of prepositions in a foreign language.[52] This has led Pauwels to state forcefully that in Belgium, with a few rare exceptions, the use of *jij/je*, far from bringing people closer together, 'immediately banishes all sense of familiarity'.[53]

But Pauwels also observed that *jij* was 'beginning to penetrate the written language'. Subsequent developments have borne out this observation, which was made twenty-five years ago. A survey of 1963 shows that at that time *jij* was already widely used in the large-circulation weeklies, children's books, etc. The same applies to the novel: in his first works, published in 1957, Ward Ruyslinck uses *gij*, but from 1968 onwards switches to *jij*.[54] It has been established that the vast majority of students use *jij* in writing to their friends. But things have not yet advanced so far with the spoken language. Already familiar with *u* as the object case of *gij*, Flemings have scarcely any difficulty in using it when addressing a stranger or a superior. As for *jij*, the 'few exceptions' Pauwels talked of have certainly set the tone, although in this case a new stratification is emerging. 'One notes that in some cases *jij* is used between friends and colleagues, while *gij* remains in use with intimates.'[55]

It is clear, then, that despite all the complications they involve, the Northern second-person pronouns are undeniably gaining ground in Flanders. This is an extremely significant fact, for it illustrates admirably the progressive orientation of Belgian ABN towards usage in the Netherlands. But there are plenty of other examples: for instance, the diminutive *-(s)ke(n)* has practically fallen into disuse in written ABN; as in the North, *-je, -pje, -tje*, etc., are the only forms used. Or again — and this is probably even more noteworthy — there is the rise of the masculine.

As we have seen, Dutch-speakers in the South keep strictly to the differentiation of the three genders, whereas the Dutch are quite happy to say: *De koe, HIJ geeft melk* (The cow, it (lit. he) gives milk). While being as conciliatory as possible, the authors of the 'Little Green Book' had set limits and prescribed that nouns with certain formal or innate characteristics should be feminine, either by preference (*kat, jeugd, wet*), or obligatory (*parochie* = 'parish', and words ending in *-ing*). This was bound to gladden Flemish hearts. And yet what do we find?

Marnix Gijsen writes of a cat: *Nu en dan trachtte HIJ... naar beneden te klauteren, maar HIJ gaf ZIJN plan onmiddellijk op* (Now and again it (lit. he) tried... to climb down, but it (he) immediately abandoned its (his) plan), and the Bishop of Gent, speaking of the modern parish, states: *HIJ wordt te weinig als centrum gezien* (It (lit. he) is seen too little as a centre). A journalist criticises *een taalwet die ZIJN uitwerking mist* (a language law which failed to have the desired effect). Similar infringements are found even in the work of a writer Flemish to the core like Teirlinck: *Is het niet normaal dat een moederloze jeugd ZIJN verlatenheid bevrijdt in een asociale samenscholing* (Is it not normal for orphaned youth to seek an outlet for its (lit. his) sense of abandonment in gathering together in asocial groups?), and in that of an experienced philologist like Pauwels: *Een taaluiting krijgt ZIJN specifieke betekenis niet alleen door...* (A speech act acquires its (lit. his) specific meaning not only through...). They are certainly not systematic or even conscious, but the very existence of these slips of the pen proves that they are a token of a real development in modern Flemish.[56]

Not everyone is convinced that this progressive adaptation of Southern Dutch, conscious or not, to the norms and sometimes even preferences of the North, is to be unreservedly welcomed. One writer claims that 57% of specifically Southern vocabulary is common to all Flemish dialects. Is it not, in that case, counter to all common sense, to try to replace these words by their Northern equivalents, which the majority of Flemings do not even understand? Would it not be preferable to construct an *Algemeen Zuidnederlands*, i.e. a cultural language specific to Dutch-speaking Belgium? The aspiration towards a degree of linguistic unity between North and South is a good thing, but 'on condition that *Algemeen Zuidnederlands* is granted a place within *Algemeen Beschaafd Nederlands*'.[57] Sometimes it is, somewhat paradoxically, a Dutchman who takes the same line. 'It seems to me,' thinks a native of Haarlem, 'that a true Fleming would never be able to speak or write supposed "ABN" without denying the most specific part of himself.' The Dutch are probably closer to the English than the Flemish; in any case their language reflects a materialistic culture. Rotterdam is a city of businessmen, The Hague a town of bureaucrats: why should they be held up as an example to those across the frontier? Certainly, Flemings should avoid Gallicisms and glaring errors, but for the rest they have retained a much purer and diversified language than their Northern neighbours. So they use words unknown or forgotten in the North? So much the better! Such words are an enrichment of the common culture. A Dutchman would never say: *De wind neuzelt in de schouw* (The wind grumbles in the chimney). Is that a reason to condemn this expression, which in no way offends against the spirit of the language, quite the reverse?[58]

These arguments are far from convincing. The second is purely emotional, the first implies a contradiction: How can one at the same time want to preserve 57% of words unknown in the Netherlands and call oneself an advocate of a degree of linguistic unity? It would be better to admit openly that one wishes to return to the particularism of the past. Moreover, Emmermann's statistics should be treated with caution. Goossens considers them 'invalid and insignificant'.[59] In practice, the specifically Flemish words common to the whole of Flanders (with the exception, of course, of those denoting specifically Belgian concepts, like *assisenhof, schepen*, etc.) are very few in number: *patat* (in the general sense of *aardappel*), *rijf* (rake), *telloor* (plate), *droogkuis* (dry-cleaning)... Equally, at the level of phonetics, there are no characteristics at once common and peculiar to Northern Belgium as a whole. This is the reason why all attempts to create an educated Southern version of Dutch, called familiarly *'schoon Vlaams'*, or more exaltedly *'AZB'*, are doomed to failure. *'"Algemeen Zuidnederlands Beschaafd"* does not exist, and nothing encourages one to expect a development in this direction.'[60] This was true in 1947, and it is even more true today.

One should, however, point to a factor which has been recently brought to light, and has since become known as the '**Brabant expansion**'. It has been noted that, with the modern communication media being in practice centralised in Brussels, Brabant dialect has begun to eat away at the others. At least it appears 'feasible that a specifically Southern variant of the articulatory base of Dutch, of Brabant (and to a lesser extent East Flemish) origin is gradually becoming the norm'.[61] And if Brabant dialect becomes a norm, it will be to the detriment of Northern Dutch. This tendency affects not only phonetics. Certain Brabant words are gaining ground over their (West) Flemish and Limburg equivalents, even in those cases where the latter turn out to be in line with Northern usage. In this way, *kapelaan* (chaplain) is gradually being replaced by *onderpastoor*, *zwager* (brother-in-law) by *schoonbroer*, *ham* (ham) by *hesp*, *van boven* (from above) by *langs boven*, and *schroef* (screw) by *vijs*. However, the discoverer of this tendency himself urges us not to exaggerate its significance. He observes with satisfaction that the centripetal tendency (rapprochement with the North) remains stronger than the centrifugal one (grouping around Brabant). In his view too, the political frontier between the Netherlands and Belgium is becoming less and less felt as a linguistic frontier.[62]

The Northern model is the obvious one, for the simple reason that there is no viable alternative. 'In the last analysis, it is always in the North that one has to seek the norm. If not, where else is one to turn?'[63] Historical circumstances have eventually obliged Dutch-speakers in the South, after having long been in the forefront, to take their cue from the North. 'It is from Dutchmen that Flemings have learnt their culture in the 19th and 20th centuries.'[64] Often, while recognising this necessity, Flemings are annoyed that the Dutch always calmly refuse to budge from their entrenched positions, with the result that all the adjustments are in one direction. This is an understandable reaction, but still they are mistaken. For when it is a matter of unifying two languages, one of which is stable and the other still evolving, it is of necessity the latter which must adjust to the former. Indeed, the Flemings need an even stricter discipline than their neighbours, for the divergences which may exist in the Netherlands are simply 'the inevitable small dose of diversity which only gives richness to unity: it is not comparable with the huge amount of diversity which with us [i.e. in Flanders] has the effect of actually undermining unity'.[65]

There is, moreover, nothing humiliating for a Fleming in taking his cue from the ABN used in the North. The latter is in fact made up in large measure of Southern elements. It should be remembered that in the Middle Ages the cultural superiority of the County of Flanders and the Duchy of Brabant enabled their language to leave an indelible imprint on the whole area. This is witnessed by the verb *zullen*, 'a word of West Flemish origin which swept the medieval chancelleries and undoubtedly owes to this its triumph in the North'.[66] Next came the refugees in the 16th and 17th centuries: without them Northern Dutch would not know *schoon, zeer*, etc.[67] Therefore, in 'imitating' ABN, the Fleming is either reclaiming what is rightfully his (hence Willems' words, cf. p. 36), or else returning a favour.

Should one nevertheless, posit as one's ideal that one day the ABN of Gent or Brugge should become completely identical to that of Utrecht or Groningen? If one asks the average Dutch person, they are very likely to reply: 'If the Flemings need the support of Northern Dutch in their struggle against linguistic Gallicisation, they should not allow any compromise. They should adopt it lock, stock and barrel or not at all.'[68] Linguists in the Netherlands, however, are much more broad-minded. Kloeke showed his understanding of those Flemings who, while opening themselves up to Northern influences, do not wish 'to go as far as a complete reconstruction of their articulatory base or to abandon their own vocabulary or syntax'.[69] Huisman considers that if Flemings have decided to adopt northern ABN, the onus is on the North 'to show tolerance with regard to Southern peculiarities of secondary importance, which do not impede communication'.[70] In 1975, Van Es, noting that linguistic integration is under way, adds: 'For the further development of this process it is not necessary to deny the Flemings the freedom to use the Dutch language in their own way to achieve their own objectives in the fields of culture, literature, science, journalism, politics and government.'[71]

The same opposition between radicals and moderates is also found among those most immediately concerned — in Flanders itself. The former used to have Grootaers at their head, and their opinions have in latter times been voiced by Grauls: 'In this area [phonetics] no half-measures are possible: sounds must be produced in as Dutch, as Northern Dutch a way as possible.'[72], by Van Coetsem[73], and by Van Nierop[74]. The last of these was replying to a famous article by Pauwels, *In hoever geeft het Noorden de toon aan?* (To what extent does the North set the tone?), dating from 1954. 'Let there be no misunderstandings', wrote Pauwels, 'the purification of the language in

Flanders will have to continue for years yet, but in imitating Northern examples too slavishly and eradicating by force deeply-rooted and quite orthodox linguistic peculiarities, one will be doing more harm than good to the cause one is purportedly defending.'[75] This has also always been Pée's position: 'If we wish to ensure the future of Dutch [in Flanders] a close collaboration with the Netherlands is an urgent necessity. This, however, does not mean that we have to adopt every-thing wholesale, and abandon our own character.'[76] And more recent-ly: 'We are,' he declared, 'acting in good faith (can anyone seriously doubt it?), but as for letting ourselves be dictated to, that we cannot do without losing all self-respect.'[77]

If one accepts this point of view, the problem will be to find a dividing-line between what is 'orthodox' (to use Pauwels' expression) or at least acceptable, and what must be mercilessly eradicated as endangering the unity of ABN.

Spelling may be left aside. It is of little consequence that Flemish usage differs a little from that of the Netherlands. The only drawback of this state of affairs is to arouse the astonishment of foreigners and the ridicule of the pro-French faction in Flanders.

'The phonetic differences between ABN as it is spoken in the Netherlands and in the Dutch-speaking part of Belgium, are often ones of nuance, which are in large part masked by the written form of ABN and do not in the slightest affect the unity of ABN' as it is used from the Scheldt to the Dollart.[78] Is the English of a Glaswegian necessarily less correct than that of a Londoner, and should one reprimand an inhabitant of Bern for not following German *Bühnenaussprache* in all respects? In addition, the Dutch are in no position to criticise Flemish pronunciation. For even within the Netherlands, probably no more than 10% of the population achieve Jespersen's ideal of speaking in such a way that one's origin cannot be detected. It is well known that the guttural *g*, often hard in Amsterdam, is always a soft velar sound in Limburg, that in Groningen final *n* is pronounced, that according to region there is a whole gamut of possible variations between *s* and *z*, *v* and *f*, and that the further north one goes the more marked the difference becomes between the open *o* of *bod* and the closed *o* of *bot*. In Jan Prins' line:

Die UIT DE kust een EIND DE zee ingaan (Those who go out to sea a little from the shore) the capitalised words will be pronounced *uide* and *einde* in the north, and *uite* and *einte* in the west.[79]

Neither need morphology and syntax present great stumbling-blocks. Why should one try to prevent Flemings from saying *leraars* rather than *leraren*, from regarding *commentaar* as masculine rather than neuter, or from preferring *doorheen het bos* (through the wood) to *door het bos (heen)*? And what is wrong with a construction like *Hij heeft daar altijd kunnen voor zorgen* (He has always been able to look after that)? It is neither obscure nor cumbersome. The effort required to eliminate such constructions would be out of all proportion to the advantage gained. Here Van de Velde's remark is particularly valid:

'The present situation, in which one is aiming at an élitist and impeccable cultural language, leads to a contraction rather than to a better use of the language... Variants should only be rejected when they endanger communication, which is not often the case. Only in this way, it seems, will the Flemings in their turn manage to achieve a spontaneous, natural and easy use of the language.'[80]

The hardest nut to crack is obviously vocabulary. If one accepts that in this case the overriding criterion should be the possibility of communication across the frontier, the following two categories of words or expressions should be outlawed:

1) Those which are totally alien to Northern Dutch: *U mag beschikken* (< vous pouvez disposer), *de brand omschrijven* (< circonscrire l'incendie), *of haar afkomst er voor iets tussen was* (< si ses origines y étaient pour quelque chose). This brings us back to the fight against Gallicisms. But this does not apply to *hesp* (ham), *telloor* (plate) or *stiel* (trade), which are no less opaque for a Dutchman than *bof* (stroke of luck), *toetje* (dessert) or *parlevinken* (talk gibberish) for a Fleming. One must not blind oneself to the fact that words of this kind are very persistent, since the majority are linked to the humble details of everyday life. Perhaps they are not so serious after all. The existence of such words as *Laib* (for *Brot* = 'loaf'), *Semmel* (for *Brötchen* = 'bread roll'), *Schmand* (for *Sahne* = 'cream'), *Esse* (for *Schornstein* = 'chimney'), and *plätten* (for *bügeln* = 'to iron'), which are very widespread in certain areas of Germany and entirely unknown in others, does not essentially harm the homogeneity of German.

2) A more difficult case is presented by words and expressions which are found throughout the Dutch-speaking area, but whose meaning or associations are not the same everywhere. *Schielijk* (swift) or *het echtelijk dak verlaten* (leave the marital home) are common coin in Flanders, but in the Netherlands they have an old-fashioned air, which is avidly exploited by humorists. The meaning, though, is at least clear. But when a Fleming says *bot* (boot) for *laars*, *lopen* (walk) for *rennen* (run), or *slechts* ('only' as general restriction) for *pas* ('only' as time restriction), he is in danger of being misunderstood. *Een merkwaardig boek* is a remarkable book in Flanders, while in the Netherlands it is an odd book. It may also happen that a word has the same semantic value in both countries but that it has an additional, different meaning in Flanders. We have already seen this in the case of *bestuurder* and *voetpad*. In the same way, *inzicht* has everywhere the meaning insight, judgement, or opinion, but only in Flanders that of intention. One can often recognise as Flemish a text in other respects well-written, from the use of *moeten* as equivalent to *hoeven (je MOET er maar zijn boek op naslaan*, 'you need only consult his book'), or else, in the form *moest*, to *mogen (MOEST ik eens ziek worden, dan zou ik die dokter roepen*, 'should I ever fall ill, I would call that doctor').

On the other hand, if one takes a moderate position, there is nothing to prevent the admission of:

1) Words which are not used by the Dutch, but which they imme-

diately grasp without any risk of misunderstanding: *steenweg* (paved road), *mistevredenheid* (discontent), *fruitboom* (fruit-tree);[81]

2) Metaphorical expressions in the same position. It is hard to see why it should be absolutely necessary to replace *ontvangen worden als een hond in een kegelspel* (receive a very cold welcome) by *als een aap in een porseleinkast, ze is zo zot als een deur* (she is as daft as a brush) by *ze is zo gek als een ui*, or *Pietje de Dood* (fam. Death) by *magere Hein*, or why in the case of *platte broodjes bakken* (eat humble pie), *appelen voor citroenen verkopen* (to hoodwink) and *groen lachen* (smile wrily), one should substitute *zoete* for *platte, knollen* for *appelen* and *zuurzoet* for *groen* respectively.[82]

Many intelligent observers think that these expressions should be not only tolerated but should become generalised in ABN, 'in such a way that Dutch would no longer be the Dutch of the North in a narrow sense, but would become a Dutch which was common to all'.[83] May one hope that this desire will one day become fact, that the time will come when Northerners will once more draw on the resources offered by Belgian Dutch? Though still a little academic, the question is raised from time to time. Certainly, it is relatively easy for a committee or a government to decree that such and such a word or stylistic custom should no longer be considered unworthy of a place in ABN, but 'incorporating them in new editions of grammars and dictionaries will serve no purpose at all, since people in the Netherlands do not learn their language from grammars and dictionaries'.[84] If one accepts this observation, should one consider as unattainable in our time any Southern input into the language of the Netherlands? Modern borrowings by the Dutch from their neighbours are indeed very few in number: they are limited to isolated words like *beiaard* (carillon) and *betoging* (demonstration) and a series of sporting terms,[85] but it is not inconceivable that the cultural development of Flanders and more frequent two-way contact between the countries will gradually change the situation. This is the scenario envisaged with both circumspection and sympathy by a particularly well-qualified Dutch observer. G. A. van Es wonders whether a complete fusion smacks of Utopia:

'or will there really be a progressive integration by way of reciprocal influences to the benefit of the whole, re-invigorating the old corpus, broadening horizons and enriching the language, which will have become truly a common language? No one can predict with certainty, at least as far as the degree of integration is concerned. Supposing that, with the support of education and practice, integration continues, there will still be a host of unresolved questions as to the nature and importance of the contribution of the two partners, although one is justified in expecting *a priori* that the cultural language of the Netherlands will continue to dominate. But I consider it inevitable and no less desirable that the increasing and fruitful influence of the South and its linguistic habits and potential will continue to grow.'[86]

1 '"Niederländisch": eine Klarstellung'. The text was first published in the journal *Leuvense Bijdragen* (Bijblad) LV (1966), p. 2.

2 Despite the theoretical inconvenience which this involves (cf. pp. 2−3), the terms 'Flanders' and 'Flemish' will be used in this chapter to refer to the whole of Dutch-speaking Belgium.

3 'Today', for in the past certain people, whose opinion could certainly not be taken lightly, voiced reservations. See A. A. Weijnen, *Het algemeen beschaafd Nederlands historisch beschouwd* (Assen, 1974), pp. 11−12.

4 K. Heeroma, *Sprekend als nederlandist* (Den Haag, 1968), p. 172.

5 P. C. Paardekooper, '"Zuid-Nederlands" woordgebruik', *De Nieuwe Taalgids*, 40, (1947), p. 194.

6 J. Goossens, 'De Belgische uitspraak van het Nederlands', in G. Geerts, *Aspekten*, p. 139.

7 E. Blancquaert, *Praktische uitspraakleer van de Nederlandse taal* (Antwerpen, 1953⁴), pp. 19−20.

8 *Geschiedenis van de Nederlandse taal*, p. 153.

9 The list is to be found in W. Pée, 'Het algemeen beschaafd Nederlands in België', *Onze Taal* (maart 1963), pp. 27−28.

10 The V.B.O. is now called *Vereniging Algemeen Nederlands* (Society for Standard Dutch) and its organ *Nederlands van nu* (Dutch Today).

11 Van Haeringen, 'Franse tussenkomst in Vlaanderen', in *Album Willem Pée* (Tongeren, 1973), pp. 419−421.

12 '...it nevertheless remains a fact that those educated during the French occupation are either no longer capable of writing Dutch or simply no longer even consider doing so, whereas in the second half of the 18th century even the upper classes...retained a knowledge of Dutch and were not ashamed to use it.' Elias, *Geschiedenis van de Vlaamse Gedachte*, I (1963), p. 119. On the specifically Flemish syntax in '...zal aan denken', see below pp. 93 ff.

13 G. Geerts, 'Nengels en Frengels', in *Taal of taaltje?*, p. 227.

14 J. Grauls, *Terug naar de oorsprong* (Hasselt, 1966), p. 28. Those familiar with G. B. Shaw's *Pygmalion* will remember a similar tendency to hypercorrection in speakers of London Cockney dialect.

15 This peculiarity is also found in the Netherlands, especially but not exclusively in the areas below the great rivers. Likewise, the *h* is unaspirated in some Zeeland, North Brabant, Overijssel, Drente and Groningen dialects. Unlike in Flanders, however, these phenomena are in the Netherlands excluded not only from the written language, but also from standard speech.

16 Cf. G. A. van Es, 'Het Nederlands van de Vlaamse (Antwerpse) schrijver Marnix Gijsen', *Tijdschrift voor Nederlandse Taal- en Letterkunde*, XCI/2 (1975), p. 101.

17 *Gramarie*, pp. 123−124.

18 'Het algemeen beschaafd in België, *Onze Taal* (maart 1963), p. 36.

19 'Het AN in Vlaanderen', in *Bijdragen en Mededelingen der Dialectencommissie van de Koninklijke Akademie van Wetenschappen te Amsterdam*, 39 (1970), pp. 5−25.

20 'De Belgische uitspraak van het Nederlands', in G. Geerts, *Aspekten*, p. 140.

21 'In hoever geeft het Noorden de toon aan?', in *Verzamelde Opstellen* (Assen, 1965), p. 77. Also in G. Geerts, *Taal of taaltje*, p. 119.

22 'ABN-dialect: een tegenstelling?', *Taal en Tongval* XXVII/1−3 (1975), p. 76.

23 F. Debrandere, 'Westvlaams en algemeen Nederlands', in G. Geerts, *Aspekten*, p. 112.

24 F. W. van Coetsem, 'De rijksgrens tussen Nederland en België als taalgrens in algemene taal', in G. Geerts, *Aspekten*, p. 114.

25 G. Geerts, *Voorlopers en varianten van het Nederlands* (Leuven, 1975), pp. 183 ff. A survey of work carried out since Meeus' study, with full references is to be found in K. Deprez, *Naar een eigen identiteit*. Resultaten en evaluatie van tien jaar taalsociologische en sociolinguïstisch onderzoek betreffende de standaard taal in Vlaanderen (Kessel-Lo, 1982).

26 F. van Coetsem, op. cit., in G. Geerts, *Aspekten*, p. 163. In Classical times, *koiné* referred to the language common to the whole of Greece, as opposed to the Achaean, Ionian and other dialects.

27 M. J. de Vriendt-de Man, *Frequentie van woorden en structuren in spontaan gesproken Nederlands* (Brussel, 1969), p. 19.

28 W. Pée, 'ABN-dialect: een tegenstelling?', *Taal en Tongval*, XXVII/1-3 (1975), pp. 76—81.

29 J. Goossens, '''Belgisch beschaafd Nederlands'' en Brabantse expansie', in G. Geerts, *Aspekten*, p. 96.

30 J. Goossens, 'De Belgische uitspraak van het Nederlands', in G. Geerts, *Aspekten*, p. 144.

31 J. Goossens, article quoted in n. 29 above, in G. Geerts, *Aspekten*, p. 105.

32 Cf. G. Geerts, *Voorlopers en varianten*, p. 148.

33 'Het A. B. in België', *Onze Taal* (maart 1963), pp. 25—26.

34 Grauls, *Terug naar de oorsprong* (Hasselt, 1966), p. 31.

35 'Hij zei dattem van niks en wist', in G. Geerts, *Taal of taaltje?*, pp. 142 ff. (The emphases are mine, P. B.)

36 G. Geerts, *Voorlopers en varianten*, p. 184.

37 K. Heeroma, *Sprekend als nederlandist*, p. 184.

38 'ABN-dialect, een tegenstelling?', *Taal en Tongval*, XXVII/1—3 (1975), p. 80.

39 *Gramarie*, p. 278.

40 See above, p. 00.

41 J. Goossens, 'De Belgische uitspraak van het Nederlands', in G. Geerts, *Aspekten*, p. 141.

42 W. Pée, 'Les divergences dans la prononciation du néerlandais aux Pays-Bas et en Flandre', *Zeitschrift für Phonetik, Sprachwissenschaft und Kommunikationsforschung*, XVII (1964), p. 278.

43 Ibid., p. 277.

44 Both definitions are taken from B. van den Berg, *Foniek van het Nederlands* (Den Haag, 1972[2]), p. 35.

45 Cf. W. Pée, 'Bilabiale w — labiodentale w', in *Spel van Zinnen* (Album van Loey) (Brussel, 1975), pp. 231—235.

46 C. A. Zaalberg, *Taaltrouw* (Noordwijk, 1975), p. 88.

47 Some examples of 'deviant' usage from a recent novel are to be found in J. Brouwers, 'Vlaamse flaters', *Tirade*, 25 (juni 1981), pp. 380—381. For an impressionistic view of language-reform in Flanders, see the same author's 'Amateurs voor pudding of: ABN in Vlaanderen', in *Mijn Vlaamse jaren* (Amsterdam, 1978), pp. 179—189.

48 But of course one can equally well say:...*ter beschikking had gesteld,...in acht had genomen*. On this subject in general, see L. Koelmans, 'Iets over de woordvolgorde bij samengestelde predikaten in het Nederlands', *De Nieuwe Taalgids* (1965), pp. 156 ff., and E. Nieuwborg, 'Woordschikking in de verbale eindgroep', in *Taal- en letterkundig gastenboek* (Album van Es) (Groningen, 1975), pp. 97 ff.

49 J. Goossens, 'Vlaamse purismen', *Tijdschrift voor Nederlandse Taal- en Letterkunde*, XCI/1 (1975), p. 125.

50 Van Haeringen, 'Wankele normen', in *Taalkunde, — 'n Lewe, feestbundel voor W. Kempen* (Kaapstad/Johannesburg, 1974), p. 138. See also M. C. van den Toorn, 'De problematiek van de Nederlandse aanspreekvormen', *De Nieuwe Taalgids*, LXX/2 (1977), pp. 520—540.

51 In some areas, notably in East Flanders, the pronoun *je* is not unknown. Some people have used this as a basis for argument. But, besides the fact that it is not found in the plural, its use is very different to that in the North.

52 C. C. Meyers, *Nu Nog*, 2 (1966), quoted in G. Geerts, *Aspekten*, p. 80.

53 J. L. Pauwels, 'In hoever geeft het Noorden de toon aan?', in *Verzamelde Opstellen*, p. 74, and in G. Geerts, *Taal of taaltje?*, p. 116.

54 Cf. G. Geerts, 'Van gij naar jij en u', in *Taal- en letterkundig Gastenboek* (Album Van Es) (Groningen, 1966), pp. 47—53.

55 Ibid., p. 51.

56 These examples, almost all of which date from the 1960s, are taken from Geerts' article, 'Hij geeft melk', in *Taal of taaltje?*, pp. 90 ff., which contains many others, with precise references.

57 R. Emmermans, 'Is de algemene Vlaamse woordenschat werkelijk zo klein?', in Geerts, *Aspekten*, pp. 74—81.

58 S. S. H. M. Boelen, 'De Nederlandse taal in Vlaanderen', in G. Geerts *Taal of taaltje?*, pp. 128−134.
59 'Algemeen Vlaamse woordenschat', in G. Geerts, *Aspekten*, pp. 82−85. Cf. J. de Rooij, 'Algemeen Zuidnederlands?', in *Bijdragen en Mededelingen der Dialecten-commissie van de Koninklijke Nederlandse Akademie van Wetenschappen te Amsterdam* XLIII (1974), pp. 5−18.
60 P. C. Paardekooper, '"Zuid Nederlands" woordgebruik', *De Nieuwe Taalgids*, XL (1947), p. 197.
61 J. Goossens, 'De Belgische uitspraak van het Nederlands', in G. Geerts *Aspekten*, p. 150. See also the same author's '"Belgisch beschaafd Nederlands" en Brabantse expansie', Ibid., pp. 95−111.
62 Goossens is here alluding to the study by F. van Coetsem, 'De rijksgrens tussen Nederland en België, een in kracht afnemende taalgrens?', in G. Geerts *Aspekten*, pp. 159−161.
63 E. De Bock, in G. Geerts, *Taal of taaltje*, p. 121.
64 J. L. Pauwels, Ibid., p. 124.
65 J. Leenen, Ibid., p. 138.
66 A. A. Weijnen, *Het algemeen beschaafd Nederlands historisch beschouwd* (Assen, 1974), p. 34.
67 See above, pp. 16−18.
68 J. Veering, 'Het Zuidnederlandse taaleigen voor het Noordnederlandse taal-gevoel', in Geerts, *Aspekten*, p. 188.
69 *Gezag en norm* (Amsterdam, 1951), p. 55.
70 *Nederlands tussen dialect en wereldtaal* (Groningen, 1965), p. 14.
71 'Nederlands uit de pen van Zuidnederlanders', in *Album Willem Pée* (Tongeren, 1973), p. 409.
72 *Terug naar de oorsprong* (Hasselt, 1966), p. 31.
73 'Over de Noord- en Zuidnederlandse taaltegenstelling', in *Handelingen van het 23ste Nederlandse Philologencongres* (1954), pp. 24−25.
74 'De roep om erkenning van Zuidnederlandse ABN-varianten', in G. Geerts, *Taal of taaltje?*, pp. 175−188.
75 *Verzamelde opstellen*, p. 74, repr. in G. Geerts, *Taal of taaltje?*, p. 116.
76 *Nu nog*, 1 (1961), quoted in G. Geerts, Ibid., p. 153.
77 'Het Algemeen Beschaafd in Vlaanderen', in *Bijdragen en Mededelingen der Dialecten-commissie van de Koninklijke Nederlandse Akademie van Wetenschappen te Amsterdam*, 39 (1970), p. 71.
78 W. Pée, 'Les divergences dans la prononciation du néerlandais aux Pays-Bas et en Flandre', *Zeitschrift für Phonetik, Sprachwissenschaft und Kommunikationsforschung*, XVII (1964), pp. 276 and 279.
79 This example is taken from C. A. Zaalberg, *Taaltrouw* (Noordwijk, 1975), p. 88.
80 'Iets over taalzuivering en taalgebruik', in G. Geerts, *Aspekten*, p. 214.
81 Flemings are often irritated by the fact that dictionaries published in the Netherlands mark these words with the sign 'ZN', which seems to them discriminatory. Would it not be better, they ask, to designate with 'NN' terms peculiar to the Netherlands? Moreover, 'ZN' is applied without distinction to words used throughout Flanders and to provincialisms (*binst, bachten*, etc.). This objection applies even to some extent to W. de Clerck's in other respects useful compilation, the *Zuidnederlands Woordenboek* ('s-Gravenhage/Antwerpen, 1981). Accordingly the authors of the 'Little Green Book' decided, having done the essential weeding out, to abandon the traditional practice. Their decision caused a great hue and cry in certain circles. Were the Dutch going to be forced to 'speak Flemish'? Such a reaction was based on a misunderstanding. No one was trying to force anyone at all to modify their vocabulary. The sole desire was to satisfy the Flemings' legitimate pride.
82 Cf. J. L. Pauwels, *Verzamelde opstellen*, p. 75.
83 W. Pée, 'Het AB in Vlaanderen', in *Bijdragen en Mededelingen der Dialectencommissie van de Koninklijke Nederlandse Akademie van Wetenschappen te Amsterdam*, 39, (1970), pp. 5−25.
84 J. de Rooij, 'Nederlands-Vlaams taalprobleem (nog eens) fris bekeken', *Neerlandica extra muros*, 10 (April 1968).
85 See, however, M. C. Godschalk's article (*Onze Taal* 44/9 (Sept. 1975), p. 43), which

attributes to Belgian radio certain shifts in journalistic vocabulary in the Netherlands and even in the pronunciation of Hilversum announcers.

86 G. A. van Es, article quoted (*Tijdschrift voor Nederlandse Taal- en Letterkunde*, XCI/2 (1975), p. 88).

CHAPTER IV

Dutch and German
or
David and Goliath

1. MISUNDERSTANDINGS AND PREJUDICES

'It always amuses me to see many people's reaction when I inform them that I study Dutch. The conversation always proceeds in the same way. At first, utter astonishment fills their faces, and could not have been greater if I had mentioned some Central African language. Having recovered from their initial surprise, they usually ask, not without curiosity: "But how did you come to do that?" Such an amazing fact demands an explanation. That someone, driven solely by the desire to extend his knowledge and enjoy great literature, should study philosophy, French language and literature, or even Dutch painting, was understandable. But for someone to be interested in Dutch language and literature, he must have been driven by some purely external motive, since — such is the idea present in the back of their minds — neither the Dutch language nor Dutch literature have anything to offer worth discovering or appreciating.'[1]

This was written in 1929 by a German scholar of Dutch, H. Schreiber. How different is the situation today? Dutch, it is true, is taught to some extent at twenty-two German universities and in a number of secondary schools. However, a short stay in the country is sufficient to make one see that things have not changed so very much.

Though deeply-rooted, this negative attitude is not **that** old. In the Middle Ages, far from scorning the language of the 'lowlands by the sea', the Germans made conscious borrowings from it. This is what some call *vloemen mit der rede*. Many of these terms derive from French, and so we find Wolfram von Eschenbach using *pardrisekin* and Gottfried von Strassburg *schapelekin*, which combine a French root (perdrix, chapel) with a Dutch suffix. The Middle Dutch *hoevesch*, a transposition of the Fr. 'courtois' (= 'courtly') becomes Middle High German *hövisch*, just as *dorper* (villain) becomes *törper*. But 'Flemish' did not only play the role of intermediary: words like *ors* (horse) and *wapen* are entirely Dutch in origin, as are *ritter* (< ridder, 'knight') and *traben* (< draven, 'to trot'). In the field of religion, long before the influence of the mystics and the *Devotio moderna* (cf. p. 11) spread throughout the Rhineland, the *Leven van Jesus*, an adaptation of Tatianus' *Harmonia* made in the 13th century by an anonymous

Limburger, penetrated into Germany and was still to have an indirect influence on Luther's language. In the 17th century, seeking a new way forward in difficult conditions, the Silesian poets look with admiration and envy at men of the stature of Heinsius and Grotius. The young Gryphius sits at Vondel's feet, while Philipp von Zesen finds in Holland the necessary inspiration for his task of purifying the German vocabulary (it is from there, for example, that *Umgang* = 'intercourse', *Sinnbild* = 'symbol', *Leibwache* = 'bodyguard' and *anmutigen* = 'to encourage' derive). His successors, impressed by the variety of the Dutch vocabulary, were to try (though in vain) to coin German equivalents for *schouwburg* (theatre), *voorspoed* (prosperity) and *tegenspoed* (adversity).

But the subsequent reversal is total. How is one to translate Homer into Dutch without travestying him, Herder seriously asks himself in his *Fragmente* (1766–1777). Sixty years later Dingelstedt is to make observations of a similar kind in discussing the Classical theatre, while A. Menzel considers that 'Dutch poetry' is a contradiction in terms. A. W. Schlegel, working as a tutor in Amsterdam, writes to Bürger in 1791: 'The language disgusts me so much that the very thought of picking up a Dutch book turns my stomach.'[2] In the following generation a man like Wienbarg, who sometimes shows a degree of sympathy for the Dutch, finds their language a veritable bog, degenerate, reduced to a series of croakings, discordant and flat.[3] Of course there are some exceptions, who are better disposed, Grimm, for example, who in 1824 does not hesitate to write: 'In general, Dutchmen and Germans should not consider their languages in terms of opposition, but as two offshoots from the same stem, which by virtue of this seems all the richer: without either the whole would be the poorer.'[4] Shortly afterwards, Hoffmann von Fallersleben devotes himself heart and soul to the rehabilitation of the masterpieces of Middle Dutch. At the beginning of this century, through his friendship with Albert Verwey, Stefan George comes to admire Dutch as, 'the noblest sister of the German language'.[5] But a few swallows do not make a summer, and it remains all too true that 'from Johannes Beckmann in 1762 down to Hausenstein and Keyserling in our own day, the dominant note in German judgements on Holland remains the same: aversion to and contempt for the country, the **language** and the national character sums up the feeling of the majority'.[6]

*   *   *   *   *

This modern German attitude is based at the same time upon impression and upon theory.

Given the indisputable and undisputed fact that German and Dutch are closely related, there is a tendency to conclude *a priori* that the latter language holds nothing of interest for the neighbouring people. There are few who, like Niebuhr, know that 'to the great perplexity of foreigners Dutch is very rich in words and phrases which are peculiar to it and are entirely separate from the two principal dialects', i.e. from High and Low German,[7] or who confess as modestly as Wilhelm Busch: 'I hope to make progress in Dutch, and to learn it as one learns English or French, but as for feeling at home in it, I shall never be able to.'[8] Usually, not to say invariably, reactions recall those described by Schreiber:

'...And this is the direction that the conversation follows. One's inter-locutors all indeed maintain that they understand a little Dutch. To back up their claim, they expound on the idea that Dutch is basically easy to learn. Anyone who knows *Plattdeutsch* will not have the slightest diffi-culty. In fact, they themselves know nothing about *Platt*, but during the First World War they were able to converse marvellously with Flemish peasants within a very short time. The implicit conclusion addressed to me is: "You must be out of your mind to devote years of study to something so simple!" If one observes that while there are correspon-dences with German there also exist some very great differences one's words will provoke a pitying smile. They know what to believe.'[9]

There is more. As a German observer noted as early as 1792: 'I believe that the Dutch language would seem less offensive, vulgar and repugnant to us if it were less closely related to our own. The majority of German words I hear strike me as deformed, rather like our language in the mouth of the rabble.'[10] This is the crux of the matter! Dutch is very similar to the north German **dialects**, and the use in a standard language of words which for them are reserved for familiar usage, strikes Germans as tasteless. Dingelstedt found that a sermon delivered in Dutch had 'an almost humorous tinge' and that 'for every German who knew *Plattdeutsch*, Dutch, however solid and worthy, would be bound to appear a little comic'.[11] Even today such words as *trekken, plaats, beest, trap, belemmeren, wat, dat, op*, etc., used 'in areas which for German sensibilities are the exclusive domain of the *Hoch-sprache* (preaching, prayer, government statements, court hearings, the theatre, lectures, etc.) are still always shocking'.[12] No doubt a primitive reaction, 'but one which is psychologically axiomatic and can only be overcome by a conscious will to recognise the legitimacy of the other language'.[13]

This will is generally lacking, and this is in consequence of a theory, or notion, as simplistic as it is widespread. Forgetting that a good part of Flanders never belonged to the Holy Roman Empire, and that the rest of the Dutch-speaking areas had only very loose links with it, the German is convinced that the Low Countries in the broad sense were once German territory and that they were very wrong to secede. Certainly the time is past when Arndt, in *Was ist des Deutschen Vaterland?* (1813), called for the annexation pure and simple of Holland and Flanders. There are no longer any discernible traces of the rancour with which this nation of renegade peoples was viewed, as was some-times the case until late into the 19th century. What remains is a vague regret that the Dutch and Flemings should have cut themselves off from their roots, a feeling which might be summed up as: 'all the worse for them'. And what applies to culture is all the more true of the language. A recent survey of the various histories of the German language currently available established that with **one** exception, 'It is certainly admitted that Dutch is today an autonomous language, but it is considered to have previously formed part of German'.[14] If the specialists, who, moreover, differ widely on the supposed date of the defection, continue to uphold this theory, what wonder if the public at large share it?

The question has so far only been discussed in its psychological context. Before looking at its factual basis, one should add the note that the German attitude to Dutch is extremely similar to that of the Dutch themselves to Afrikaans, as has often been pointed out. For the Dutch, with a few exceptions to be sure, Afrikaans will always have an air of the stables and the kitchen, and the abandonment of Dutch be regarded as the result of irritating stubbornness. The same two elements are present: a gut reaction and a more or less conscious theory. The difference is that the language of the Boers is without question the emancipated daughter of Dutch, whereas Dutch, as we shall try to show, is in no way a product of German.

2. DAUGHTER OR SISTER?

Deutsch is a very ambiguous term, and German philologists have up till now scarcely concerned themselves with removing the ambiguity. 'Hundreds of pages have been filled with the history of the word *Deutsch*, but one will look in vain in the textbooks for a definition of what is meant by German.'[15] Originally, as we have seen, the word denoted the vernacular as opposed to Latin (c.f. p. 2), and it took ages before it acquired its present meaning. In Germanic times there existed neither 'German' nor 'Dutch', but a group of more or less closely related dialects, which linguists group under the name of 'West Germanic'. If one, in talking of these remote periods, were to replace *Deutsch* by (*Kontinental-*) *Westgermanisch*, the problem would disappear immediately.

From this West Germanic, two languages gradually emerged, German and Dutch. There is no reason to suppose that one of these (German) represents the culmination of a normal development from which the other (Dutch) at a given moment departed. To try to lump Dutch together with German in this way would be no less absurd than the reverse: if it seems otherwise, it is solely because of the numerical disparity. 'In fact, it is a case of "cellular division": German and Dutch are sister-languages.'[16] The former developed from the Southern dialects, the latter from the North-western dialects.

One can, even, maintain without paradox that Dutch shows a greater degree of continuity in its development, and from two points of view. The long effort of the 'Netherlanders', from generation to generation, to create a cultural language beyond dialect, is not only comparable with parallel efforts made by Germans, 'but is superior to them in its uninterrupted development'.[17] However, the essential developments took place long before such preoccupations were relevant. In fact, if there is any language, in talking of which the terms 'rupture' and 'schism' are appropriate, it is not Dutch, but German. The latter derives from dialects which, at the beginning of the Middle Ages, underwent a profound transformation and which by virtue of this set themselves apart from all the rest of the Germanic area — hence also from the dialects from which Dutch was later to emerge. Such was the effect of 'second sound shift'.[18]

In broad outline, the sound shift operated as follows: the shift applies to the unvoiced occlusives, *p, t* and *k* on the one hand and the dental *d* on the other.

At the beginning of a word, *p* and *t* become *pf* and *ts* (in today's spelling *z*) respectively:

Dutch	German
paal	*Pfahl*
pijl	*Pfeil*
pijp	*Pfeife*
pond	*Pfund*
tam	*zahm*
tin	*Zinn*
tien	*zehn*
teen	*Zehe*

The same applies in the body of a word, if the occlusive follows a consonant: *hart/Herz, hout/Holz, kamp/Kampf* (however, after *r* and *l* the development has been carried a stage further, and the fricative *pf* becomes *f: helpen/helfen, werpen/werfen*). The same applies to geminates: *appel/Apfel, zitten/sitzen*.

Everywhere else *p* becomes *f* and *t* becomes *s: aap/Affe, roep/Ruf, eten/essen, water/Wasser*. The third unvoiced occlusive, *k*, which in the above-mentioned cases remained stable, elsewhere becomes a *ch*, either a guttural as in *week/Woche* or velar as in *ik/ich*.

Finally, Germanic *d* becomes German *t: dood/tot, deur/Tür, dochter/Tochter*.[19]

These various transformations did not all have exactly the same geographical distribution. None of them, in any case, extends northwards of the line Venlo−Benrath−Kassel−Frankfurt-an-der-Oder.

But, if the second sound shift did not affect the Low German dialects, the *Hochdeutsch* to which it gave birth gradually became the **cultural language** of the whole of Germany, being superimposed on the local dialects in the countryside and wiping them out in the towns. This process goes back a long way. It begins with the literature of chivalry, but soon extends beyond poetry. The Franciscan Berthold von Regensburg (1220−1272) is certainly not referring only to aristocratic circles when he observes '*daz manic niderlender* (that there many

North Germans who are adopting South German speech) *ist, der sich der oberlender sprâche an nimet'.*[20] In 1336, the towns of Göttingen, Minden and Northeim conclude an alliance couched in High German. There were of course reactions here and there, but in the 16th century the combination of the Reformation, Humanism and dynastic forces were to deal a death-blow to Low German. It is not necessary to go into too much detail. What concerns us is the fact that this patient, but apparently irresistible advance of High German stopped short of the Dutch-speaking area. It never stood the slightest chance of penetrating, much less of becoming dominant in Flanders, Brabant, Holland or even in Gelderland. Once more David triumphed over Goliath, or rather showed himself so resolute that the giant did not force the issue. This resistance is the best proof of the vitality of Dutch and of its autonomy within Germanic.

Where did this strength derive from? If Low German did not manage to survive as a cultural language, it is in part and at a certain period because of the decline of the Hansa, but above all it is because 'in the area there was a lack of creative literary spirits, who might have given greater support to the indigenous language'[21] and counteracted the pull of the South. The Netherlands, however, had no need to import a *Hochsprache*. They had one of their own. Not only had a flourishing literature developed there from at least the beginning of the 12th century, but *diets* served as a vehicle of an intense cultural life. And when Flemings and Brabanters, as they often did, looked beyond their own area, it was not to Thuringia or Bavaria that they turned, but to France. As for the Reformation, this also came from France, in its Calvinist version; moreover, even if it had come from Germany, the example of Denmark is proof enough that a small country adjacent to Germany, but with a culture of its own, could assimilate Lutheranism without adopting, as did the North Germans, the language of Luther.[22] In the Netherlands, the Southern provinces were subsequently eclipsed by Holland, but that is immaterial. It was not during the height of the Golden Age that the language was in danger of losing its identity. Never, on the contrary, was Europe better able to realise that Dutch, in the words of Bakhuizen van den Brink, who was addressing himself explicitly to Arndt, is 'an independent tree, with its own roots in the earth, with its own top in the clouds, nay, in the heights!'.[23]

3. CONFRONTATIONS

As sister-languages, Dutch and German have obvious family resemblances. A German or Germanist beginning the study of Dutch has the feeling of being on familiar ground, and indeed, coming across a sentence like: *Ik weet dat dit slot in 1640 door de koning gebouwd (geworden) is* (I know that this castle was built by the king in 1640), he will be delighted to be able to understand it without difficulty (although it diverges on three points from the corresponding German sentence: *in* introducing a date, *door* used for the agent of the passive, *geworden* instead of *worden*). But if one confronts him with the following, hardly less complicated sentence: *Al was het reeds vrij laat, toch zijn ze nog even in de tuin gaan praten* (Even though it was already quite late, they still went and talked in the garden for a moment), he may, if an English speaker, be able to guess the meaning of *laat*, but he will have no idea what *tuin* or *praten* mean, and is in danger of being very wrong about *al*, *vrij* and *even*. Or consider the Dutch word *bericht* and the German word spelt in the same way. There is a threefold difference between them: of meaning (nine times out of ten, *bericht* is closer to *Nachricht* than to *Bericht*); of gender (masculine in German, neuter in Dutch); and finally of pronunciation (the first syllable of *bericht* is a neutral sound like that in English 'harbour', though with lip-rounding, while the *be* of *Bericht* tends towards that of 'berry'; the *i* is impure, i.e. intermediate between *i* and *e* in the Dutch word, and pure in the German; *ch* is guttural in the first case and velar in the second).

The divergences, large and small, are therefore numerous, and it is on them that we wish to focus attention below, albeit rather through characteristic examples than in systematic form, and not before having stressed once and for all that modern German is a much more highly-structured language than Dutch. One only rarely finds in it the same margin of uncertainty, the same variable norms, whose advantages and disadvantages can be weighed against each other, but which without the shadow of a doubt constitute an essential feature of Dutch.

A. Phonetics

The most striking feature, of course, consists in the total absence in German of certain sounds current in Dutch and vice versa. German does not have the *g* of *zeggen*, nor does Dutch have the *sp* of *spülen* or the *st* of *Stuhl*. The diphthongs *eeuw, ieuw, ooi, oei* do not exist in German, and beginners in Dutch are hard put to it not to confuse Dutch *ei* (or *ij*) with German *ei*, and not to produce the same sound in *koud* and *Haut* or in *huizen* and *Häuser*. Even when the sound is essentially the same, there are often slight shades of difference. *K, p* and *t* are explosive in German, but not in Dutch. In his respect too, *Tafel* and *tafel* are not identical, and whereas the *k* of *Kanone* seems like the report of a gun, the first consonant of Dutch *kanon* has a sound much closer to English 'cannon'. The same differences are found in vowels. Except before *r* Dutch long vowels are a little less long than the corresponding German ones. The *e* in the root of *nemen* is shorter than that of *nehmen* (and moreover, slightly diphthongised, at least in the Netherlands, while in the German verb the vowel is a pure monophthong).

Pronunciation is not, however, simply a matter of isolated sounds. A fundamental principle of German pronunciation is the *Silbentrennung* or glottal stop. In the introduction to the *Aussprache-Duden* one can find a whole exposition on the subject, in which the author gives no less than fourteen practical rules, while still denying any claim to exhaustiveness! It is important, in effect, to separate in speaking not only words but elements within the same word[24] so that one says *ent-arten* and *Reichs-amt*. In Dutch, quite the reverse happens. In the face of all etymology, one tends to pronounce *on-taarden* and *rijk-sambtenaar*. The German-speaker takes great pains to separate two consecutive identical sounds, for instance in: *um-mähen, kopf-faul* or *ab-passen*. The Dutch-speaker, on the other hand, 'assimilates' to the hilt (see pp. 59 ff.), pronouncing only one *s* and one *t* in *vaststaan*. What is more, assimilation operates between one word and another, which would be unthinkable in German. As a result, German speech has a clipped and jerky quality to Dutch ears, while a German-speaker drowns in the uninterrupted flood of Dutch pronunication. In addition, 'compared to that of Dutch, German pronunciation is characterised by noticeably more articulatory energy and significantly more muscular tension'.[25] Since on the other hand wordstress is more marked in their language than in Dutch, Germans, according to some observers, have more difficulty in lowering their voices in polite company.[26]

B. Morphology

Between Dutch and German there is all the difference between a language which is already very analytical and one which has remained essentially synthetic:

> 'The characteristic of a synthetic linguistic system is the wealth of possibilities of grammatical expression, and consequently the high degree of autonomy of each form independently. A Gothic nominal form like *anstais* (of the favour) expresses simultaneously, quite apart from any insertion in a sentence, several grammatical categories: part of speech, case, number and class. The same applies, *mutatis mutandis*, to a verb form like *habaidedeina* (they would have had): part of speech, tense, mode, number, person and class.
>
> In an analytical system, the forms by themselves have much less autonomy: it is only to the group of words and the sentence of which they form part that they owe their grammatical value. The more morphology is simplified, the more the grammatical centre of gravity moves towards syntax.
>
> Simplification of inflection and the concomitant weakening of unstressed vowels and even syllables (sometimes leading to their complete disappearance); increased grammatical importance of syntax in the widest sense: there are the main lines along which the Germanic languages have developed, at varying tempos and in varying areas of grammar.'[27]

That Dutch has advanced much farther along this path than German is evidenced by the large number of monosyllables, like the following twelve in a quite ordinary sentence: *Ze heeft dan ook nooit iets van dat plan aan haar broer verteld* (And so she never told her brother anything about that plan); the corresponding German sentence would contain only seven. One finds them at the level of inflection (*neem/nehme*), and at a lexical level (*eer/Ehre, trouw/Treue*). Unstressed *e* has survived, with the exception of archaisms like *ere* and *vreze*, only in precise cases: to safeguard a suffix (*breedte, dikte*), to prevent homonymy (*aarde/aard*), or to mark a different shade of meaning (*proeve* = 'attempt', as opposed to *proef* = 'test').

Dutch **conjugation** is more complicated than German on three points, which are easily listed:

1) in the second-person singular of the present tense, the *t*-ending is dropped when the subject follows the verb: *je slaapt*, but *slaap je?*;

2) the preterite of weak verbs has the ending *-te(n)* when the root of the verb ends in an unvoiced consonant (they are all found in the well-known mnemonic *'T KoFSCHiP*), and in other cases the ending *-de(n)*; hence: *werken/werkte* but *roeien/roeide*;

3) in the preterite of certain strong verbs there is an alternation between short and long vowels which in German has been levelled out by the operation of analogy *lag* (short)/*lagen* (long).

Nevertheless, Dutch conjugation as a whole is still much simpler than German. In German, roughly one in five of strong verbs has irregularities in the singular of the present tense. Apart from the special cases of *sein, haben* and the modal auxiliaries, they fall schematically into two groups: *du fährst, er fährt; du gibst, er gibt*. Dutch has a mere seven verbs with irregularities in the present tense: *zijn, hebben, komen, kunnen, mogen, willen* and *zullen*.

The greatest difference is of course the subjunctive, which has a considerable place in the theory and practice of German. For Dutch, the first thing to note is that, except for set expressions like *als het ware* (as it were), the past subjunctive no longer exists.[28] Its use in the present is to a certain extent parallel with that in German. The subjunctive may express a wish (*Leve de Koningin!* = 'Long Live the Queen!'), a concession (*wat er ook van zij* = 'be that as it may'), a possibility (*we moeten volhouden, er kome van wat wil* = 'we must persevere, come what may'), or a directive (*men wende zich tot de secretaris* = 'enquiries should be addressed to the secretary'). These forms, as in German, are largely confined to written usage, but even in writing, Dutch-users are much less inclined to use the subjunctive than are their German counterparts. The German sentence *Als Staatsmann beurteile ihn jeder wie er mag* (Let everyone judge him as a statesman as they think fit) may certainly be rendered literally as: *Als staatsman beoordele iedereen hem zoals hij wil*, but equally well as: *Laat als staatsman iedereen hem beoordelen zoals hij wil*.

However, this is not where the main difference lies, which is that Dutch never uses the subjunctive to indicate indirect speech, whereas this is the most natural thing in the world in German, with or without *dass*. In most cases, it is sufficient to replace the German subjunctive by a Dutch indicative. *Das Gerücht verbreitete sich, er SEI erschossen worden* (The rumour spread that he had been shot) becomes quite simply: *Het gerucht verspreidde zich, dat hij doodgeschoten was.* When the German sentence does not contain a word such as 'say', 'think', etc., it is sometimes necessary to insert one in Dutch, precisely because the verb form does not indicate that one is dealing with indirect speech. *Ein Diener trat ein und überreichte ein Schreiben. Ein Kornet HABE es gebracht* (A servant entered and handed him a letter, (saying that) an ensign had bought it) will be rendered as: *Een dienaar trad binnen en gaf een schrijven af, MET DE WOORDEN dat een kornet het gebracht had.* Or else Dutch will have recourse to a conjunction, as for example in: *Der Wirt munterte ihn auf, noch einen Löffel zu nehmen, das SEI gut bei dem rauhen Wetter/De waard spoorde hem aan nog een lepel te nemen, OMDAT dat goed was bij het gure weer* (The landlord urged him to have another spoonful, saying that it would do him good in the harsh weather).[29]

The formation of the **plural** in German is of frightening complexity: ¨, *e*, ¨*e*, *er*, ¨*er*, *en*, *s*, not to mention invariable nouns. Dutch, on the other hand, is delightfully simple. Apart from a few words which form their plural in -*eren* (*eieren* = 'eggs', *kinderen* = 'children'), and a few words of foreign origin (*musea* is more frequent than *museums*), there are only two classes of plural, -*en* and -*s*. It should be added that in a certain number of nouns the root vowel of the singular is modified: *stad* (town)/*steden*, *smid* (smith)/*smeden*, *dak* (roof) and *hol* (cave, den) have a short vowel, *daken* and *holen* a long one. But these special cases are quickly summed up.

The **declensions** are as alive as ever in German, and are indeed the principal headache of the would-be Germanist. They affect not only the articles but also adjectives, whose inflection varies according to whether or not they are preceded by an article, and if so, what kind of article, and finally the class of the noun. The latter takes an -*s* in the genitive masculine singular (unless it is a weak noun, in which case it takes the ending -*en* throughout), and in the genitive neuter singular. Not forgetting the obligatory -*n* in the dative plural. And so on and so on. In Dutch, all this has disappeared. Inflection survives only in the adjective, which in certain cases takes the ending -*e*. Remnants of the old case system are to be found in numerous set expressions and formulae: a masculine genitive in *schrijver dezes* (I, the undersigned), a feminine genitive in *onverrichter zake* (without achieving one's aim), and a neuter dative in *in koelen bloede* (in cold blood). The formal written language retains the use of the Saxon genitive (*Vestdijks werk, Maria's hoed*) particularly in the forms *wiens, wier, welks: de buurman, wiens huis* (= *van wie het huis) hier staat* (the neighbour whose house stands here). It should be noted also that the form *der* (fem. genitive sing. and masc./fem./neut. genitive plural) is quite common in writing, since it is a convenient way of avoiding strings of *van*'s: *besluit ter uitvoering van artikel 15 DER wet van 20 januari* is clearly more elegant than . . . *van de wet* . . . It may even happen that *der* is used when the noun in question is not either feminine or plural. A school pupil who (with good reason) would roar with laughter at the idea of using *des stoels* or *des bergs*, will quite calmly write: *ter opluistering DER feestavond* (to brighten up the evening festivities) or *de gevolgen DER sterke aandrang* (the result of the great crush) — a further illustration of the tendency to confuse grammatical genders (cf. pp. 66–67).

The only area in which one can freely talk of declension in Modern Dutch is that of personal pronouns (even though it does not apply to all pronouns, as *je, het, zij* and *jullie* are not affected), where there is a very precise distinction between subject and object case. To this extent Dutch is close to German. However, an essential difference is immediately apparent, in that Dutch has only one form for dative and accusative (the distinction between *hun* (dat.) and *hen* (acc.) in the 3rd-person plural is a somewhat artificial one, and often disregarded in practice). The psychological motivation for this merger of cases extends far beyond the use of pronouns. The following was written by a linguist of repute: *De taal is hetgeen DE MENS in staat stelt te denken en door het denken de macht geeft over de dieren* (Language is what enables man to think and through thought gives (him) power over animals).[30] The author has taken the liberty of implying *de mens* in the second part of the sentence, although the noun obviously has a different function than in the first part.

Dutch is also inclined, in a much more limited but definite manner, to confuse nominative and dative. From *MIJ werd (de deur) door de concierge opgengedaan* (The porter opened the door to me; lit: The door was opened to me by the porter) it is a short step to *IK werd door de concierge opengedaan* (lit.: I was opened by the porter), and only purists would take offence at a sentence like: *Daarop werd HIJ door de anderen de mond dichtgestompt* (Thereupon he was forcibly shut up by the others). To return to the pronouns, one can, for emphasis, say (perfectly correctly): *Als ik JOU was* (If I were you) and even, without emphasis: *Dat is 'M* (That's him). The last example borders on incorrectness, while *HUN moeten altijd gelijk hebben* (lit.: Them always like to be in the right) is clearly substandard, but the very existence of such constructions in popular speech is a clear indication of the direction in which the language is moving. Needless to say, one will look in vain for an equivalent in German.[31]

The relatedness of Dutch and German is particularly clear in **compounds**. There are certainly some minor disparities: the equivalents of *stadSwal* (town wall) and *woningprobleem* (housing problem) and *Stadtwall* and *WohnungSproblem* respectively; bishops in the Netherlands attend a *bischoppENconferentie* (episcopal conference), their German colleagues a *Bischofskonferenz*. But the broad outlines of compounding are the same, whether in a combination of two nouns, as in the above examples, or of a verb root and a noun as in: *rijweg* (carriageway), *wandelpad* (footpath), *maaimachine* (lawnmower), *vechtwagen* (tank), etc.[32]

Having said this, even a cursory comparison reveals that Dutch is not as fond as German of very long compounds. While in German there is nothing abnormal about *Reisebücherverlag* or *Auswanderungs-vermittlungsstelle*, Dutch recoils at *fotografiebenodigdhedenmagazijn* (photographic equipment store), and *gemeentereinigingsroltrommel-huisvuilophaalautos* (municipal sanitation domestic dustbin collection vehicles) remains just a curiosity. In fact, the length of some compounds is masked by writing conventions. *Vreemde-talenonderwijs* could be written as one word (although the hyphen is a means of representing the underlying grammatical structure of the compound, cf. Eng. 'foreign-language teaching'), as could *lange afstandspatrouille vliegtuigen* (a very unsatisfactory way of writing the compound, though hard to improve on). An extreme case of compound-splitting (which is becoming increasingly common, possibly under the influence of English) is: *openbare lagere schoolonderwijzeres*, instead of *openbare-lagere-schoolonderwijzeres*, or better still, *onderwijzeres aan een* [or: *aan de*] *openbare lagere school*.[33]

Short or long, there are fewer compounds in Dutch than in German. The examples are legion: *koperen lamp/Kupferlampe, volledig pension/ Vollpension, halve laarzen/Halbstiefel, voorstel tot wijziging/Abän-derungsvorschlag*. And one is hard put to find Dutch equivalents for *Sprachraumforschung, Werthaftigkeit* or *Mehrsilber*. There is a very simple explanation: resorting to compounds is a way for German to compensate for complexity of its inflections, and Dutch has correspondingly less need of them. 'While one can say that Dutch, morphologically speaking, is far in advance of German as far as rational simplification is concerned, German makes far better use than Dutch of the possibilities of compounding.'[34] To this is added a not insignificant psychological factor: the desire felt by Dutch-speakers to keep their distance from their powerful neighbour. This distrust can sometimes reach the point of phobia: a dogged rearguard action was fought, for example, against *nieuwbouw* (< *Neubau*), now quite current, while umpteen localities in the Low Countries are called *Nieuwstad, Nieuwpoort*, or have a *nieuwmarkt*. Why do lexicographers mark *hoogbouw* (high-rise buildings) and *rauwkost* (raw food) with a 'Du[its]', when *witkiel* (luggage-porter) and *blauwkous* (bluestocking) are formed on precisely the same model? In fact, whether or not such compounds derive from German, they are in no way contrary to the spirit of the Dutch language. But theory and usage are two different things.

C. Vocabulary

What was said of compounds also applies to derivatives (the operation of prefixes and suffixes) and to vocabulary in general: the common origin of the two languages is recognisable at every turn. This makes the differences all the more interesting. These relate either to gender or to meaning or to both at once: the case of *bericht/Bericht* cited above, is in no way exceptional.

Certain nouns, neuter in Dutch, have a different gender in German: *het zand/der Sand, het deel/der Teil*. Conversely, *knie* and *oever* are 'de-words', while German has *das Knie* and *das Ufer*, and the same is true of a great many technical terms: *auto, radio, telefoon*, etc.

As for derivatives, the suffixes usually have the same effect in both languages: words ending in -*ij* (except for *schilderij*, which may also be neuter), -*heid* and -*ing* are feminine, like German nouns ending in -*ei*, -*heit* and -*ung*. But whereas one finds in German *die Bedrängnis* and *die Betrübnis* alongside *das Ereignis* and *das Gefängnis*, Dutch nouns ending in -*nis* (apart from *getuigenis* and *vuilnis*, which have dual gender) are all feminine. On the other hand, -*schaft* raises no problems in German, since all nouns formed with this suffix are feminine, whereas Dutch -*schap* is full of traps. One can immediately grasp the difference between *de priesterschap* = 'the clergy' (collective) and *het priesterschap* = 'priesthood' (vocation). But why are *vriendschap* and *gemeenschap* feminine, while *vaderschap* and *genootschap* are neuter? The criteria in this case become so nebulous that the foreigner must appeal to the dictionary for enlightenment. A last, though somewhat special example is the suffix pair Du. -*isme*/Germ. -*ismus*: Dutch nouns formed with it are neuter, German ones masculine.

Three prefixes in Dutch have a decisive influence on gender. Provided they are bisyllabic, all nouns beginning in *be-, ge-* (except for *gezant* and *gezel*) or *ver-* (except *verkoop, verhuur* and *verbouw*) are neuter: *het beroep, het geduld, het verdrag*. No such thing in German: in the vast majority of cases the corresponding nouns are masculine (*der Beruf, der Vertrag*) or feminine (*die Geduld*).[35] These nouns are very numerous, but obviously cause difficulty mainly to those passing from Dutch into German.

A canny teacher once coined the term '*faux amis*' to describe those English words (like 'assist') which immediately evoke a French word, but actually mean something entirely different. The term caught on. In the Netherlands teachers of German list the dangerous words of this type among the 'schwere Wörter', of which there are many collections. The few examples below have been ranked in order of their approximate degree of difference, that is, those at the top are separated from their apparent equivalents by a simple nuance (which may nonetheless be significant), while those at the bottom have more or less opposite meanings:

German		Dutch	
Andacht	'devotion, prayers'	*aandacht*	'attention'
ruchlos	'wicked'	*roekeloos*	'reckless'
seltsam	'odd'	*zeldzaam*	'rare'
geistig	'spiritual, mental'	*geestig*	'witty'
fast	'almost'	*vast*	'fixed'
eben	'just, precisely'·	*even*	'for a moment'
Laster	'vice'	*laster*	'slander'
redlich	'honest'	*redelijk*	'reasonable'
schlimm	'bad'	*slim*	'cunning, clever'

wie	'how'	*wie*	'who'
Ausfahrt	'motorway exit-road'	*uitvaart*	'funeral'
absichtlich	'deliberate'	*afzichtelijk*	'hideous'
versuchen	'to try'	*verzoeken*	'to request'
hochherzig	'magnanimous'	*hooghartig*	'haughty'
einstellen[36]	'to call off'	*instellen*	'to institute'

In addition, the modal auxiliaries, so basic to both languages, are far from always having the same use:[37]

Dutch	German
Hij DURFDE niet (te) spreken (He did not dare speak)	Er WAGTE nicht zu sprechen
KENT U Frans? (Do you know French?)	*KÖNNEN Sie französisch?*
U had mij de waarheid MOETEN zeggen (You should have told me the truth)	*Sie hätten mir die Wahrheit sagen SOLLEN*
LAAT hem komen! (He is to come!)	*Er SOLL kommen!*
Wat MOET ik nu doen? (What am I to do now?)	*Was SOLL ich jetzt tun?*
MAG ik U onderbreken? (May I interrupt you?)	*DARF ich Sie unterbrechen?*
MOCHT U thuis zijn... (Should you be at home...)	*SOLLTEN Sie zu Hause sein...*
WIL ik U helpen? (Shall I help you?)	*SOLL ich Ihnen helfen?*
Hij ZAL komen (He will come)	*Er WIRD kommen.*
Hij ZOU komen (He was to come/ He would come)	{ *Er SOLLTE kommen* { *Er WÜRDE kommen*
Hij ZOU gestorven zijn *Hij MOET gestorven zijn* (He is supposed to have died) }	*Er SOLL gestorben sein (= man sagt, er SEI gestorben)*
We ZULLEN eens opstappen (We'll be going)	*Wir WOLLEN mal aufstehen*
Dat ZOU wel het einde KUNNEN zijn (That is probably the end)	*Das DÜRFTE das Ende sein.*
Dat KAN niet (That is impossible)	*Das ist unmöglich*
Het MAG niet (It is not allowed)	*Es ist verboten*
't MOET (It is imperative)	*Wir können nicht umhin*
't ZAL wel (zo zijn) (I expect so)	*Wahrscheinlich*

D. Syntax

Gisteren is ze voor de tweede keer in de hoofdstad geweest (Yesterday she went to the capital for the second time).

Het horloge, dat ik verleden zomer op mijn reis naar Zwitserland kocht, loopt uitstekend (The watch that I bought last summer on my trip to Switzerland, keeps excellent time).

Such sentences as these can be rendered literally in German. The basic rules of inversion and subordination are the same in both languages.

However, Dutch takes liberties with the rules, which modern German does not allow itself. This is an obvious fact. Except with careless writers or those who are out for unusual effects, one scarcely finds in German constructions like those analysed above (pp. 56 ff.). There is no choice between 'red' and 'green' constructions: 'red' is ruled out. Neither in foregrounding a particular element, nor in giving the sentence more balance, nor in bringing the antecedent closer to the relative, does German show the same flexibility as Dutch — and this is a fundamental difference.

Does this mean that German is necessarily more cumbersome? Certainly Dutch has the choice between: *De angsten die ik tussen het eerste en het tweede deel van mijn examen uitgestaan heb* (The terrors I went through between the first and second part of my exam) and... *die ik uitgestaan heb tussen het eerste en het tweede deel van mijn examen*, whereas German is forced to choose the first formulation, which needs more breath. But if one takes the following sentence, from the 19th-century collection of humorous sketches by Nicolaas Beets, the *Camera Obscura*: ...*indien ik had kunnen besluiten al de zes karaffen, die er met haar bijbehorende gezelschap van glazen, ineens werden uitgelicht, na elkander leeg te drinken* (...if I could have made up my mind to empty the six carafes which were suddenly produced, together with their accompanying array of glasses, one after the other), and tries to transpose it into German as it stands, the result will be painfully awkward. If the reader objects that Beets' style is archaic, and that the convolutions are deliberate and intended to amuse, take the following two sentences by Jacques Hamelink, a modern writer who in no way sets himself up as a humorist:

> *De vrouw wist dat de twist elk ogenblik opnieuw en heviger dan totnogtoe het geval was geweest ontvlammen kon* (The woman knew that the quarrel might flare up again at any moment, and more violently than it had done up to now).
> *Ze had amper naar het gepraat waarin zich de begeerte naar het goud openbaarde en verhulde, dat hun stemmen fel en kwaad en verheugd tegelijk deed klinken, geluisterd* (She had scarcely listened to the chatter in which the lust for gold was both revealed and concealed, and which gave their voices a ring at once passionate, angry and joyful).

While the first could, at a pinch, be put literally into German, the second would be horrific. However 'literary' such sentences may be, they reveal a tendency which is found even in the most ordinary written language. Instead of *Ken je het boek waarvan de titel opgegeven werd door de leraar die gisteren zijn cursus begon?* (Do you know the book, the title of which was given out by the teacher who began his course yesterday?) there is nothing to stop one saying: *Ken je het boek waarvan de titel door de leraar die gisteren zijn cursus begon, opgegeven*

werd? In German, the first construction would be incorrect, and preferable to the second would be: *Kennst du das Buch, dessen Titel von dem
Lehrer angegeben wurde, der,* etc.

The following observations concern only points of detail, but these
derive their importance from the fact that they constantly recur.

1) 'A single subordinate clause can refer to several following
coordinate main clauses; in this case there will be inversion in all the
main clauses':[38] *Toen de storm met volle kracht woedde, werden bomen
uitgerukt, vlogen muren omver en braken dijken door* (When the storm
was at its fiercest, trees were uprooted, walls demolished and dykes
breached). This is contrary to German usage. Certainly it is not
impossible to say: *Toen de storm met volle kracht woedde, werden bomen
uitgerukt; muren vlogen omver en dijken braken door,* but it is
symptomatic that the second comma is instinctively replaced by a
semicolon.

2) Dutch does not tend, as does German, to place personal pronouns
as early as possible in the sentence.

Vroeger heeft mijn zuster ONS een pakje gestuurd (In the past my sister
sent us a parcel) (Germ.: *Früher hat UNS meine Schwester...*)
Als de gelegenheid hiertoe ZICH voordoet (If the opportunity presents
itself) (Germ.: *Wenn SICH Gelegenheit dazu bietet).*

3) In a subordinate clause containing an embedded clause, the
subject-pronoun can easily be put after the embedded clause in Dutch,
whereas in German it always precedes it: *Je vader zei dat, als je carrière
wilde maken, JE dan hard zou moeten werken)* (Your father said that if
you wanted to make a career, you would have to work hard) (Germ.:
...dass DU, wenn du...).

4) When the auxiliary relates to two participles or two infinitives,
German always suppresses the auxiliary in the first case: *Das sind
Menschen, mit denen ich lange korrespondiert, die ich aber nie gesehen
HABE.* The Dutch-speaker will say: *Dat zijn mensen met wie ik lange tijd
HEB gecorrespondeerd, maar die ik nooit gezien HEB* (They are people I
have corresponded with for a long time but have never met).

5) Even when it could use a preterite instead of a conditional, Dutch
prefers the compound form, and this has repercussions on written
style. The preference can be justified when the use of the preterite
would lead to ambiguity: *Ik weet niet hoe eenvoudige boeren zo iets
ZOUDEN KUNNEN realiseren* (I do not know how simple farmers
could achieve something like that). Here the use of *konden* might
suggest that something had indeed been achieved. But the preference
is also clear when there is no danger of misunderstanding:...*hoe
vader en moeder gereageerd ZOUDEN HEBBEN als se ZOUDEN HEBBEN
geweten dat hun zoon de gelijke van Einstein was* (...how father and
mother would have reacted if they had (lit. would have) known that
their son was the equal of Einstein). The writer of this sentence, the
novelist Willem Frederik Hermans, could just as well have written: *als*

ze HADDEN geweten, but the repetition of *zouden* raises no eyebrows. In German, however, one would have had to write: *wie Vater und Mutter reagiert haben würden, wenn sie gewusst HÄTTEN, dass*, etc.

The monotony to which this predilection for compound forms might lead is in part offset by the freedom which Dutch enjoys with regard to the position of the auxiliary. This applies equally to 4) and 5). By putting *heb* before *gecorrespondeerd*, but after *gezien*, one breaks the parallelism. In the same way, after *gereageerd zouden hebben*, Hermans is careful not to write: *geweten zouden hebben*.

E. Miscellaneous

We should like to group here a few remarks regarding phenomena which exist in both languages, but whose development seems to have been arrested in one while continuing in the other.

In at least two respects, German goes further than Dutch: diphthong-isation of long *u* and vowel-mutation (*Umlaut*).

It will be remembered that at the beginning of the 17th century long *u* and *i* became *ui* and *ij* respectively (cf. p. 17). The same phenomenon occurred in German but on a much larger scale. In Dutch, long *u* in fact escaped diphthongisation when followed by *r*, whether in a Germanic word like *zuur* or in words of foreign origin like *muur* or *duren*. In German there are no exceptions, hence *sauer, Mauer, dauern*.

Vowel-mutation continues to play a huge part in German. With nouns it helps to determine the number (*Mutter/Mütter, Sohn/Söhne*); with verbs, person and number (*ich nehme, du nimmst, er nimmt*), and even mood (*war/wäre*); with adjectives, the degree of comparison (*gross, grösser, am grössten*). Vowel-mutation existed to a degree in Middle Dutch and there are remnants of it today: *stad/steden, tam/temmen, vol/vullen, goud/gulden*. But these alternations represent only a few isolated cases. 'In Dutch (unlike German) *Umlaut* has not become a significant morphological feature.'[39]

Displacement in word-stress under the influence of certain suffixes, use of positional verbs, and 'double infinitives', are three areas in which German has not taken things as far as Dutch.

As has been seen, the suffixes *-ig, -(e)lijk, -isch, -baar* and *-zaam* involve a shift in the stress (cf. p. 60). In German, this also happens, as for example, in: *Abscheu/abschéulich, Vórzug/vorzüglich*, and similarly in *vortréfflich* and *barmhérzig*. But what in Dutch is an absolute rule, here becomes sporadic and problematical, and the opinions of specialists differ. Should one say, can one say, *áusführlich* or *ausführlich, úrsprünglich* or *ursprünglich*? As far as theory is concerned, Duden does not even mention the phenomenon under the heading 'Abweichende Betonung' (though it calmly asserts, speaking of Dutch in general, that 'the pronunciation is more or less the same as in German'.).[40] H. H. Wängler observes 'in compounds and derivatives, there is quite often a shift of stress towards the end of the word' and vaguely invokes 'rhythmical reasons'. He does point out that

unausstéhlich, unberéchenbar and *unerbíttlich* have the principal accent
on the root but he attributes this anomaly to the coexistence of *un-* and
a second prefix.[41] T. Siebs is a little more precise: according to him,
North Germans have an annoying tendency to displace the accent in
compounds. He is also aware of the special case of adjectives beginning with *un-* and containing one of the suffixes *-lich, -ig, -sam, -bar*
and *-haft*, and draws up a list of some three hundred.[42] But in the
main, one does not get the impression that German scholars have ever
considered the question of the influence of suffixes of word-stress in
their language worthy of in-depth study.

The thesis has been defended that German inclines more to
abstraction than Dutch. By way of proof it has been pointed out that it
is difficult to render into German such expressions as: *een kruiwagen
hebben* (be able to 'pull strings'), *spijkers op laag water zoeken* (to split
hairs) or *het loopt de spuigaten uit* (that's the last straw), and that,
conversely, Dutch has no equivalent for: *aufs Tapet bringen, ad acta
legen, etwas durch die Blume sagen*. The latter images are indeed less
colourful, less 'realistic'.[43] The discussion remains open and is in
danger of remaining so, given the subjective nature of this kind of
judgement. On the other hand, no one will dispute that Dutch and
German have in common the very frequent use of positional verbs.
Where English has 'in the hall there is a hallstand', Dutch is naturally
more specific: *In de gang STAAT een kapstok*, as is German: *Im Gang
STEHT ein Kleiderständer*. The Dutch *In het bestuur ZITTEN* has a
German equivalent in *Im Präsidium SITZEN* (cf. Eng. 'Be on the executive'). Nor will a German-speaker be surprised to read: *De kast
HING vol kleren* (The cupboard was [lit. hung] full of clothes), however
'illogical' such a construction might appear at first sight.

But beyond this, in opposition to German this time, Dutch is fond of
combining positional verbs with an infinitive:

> ze *LAG* de hele nacht *TE DROMEN* (She dreamt all night long)
> Ik *STOND* aan de deur *TE BELLEN* toen...(I was ringing the doorbell,
> when...)
> De raven *ZITTEN TE KRASSEN* (The ravens are croaking)

German would have simply: *Sie träumte die ganze Nacht; ich klingelte an
der Tür, als...; die Raben krächzen*. The Dutch construction, so frequent
that it is virtually impossible to read a page of Dutch without coming
across it, nevertheless does not, oddly enough, date back further than
the 17th, indeed the 18th century. Before then, the second verb was
not put in the infinitive, but in the same tense as the positional verb:
ic sta ende wachte (= *ik sta en wacht*, 'I stand and wait'). This construction, which has not altogether disappeared from present-day
Dutch, is not inconceivable in German: *sie sass und schaute ihn lange an*
(She sat and looked at him for a long time). But just as one finds no
equivalent in modern German to *Ze ZAT uien TE SCHILLEN* (She sat
peeling onions), so older German has nothing to approximate the

famous line from Jacob Cats: *Een waterlantsche Trijn SAT eens ajuyn EN SCHELDE* (A lass from Waterland once sat peeling onions).[44]

The double infinitive, or in more scholarly terms, the *infinitivus pro participio*, describes the fact that when compound forms on the perfect and pluperfect form a fixed syntactical unit with an infinitive, an infinitive form may appear instead of the past participle.[45] 'I have not been able to read this book' is rendered in Dutch as: *Ik heb dit boek niet KUNNEN lezen*, and in German as: *Ich habe dieses Buch nicht lesen KÖNNEN*. Apart from the fact that the infinitives are not in the same order, the two sentences are entirely parallel, and the same remains true in a subordinate clause: *Het spijt me dat ik dit boek niet HEB kunnen lezen* (I am sorry that. . .), *Es tut mir leid, dass ich dieses Buch nicht HABE lesen können*. In both cases one finds the same departure from the usual construction.

Having said this, a first difference consists in the choice of auxiliary. Corresponding to the German *Er HAT sofort abfahren wollen*, Dutch has either *Hij HEEFT dadelijk willen vertrekken*, or (more frequently): *Hij IS dadelijk willen vertrekken*. Some consider that *hebben* is used when the weight of the sentence falls on *willen*, and *zijn* when it falls on *vertrekken*. One does indeed say *hij heeft gewild*, but *hij is vertrokken*. Nevertheless, this ingenious criterion is far from being universally accepted.

There is, however, no hesitation (except perhaps from some Flemings) about *Ze IS haar spullen komen halen* (She has come to fetch her things) or *Hij IS blijven staan* (He went on standing there; he stopped). In this case the auxiliary is that of the first. But there is no question of a comparison with German, as there is no possibility of a double infinitive construction with either *kommen* or *bleiben*. Here we touch on an important point: the very wide field of application of the double infinitive in Dutch. In German, it is limited to modal auxiliaries, verbs of sensation (*sehen, hören, fühlen*) and a very few others,[46] i.e. verbs which when governing an infinitive do not require a preceding *zu*: *Ich höre ihn sprechen; ich habe ihn sprechen hören*. In Dutch this category is much wider; it includes, notably, *doen, gaan* (frequently used as a semi-expletive: *Het type school, dat later H. B. S. is GAAN heten*, 'The type of school which later came to be known as H. B. S.), and *blijven* (in the sense of 'continue to': *Ik ben de hele dag BLIJVEN werken*, 'I went on working all day'). But other verbs also obey the double infinitive rule, either compulsory like *weten* (*Hij heeft zijn doel weten te bereiken* 'he managed to achieve his aim', Germ. . . . *zu erreichen gewusst*) and *hoeven*,[47] or optionally like *beginnen* and *proberen* (*Ze hebben de vijand proberen te vernietigen* 'They tried to destroy the enemy' or: *Ze hebben geprobeerd de vijand te vernietigen*). As can be seen, in such cases (and there are many others) the *te* is retained, and is inserted between the two infinitives. Positional verbs occupy in this respect an intermediate place between *doen*-types (no *te*) and *weten*-types, in the sense that the *te* is used when the verb is a simple tense and disappears when the verb is perfect or pluperfect: *We stonden op de tram TE wachten/We hebben op de tram staan wachten* (We stood waiting for the tram).[48]

The frequency of the 'double infinitive' on the one hand and the predilection for compound verb forms on the other can lead to strings of infinitives with which other languages, and German in particular, are unfamiliar, and from which they shy away. *Een artieste die hij zou hebben kunnen horen zingen* (A performer whom he might have been able to hear sing), *Zo'n boek zou men beslist hebben moeten laten vertalen* (They should certainly have had a book like that translated), are two quite normal sentences, which are, at a pinch, transposable into German, provided that one substitutes *hätte* for *zou hebben*, thus saving one infinitive out of four. To render *U zult mijn man toch wel eens meer in de tuin hebben zien staan harken?* (I expect you've seen my husband raking in the garden quite often before, haven't you?) one will have to say: *Sie haben meinen Mann sicher schon mal im Garten harken sehen?*, i.e. to simplify the verb form and drop *staan*. As for *Een stomme beslissing waardoor zij urenlang zou hebben kunnen blijven zitten wachten* (A stupid decision as a result of which she might have gone on sitting waiting for hours), the five infinitives tagging along behind each other are something of a record, but are in the normal run of the language. Let the foreigner try to make head or tail of this...and the translator rescue himself as best he can.

---

1 *Die niederländische Sprache im deutschen Urteil* (Heidelberg, 1929), p. 3.
2 References in E. F. Kossmann, *Holland und Deutschland, Wandlungen und Vorurteile* (Den Haag, 1901).
3 L. Wienbarg, *Holland in den Jahren 1831–1832* (Hamburg, 1833), I, pp. 21 and 68, quoted in H. Schreiber, op. cit., p. 6.
4 A. Reifferscheid, *Briefe von Jakob Grimm an H. W. Tydeman* (Heilbronn, 1883), p. 78.
5 Quoted in H. Combecher, *Uber niederländische und deutsche Sprache*, herausgegeben vom Arbeitsausschuss der deutsch-niederländische Arbeitsgemeinschaft Niederrhein-Limburg (1966), p. 13.
6 J. Huizinga, *Verzamelde Werken* (Haarlem 1948–1953) Vol. II, pp. 329–330 (My emphasis, P. B.) The passage from Keyserling to which Huizinga is alluding is as follows: 'Its [the Dutch language's] foundation is heaviness. One realises the deep-seatedness of this heaviness from the special way Dutchmen have of speaking and writing bad German.' It is true that the context of these remarks encourages one to take them with a pinch of salt.
7 'Circularbriefe aus Holland von 1808', in *Nachgelassene Schriften nicht philologischen Inhaltes*, pp. 104–105, quoted in H. Schreiber, op. cit., p. 18.
8 *Wilhelm Busch an Maria Anderson, Siebzig Briefe* (Rostock, 1908[5]), pp. 17–18, in H. Schreiber, op. cit., p. 5.
9 H. Schreiber, loc. cit.
10 Quoted in H. Schreiber, p. 8.
11 *Jusqu'à la mer. Erinnerungen an Holland.* (Leipzig, 1847), pp. 201–202, quoted in H. Schreiber, p. 6.
12 H. Combecher, op. cit., pp. 12–13.
13 K. Heeroma, *Sprekend als nederlandist* (Den Haag, 1968), p. 148.
14 J. Goossens, *Was ist Deutsch — und wie verhält as sich zum Niederländischen?* 'Nachbarn', Königliche Niederländische Botschaft (Bonn, n. d.), p. 22. See also the

examples quoted in C. Soeteman, *Het Nederlands, een dialect van het Duits?* (Groningen, 1956).

15 J. Goossens, op. cit., p. 21.

16 Ibid., p. 23.

17 T. Frings, in a report of 1943 to the Sächsische Akademie, cf. C. Soeteman, op. cit., p. 4.

18 The first, much earlier, consonantal shift, gave Germanic its own character vis-à-vis the other Indo-European languages.

19 This does not mean that Dutch *d* always corresponds to German *t*. Germanic did indeed have a plosive which at a certain moment became voiced as *d*. But this pheonomenon only took place in the 8th and 10th centuries, hence too late for this new *d* to undergo the second sound shift. On the other hand, it won out in all the continental Germanic tongues, and only in them. Hence the following parallels:

English   Dutch   German
brother   *broeder*   *Bruder*
thank   *dank*   *Dank*
thorn   *doorn*   *Dorn*

20 Quoted in A. Bach, *Geschichte der deutschen Sprache* (Heidelberg, 1949[4]), p. 140.

21 Ibid., p. 166.

22 This remark is H. Combecher's in 'Netherlands in duitse, Duitsers in nederlandse ogen', *Ons Erfdeel*, XI (1972), p. 60. Of course, this analogy is not conclusive. Danish was less exposed than Dutch, since as a Scandinavian language, it does not belong to the same branch of Germanic as German and Dutch.

23 *Briefwisseling van Bakhuizen van den Brink met zijne vrienden gedurende zijn ballingschap* (Haarlem, 1906), p. 158, quoted in H. Schreiber, op. cit., p. 13.

24 *Der grosse Duden*, Band 6, Aussprachewörterbuch (Mannheim/Wien/Zürich, 1962), p. 37.

25 J. van Dam, 'Nederlands en Duits', *Levende Talen* (1932), p. 148.

26 E. Kruisinga, *Nederlands en Duits* (Groningen/Batavia, 1947), p. 18.

27 Van Haeringen, *Gramarie*, p. 319. Van Haeringen is careful to add that the development defined in this way is only observable in general terms, and does not exclude different tendencies.

28 Of course, when a Dutch-speaker exclaims: 'HAD hij dat maar eerder geschreven' (If only he had written that earlier) *had* has exactly the same value for him as *hätte* would have for a German-speaker in the corresponding sentence, but *had* is not formally a subjunctive.

29 These examples are taken from or inspired by M. J. A. de Leur, *Duitse grammatica* ('s-Hertogenbosch, 1967), pp. 41–42.

30 E. Kruisinga, *Het Nederlands van nu* (Amsterdam/Antwerpen, 1951[2]), p. 15. The grammaticality of this sentence is doubtful and many would consider Kruisinga guilty of a *'Tante Betje'*, as this kind of solecism is popularly known.

31 Dutch is in this respect much closer not only to English (*I was given the book. If I were HIM*), but also to French (*C'est MOI, EUX veulent toujours avoir raison*).

32 To this series may be added words like *slaapkamer* and *leergeld*, in which the first element, originally a noun, is today felt to be a verb root.

33 Cf. C. A. Zaalberg, *Taaltrouw*, p. 167.

34 Van Haeringen, *Gramarie*, p. 242.

35 It is curious to note in this regard that of the words denoting the five senses in both Dutch and German, three are neuter and two masculine. The latter, however, have no prefix in Dutch (*reuk* and *smaak* as opposed to *Geruch* and *Geschmack*).

36 In the sense of: *eine Untersuchung einstellen*.

37 *Kennen, laten* and *durven*, which figure in these examples, are not strictly speaking modal auxiliaries, but the first two are rendered by a German modal in the cases in question, and the third is formally the same as the German modal *dürfen*.

38 J. L. Pauwels, *Les difficultés de la construction néerlandaise*, p. 30.

39 J. Goossens, 'Konstituierendes in der Herausbildung der niederländischen Sprache', in *Akten des Internationalen Germanisten-Kongresses, Cambridge 1975* (Frankfurt/München, 1976), p. 68.

40 *Aussprache-Duden*, pp. 39 and 86.

41 *Grundriss einer Phonetik des Deutschen* (Marburg, 1967^2), p. 192.

42 *Deutsche Aussprache* (Berlin, 1969^{19}), pp. 117 and 124.

43 Van Dam, op. cit., pp. 153—154.

44 A similar difference between the two languages (no longer concerned with positional verbs) is that while *Hij was aan 't schrijven* does have a German equivalent: *Er war am Schreiben*, the latter is 1) colloquial in register, and 2) cannot take a direct object, while in Dutch there is nothing odd in saying: *Hij was een brief aan 't schrijven*.

45 Cf. J. P. Ponten, 'Le participe passé à forme d'infinitif, un problème des syntaxes allemande et néerlandaise', in *25 ans d'études néerlandais à Lille*, Université de Lille III (Lille, n. d.), pp. 61—78.

46 Six to be precise: *lassen, heissen, machen, lehren, lernen* and *helfen*. Moreover, it should be stressed that outside the model auxiliaries 'the use of these verbs may indeed involve an *infinitivus pro participio*-construction, but this is not obligatory (Ponten, op. cit., p. 62).

47 Germ. *brauchen*, which means the same as Du. *hoeven*, also sometimes has the construction: *Du hättest das nicht (zu) tun brauchen.*

48 *We hebben de voorbijgangers staan TE bekijken* is correct, but unusual.

Appendix: Afrikaans

The events of Soweto in 1975 focused the attention of the whole world on Afrikaans, the language used at present, according to 1970 statistics, by 60% of the 3,750,000 whites living in the Republic of South Africa, and by all the more than two million Coloureds.[1] The schoolchildren of Soweto undoubtedly had their reasons for opposing the expansion of Afrikaans in black education. The language in itself is nevertheless of great interest, as it is quite unique: it is the only language of Germanic origin which is spoken exclusively outside Europe. This makes it worth looking, however briefly, at how Afrikaans has managed to preserve its identity *vis-à-vis* English, in what ways it differs from Dutch, and what problems are raised in trying to trace its origin and development since the 17th century.

Either coming from Holland or under the command of Hollanders, the first colonists landed at the Cape of Good Hope in 1652. Until the end of the 18th century the Cape and the surrounding territory were the property of the Dutch East India Company. From the date of their final takeover in 1814, the British did their utmost to impose their language on the colony. Specifically, a decree issued by the Governor, Lord Somerset, in 1822, made the exclusive use of English obligatory in offices, courts and schools. Even in the church, the new administration tried to make its measures felt, by attempting to introduce Scottish clergymen. Of course all these measures were directed at Dutch, not Afrikaans, which was held in complete contempt, not only by the British but by other whites. When the Boers, who had settled in the north after the Great Trek of 1836, founded their two independent Republics in 1852–1854, they did not dream of adopting the language they spoke every day as their official one, but returned to Dutch (or *Hollands*, as they called it). For their part, intellectuals scoffed at the Boers' *kombuistaaltje* (cookhouse lingo): the first quotations in Afrikaans, dating from about 1825, are used for comic or picturesque effect. In church, both preaching and singing were in Dutch. It created a furore when in 1872 Arnoldus Pannevis, a Dutchman who had settled in the Cape, suggested that the Scriptures should be translated into Afrikaans; the Bible societies to whom he addressed himself replied that they did not feel the time was ripe.

But Dutch had become virtually a foreign language for the vast majority of the population, and the triumph of English would have been in no doubt had there not been a revival of Afrikaans.

Two separate phases must be distinguished in this revival. On

14 August 1875 the *Genootskap van regte Afrikaners* (Society of True Afrikaners) was founded, and this marked the beginning of the 'First Afrikaans Movement', whose concerns, however, were not exclusively of a linguistic nature. 'The aim of our movement', article 2 of its statutes declared, 'is to defend our language, our nation and our country.' In 1876 S. du Toit launched a monthly journal called *Die Patriot*, which enjoyed a huge success: within a few years the number of subscribers had risen to 3,000, a remarkable number for the time. What should be remembered is that the First Movement was not aimed at the educated section of the population, either won over by the 'enemy' or living in the past. 'There are three kinds of Afrikaners: those whose heart is English, those whose heart is Dutch, and those whose heart is Afrikaans.' This extract from a manifesto is typical of the tone, but the polemical tracts and light reading-matter produced at this time have no lasting value.

After the Boer War, the British renewed their efforts. The 1902 treaty did establish a degree of bilingualism in schools and courtrooms, but the concession was a conditional one and in any case did not take any account of Afrikaans. It was at this moment that the Second Movement was organised. Like the pioneers of the preceding generation, its supporters were concerned with the necessity of fighting English not with Dutch but with Afrikaans. But they realised that to be able to hold one's ground against one cultural language one must have an alternative cultural language, and that they were faced with the choice between going under and 'Africanising' religious life, scholarship and literature. Such were the ideas expressed in 1905 by G. J. Preller in a resounding speech, 'Laat 't ons toch ernst wezen' (Let us set about things in earnest), and the practical consequences were: 'Afrikaans schrijven en spreken, Hollands lezen, albei leeren' (Speak and write Afrikaans, read Dutch, learn both). It is clear that the programme involved no hostility towards Dutch, the mother-language of Afrikaans, but this did not prevent some people from vociferously proclaiming that if the choice was between English and Afrikaans, they would choose English.

But resistance gradually crumbled before the Movement's successful advance. Preller's address had been followed by the setting up at Pretoria of the *Afrikaanse Taalgenooskap* (Afrikaans Language Society), soon followed at the Cape itself by the *Afrikaanse Taalvereeniging* (Afrikaans Language Association). 1909 saw the foundation of the South African Academy, followed twenty years later by the Federation of South African Cultural Associations, which took as its motto: 'Preserve and build'. This was not simply a programme, but a statement of what had already been achieved. It is impossible to go into great detail here, but suffice it to say that today there is no intellectual field into which Afrikaans writers have not ventured, and that literature in particular is flourishing.

The necessity of conducting church services in Afrikaans was recognised in 1916 and this was accomplished by 1924; an Afrikaans

Bible appeared in 1932, followed by a prayer-book. Elsewhere, the fairly rapid improvement in relations between British and Boers made it possible for legislation to be brought into line with the new situation. In 1925 Afrikaans was admitted in parliamentary debate instead of Dutch, which it had already replaced in primary schools in 1914 and in secondary schools in 1917. At present, five of the ten 'white' universities have Afrikaans as their language of instruction and one is bilingual; the Coloured university is naturally Afrikaans-speaking.

One need only glance at an Afrikaans text to realise the extreme simplification which Dutch underwent at the Cape, both phonetically and grammatically. 'Simplified Dutch' is not an adequate definition of Afrikaans, but this aspect is undoubtedly a very striking one, and a few examples will provide a cursory illustration:[2]

— Phonetically, the changes may be grouped under three headings: syncope, assimilation and apocope.

Syncope of intervocalic g: *vogel* > *foël* > *fool* (bird); *leugen* > *leuën* > *leun* (lie), and of intervocalic v: *over* > *oër* > *oor* (over); *avond* > *a'end* > *aand* (evening).

Assimilation of g after a consonant: *volgens* > *follens* (according to); *berge(n)* > *bêre* (to store), and of d between n or l and neutral s: *kinders* > *kinners* (children); *zolder* > *soller* (loft).

Apocope, in the infinitive: *plagen* > *plaag* > *pla* (to tease); *zeggen* > *sê* (to say); *leggen* > *lê* (to lay), and in words ending in t: *lust* > *lus* (desire); *acht* > *ag* (eight).

— Conjugation is reduced to maximum simplicity: the root of the verb serves for all tenses for all persons, singular and plural. Hence there is no distinction between 'strong' and 'weak' verbs, since the latter have no preterite-suffix and the former, with the exception of a few remnants such as *had, sou, kon, werd* or *wou* (infinitive forms: *het, sal, kan, word, wil*) have no vowel change. Where Dutch has *ik nam*, in Afrikaans one must use either *ek neem* (historical present) or *ek het geneem* (present perfect).

— There is no trace of declension. The genitive with proper nouns has been replaced by a construction with a possessive adjective: instead of *Jans hoed*, one has *Jan se hoed*.

— Apart from the third-personal pronouns (*hy, sy, dit*), there is only one gender, with the definite article *die*.

Afrikaans, therefore, has carried the process of reduction, which characterises the Germanic languages generally (see above, pp. 114 ff.), a very long way. Its uniqueness resides in the fact that its starting point is a modern Germanic language, 17th-century Dutch.

There are complications in virtually only two respects. Firstly, the plural of nouns is usually formed with -*e*, but sometimes also in -*s*, and there are also some double plurals like *kinners, kalvers, eiers* (cf. Du. *kinderen, kalveren, eieren*), and even *ruggens*, pl. of *rug* (instead of Du. *ruggen*). A second and much stranger feature is the repeated negative. 'I cannot do it' becomes *ek kan dit nie doen nie*, and 'not without great success' *nie sonder 'n groot sukses nie*. This feature will be dealt with below.

Given the close relationship between the two languages, one might suppose that 'a Dutch person or Fleming can converse with an Afrikaner without much difficulty' and that 'they can quite easily read each other's languages'.[3] One could be correct, provided one does not overlook the qualified caution in these remarks. All the same, some 5% of the Afrikaans vocabulary derives from non-Dutch sources, and this includes not only specialised terms like *onbietjie* (a kind of antelope) and *nartjie* (a kind of tangerine), or popular ones like *gogga* (vermin, bogey), but also some of the most common words: *baie* (many, much, very), *nooi* (girl) and *dalk* (perhaps). In addition, certain Dutch words have changed their meaning: *boerderij*, for example, means farming in general, and *plaas* is used to refer to an individual farm. Finally, much depends on whom one is talking to, as an Afrikaans-speaker obviously needs a minimum of linguistic training to be able to recognise *ons is* (we are) in Dutch *wij zijn* or *hulle het* (they have) in *ze hebben*, and vice versa.

The existence and characteristics of Afrikaans have been a source of fascination for philologists, both on the spot and in the Netherlands and Flanders.

'Almost all the theories constructed to account for the origin and development of Afrikaans are based on an incredible indifference to the findings of Dutch dialectology,' wrote a specialist some sixty years ago.[4] Indeed, if one thinks of the state of flux which official Dutch was in during the 17th century, and of the importance retained to this day by regional speech in the Netherlands and Flanders, despite the smallness of the language-area, one can appreciate of what enormous interest it would be to be able to determine what dialects formed the basis of Afrikaans.

A difficult question, to be sure. Nevertheless, we are well informed about the original composition of the Cape Colony. We have at our disposal the 'monsterrollen', or census lists, which are very valuable, since they almost always give the place of birth of the pioneers. Thus, of 264 persons whose birthplace can be established from the list for 1664, 34 are from North Holland, 24 from South Holland, 147 (including the Hollanders) are Netherlanders and 82 are German. It may be assumed, given the origin of the settlement and the political situation, that despite the presence of a sizeable foreign minority, the Netherlanders in general and the Hollanders in particular set the tone. But what Hollanders precisely? It might be advisable to apply qualitative rather than quantitative criteria. It should not be forgotten how heterogeneous this community was, both as regards cultural level and origin, and above all how restricted the group in question was whose members, to begin with, stayed clustered around the fort which protected them. Such conditions favoured the influence of a few powerful personalities, and if we look at the directorate of the original colony we find that all its members came from South Holland. Take Jan van

Riebeeck himself:[5] he was born in Culemborg, which if not technically in South Holland is within a few miles of it; his mother came from Rotterdam, and he was brought up in Schiedam. A study of his journal leaves us in no doubt as to his language. Riebeeck was careful to surround himself with men from the same area like his brother-in-law Van der Stael from Rotterdam and the Hague merchant Gabbema, and to confer high office on them. Is it not tempting to see this combination of circumstances (which was never to repeat itself) as decisive? This would amount to saying that three or four families were sufficient to shape the structure of a language which is today spoken by several million people.

This is the line taken by Kloeke in his book on the subject,[6] which in spite of all the criticism levelled at it remains a masterly work. He sees, in his discussion of the founding fathers, a confirmation of the conclusion to which he has been led by extensive research into dialect: the principal starting-point for Afrikaans is to be found in the dialects of South Holland. But just as before Kloeke some investigators had extended the region to take in a circle with Gouda as its centre and the line Gouda–Amsterdam as its radius,[7] so after him others still believed that it covered the whole of Holland south of the River IJ and even the western part of the province of Utrecht.[8] And besides, is it quite certain that *Holland* played such a decisive part? The South African philologist H. van der Merwe goes so far as to believe that 'a broader study of the *Flemish* dialects would provide proof that the Southern Netherlands contributed much more to the formation of Afrikaans than the North. To convince oneself of this, it is sufficient to travel around Flanders with one's eyes and ears open'.[9] The same impression is shared at the other end of the line. 'We Flemings,' writes Pauwels, 'are well aware of our linguistic relatedness to the Afrikaners. We are constantly struck by the fact that their language has for us a ring at least as familiar as that of a Dutchman from above the Moerdijk[10] and their way of speaking, sentence-melody, for example, is very like our own.'[11] The dialectologists still have plenty of work to do.

Was Afrikaans formed rapidly or through a series of imperceptible transitions? The reason that this question poses itself is because for centuries the colonists wrote exclusively in Dutch. The first Afrikaans book dates from 1854. We know virtually nothing about the everyday **spoken** language of the time. Kloeke believes (and many support him in this opinion) that a few decades were sufficient for Afrikaans to become, in essence, what it is today. But, whether slow or almost immediate, the question remains as to what influences the process was subject to, and on this point the arguments have been going on for more than half a century.

The first thought that comes to mind is to attribute the transformation of *Hollands* to foreigners, who were so numerous from the outset. In 1664, as we have seen, Germans accounted for almost a third of the colony and while their relative importance decreased subsequently, they were to continue arriving throughout the 18th century. Groups of French Huguenots sought sanctuary at the Cape in 1687 and 1688: there were 150 of them, at a time when the whole population numbered not more than 600 people. Though there was scarcely any further French immigration, the original group was very prolific, as can be seen today from the telephone directory of any large town, which will contain whole pages of Du Plessis's, Du Toits and Malherbes. Ingenious statisticians have calculated that around 1806 the white population had 50.4% Dutch blood in its veins, with German, French and others representing 27%, 17.25% and 5.5% respectively.[12] It is, however, no longer disputed by anyone that French had **no** influence on the formation of Afrikaans, even in the field of vocabulary: words borrowed directly from French amount to four horticultural terms! Similarly, German provided a mere twenty or so words (*laer < Lager* = 'camp', *verfoes < verpfuschen* = 'to bungle', *jaarhonderd < Jahrhundert* = 'century'), and may have contributed to the substitution of *die* for *de* as the definite article. But that is all.

It is, however, permissible to surmise that a tendency common to all the foreigners, whatever the nature of their original language, was to simplify as much as possible. The points listed above show that the objective spontaneously striven after has been achieved. Another striking example of this kind is that of the two forms of a number of personal pronouns in Dutch, one stressed the other unstressed (see above p. 51), only the first has been retained in Afrikaans. Nothing could be more natural from the point of view of foreigners: why bother with two words, when one is enough? And if one has to choose, why not opt for the clearer form, most easily comprehensible by a foreigner?

However, such generalities are insufficient in themselves: Afrikaans is not purely and simply a kind of 'basic Dutch'. It has a pronounced character of its own, and the question is: from where does this derive? One well-known theory stresses the importance of a sort of *lingua franca*, made up of Portuguese and Malay, which, having originated in the Indies during the Portuguese occupation, was spread in Southern Africa through the agency of sailors, traders and servants and did not finally die out till the beginning of the 19th century. Through contact with this *lingua franca*, it is claimed, Dutch became 'creolised'. There are indeed obvious traces in Afrikaans of Portuguese (*tamaai < tamanho*, 'enormous'), and Malay (*boetie < boedjan*, 'brother')[13] and Hindi (*katel*, 'bedstead'). This theory, first launched by the Dutchman D. C. Hesseling[14] has recently been given a new lease of life thanks to another Dutchman, M. F. Valkhoff.[15] On the other hand, it has always encountered bitter opposition from South African linguists and also from some Europeans. In their view, Hesseling and his followers 'have let themselves be misled by the differences between Afrikaans and official, written Dutch, which they regarded as specifically African, and since they were concerned precisely with **deviations** from Dutch, they looked for explanations everywhere except in that language'. This was to forget that the overwhelming majority of the 17th-century colonists spoke a language which was neither refined nor uniform. 'A very large number of the so-called characteristic features of Afrikaans have their counter-parts in one or more Dutch dialects. The parallels are often so striking that one can be in no doubt as to their origin: the majority of Africanisms were imported from the European homeland!'[16]

One particularly illuminating example of this dispute concerns the 'double negative'.[17] This means that 'when an idea, an action, a state, etc., are negated, the main clause or subordinate clause will almost always end in *nie*'.[18]

Waarom doen jy NIE die werk soos die onderwyser jou geleer het NIE?
(Why don't you do the work like the teacher taught you?)
Dit het begin lyk asof die Transvaalse regering GEEN stap waarby die belange van die uitlanders, in watter verwyderde sin ook al, gemoeid was, sou kan doen sonder om te vra wat Brittanje te sê het NIE.
(It began to look as though the government of the Transvaal would not be able to do anything which affected the interests of the foreigners, however remotely, without asking what Britain's attitude was.)

One wonders if there are any limits to the length of the clause. All the grammarians say is that 'when the clause is so long that the repetition of *nie* would be felt as unexpected or unnatural, the second *nie* may be dropped'.[19] But modern Afrikaans makes less and less use of this degree of latitude. The paradoxical fact is that the final *nie*, so absolutely indispensable in 99% of cases, carries **no** stress, either primary or secondary, but is there solely to sound off the sentence. This means that one is not dealing with a double negative in the strict sense.

This is one of the reasons (in fact, the main one) why this feature cannot, as was thought at the end of the last century, derive from French *ne...pas, ne...jamais*, etc. In French, the second particle is stressed and contributes so much to reinforcing the meaning that it has eventually become the essential element: hence such colloquial constructions as *J'sais pas*, and even perfectly regular ones like *Qu'as-tu vu? — Rien*. Exactly the opposite, that is, of what happens in Afrikaans.

A. C. Bouman's attempt at an explanation is of an entirely different order.[20] He notes the existence 'in Coloureds and whites of all classes, and even among English-speaking South Africans', of a 'double hiccup ($\wedge$)' which puts negative sentences into relief, and which without any doubt derives from indigenous languages, and specifically from Hottentot. The negative answer to the question: *Weet jy waar Langenhoven woon?* (Do you know where Langenhoven lives?), is: $\wedge$ or: $\wedge$, *ek weet niet*. Being somewhat disagreeable to white ears, the hiccup, Bouman suggests, was often replaced by *nee: NEE, ek weet NIE*, so that it is a simple matter of substitution. Going a step further, the transition from *NEE, ek sê dit NIE* (I don't say) to *Ek kan (dit) NIE sê NIE* (I can't say) is an easy one, the more so because of the presence of the modal auxiliary. In reply to this thesis it has been pointed out that a construction like *NEE, ek ken kom NIE* is a polite tautology found in all languages: *No, I can't tell you; Nein, das weiss ich nicht.*

One of Bouman's opponents, D. B. Bosman, suggests a very different explanation. In his view it is not a matter of substitution but of contamination. Bosman links *nie...nie* with constructions like *Hy is AL lank AL weg* (He is long gone) or *Hy loop UIT die huis UIT* (He goes out of the house), which, moreover, have near-equivalents in Dutch. Looking at the following sentence: *Ek sal NIE gaan NIE* (I will not go), he regards it as a fusion, so to speak, of *Ek gaan NIE and Ek sal NIE gaan.*[21] This theory is a rather tenuous one. Bosman has chosen an ideal example: nothing proves that sentences of the type *Ek sal NIE gaan NIE* are older than *Ek sien NIEMAND NIE* (I see no one) or *NIET die man NIE, maar die vrou, was die skuldige* (Not the man, but the woman was the guilty one), cases in which contamination seems very improbable. Nevertheless, Bosman's theory had the merit of introducing a new explanatory principle. By presenting 'double negation' as having issued from an internal development, he opened up a very fruitful avenue of exploration. Almost simultaneously, the great Flemish philologist Blancquaert joined in the debate in a paper which has remained famous, in which he expressed his conviction that 'double negation is not at all specific to Afrikaans, but is equally European and Dutch, and there is no need to look very far afield to find it'.[22] Of course, Blancquaert could only generalise from sporadic observations, and we are still waiting for the systematic survey, across all the dialects of North and South, which he called for. One at least has been done in very great detail by his younger colleague Pauwels for the locality of Aarschot in Belgian Brabant.[23]

There is an extraordinary symmetry between the use of the expletive negative by the inhabitants of Aarschot and by Afrikaners, though the use is not absolutely identical. The enormous gaps between the two elements found in Afrikaans do not occur in Brabant, and, moreover most importantly, the expletive *nie* is never obligatory in the Aarschot dialect. Having said this, the syntactical ordering is exactly the same: *De dokter is NIET geweest NIE* (The doctor hasn't been); *ze heeft er geen plezier aan beleefd NIE* (She got no pleasure from it), as is the semantic nuance: the Aarschot final *nie* has no other function except to indicate rhythm, and in consequence never carries any stress.

If then, on the basis of facts of this kind, one accepts that 'double negation' is of Dutch origin, it still remains to be seen why and how in South Africa the phenomenon acquired such a general and regular character, why this humble seed flourished so profusely. Must it not be that it found a particularly favourable environment there? One thinks immediately of the Hottentots, who unlike the Bantu tribes, whom the whites scarcely encountered before the end of the 18th century, had close contacts with the Hollanders from the moment of

Van Riebeeck's first landing. The number of Hottentots living within the boundaries of the colony in 1800 has been put at 15,000. By this time they had virtually abandoned their own language and spoke, after their own fashion of course, that of the whites.[24] In Nama, one of the two dialects spoken by the Hottentots and the only one of which we know anything, negatives almost always follow the verb, and are often placed both before and after it. The following are two sentences in Nama transposed literally into Afrikaans: *NIEMAND mos huur ons — NIE* (lit.: No one must hire us, not); *So jy mag NOOIT handel — NIET* (lit.: You must never act like that, not). In making these observations, G. S. Nienaber in fact rejected the idea that the adoption of final *nie* by the whites, prompted as it were by the Hottentots, could have been facilitated by a predisposition in Dutch. He considered any possible similarity between Afrikaans and Dutch with regard to double negation 'more apparent than real'.[25] But these words were written three years before Pauwels' work appeared, and the Leuven professor's findings lead one on the contrary to the view that this is to a certain extent a case of resurgence, and that it confronts us with a strange 'linguistic encounter'.

While he knows Nienaber's work and even quotes him, Valkhoff uses the term **linguistic encounter** in a quite different context. This successor of Hesseling's observes that pidgin Portuguese, which with a varying admixture of Malay once served as a *lingua franca* at the Cape and which still survives elsewhere, for instance on the Luango coast, also has double negation: *Estas doente?* ('Are you ill?') — *NÃO esta NÃO!* This, in Valkhoff's view, is the direction in which we must look for the explanation of final *nie* in Afrikaans. It is the only direction, not because he discounts any Hottentot influence, for example, but to the extent that he sees any parallels with Dutch dialects, even that of Aarschot, as purely fortuitous. He is quite prepared to admit that constructions like *ma se hoed* (mother's hat), or even *'n sjieling se koek* (a shilling cake) derive at once from colloquial Dutch (*vader z'n hoed* instead of *vaders hoed* or *de hoed van vader*), and from a process of creolisation. But in the parallels between constructions quoted by Pauwels and the corresponding ones in Afrikaans he sees only 'rapprochements' without significance. He writes in this connection:

> 'It is not enough to discover a *rapprochement* (aanknopingspunt) for an Afrikaans characteristic in some dialect of the Low Countries; one has to prove why this phenomenon, **and not another**, became the vogue in Afrikaans. Since the Nederlandicist [sic] is unable to give this answer, the specialist in Creole steps in and points at a **linguistic encounter** with, or even purely and simply an adoption from, one of the main languages with which Dutch came into contact'.[26]

It must be admitted that the last sentence is not particularly clear, as it would be if Valkhoff had written simply: '...the specialist in Creole steps in and points at an adoption from...'. For does not to talk of a 'linguistic encounter' mean to admit that the same effect may be due to the interplay of two heterogeneous elements, to wit, in the case under discussion, a tendency inherent in the Dutch of the colonists, **and** the influence of one or more local languages? Perhaps in the last analysis the wisest course would be to apply to double negation also the principle that Valkhoff himself expressed so felicitously when talking of certain items of vocabulary:

> 'This may be a lesson, that we should not be too doctrinaire or too rigorous in matters of linguistics. It is not always **either** one thing **or** another in the evolution of such a delicate social phenomenon as speech or language. Hence, in the history of Afrikaans, too, it was not always **either** Dutch **or** Creole, but the two linguistic currents may well have met and the latter may have stimulated the development of the former.'[27]

However wide, the rift driven by circumstances between Dutch and Afrikaans has never become unbridgeable.

Contact has, in fact, never been broken at any period. As the language of the administration for a century and a half and of church and school until recently, *Hooghollands* has always enjoyed the prestige attached to literary languages. Though powerless to change anything in the basic structure of Afrikaans, its influence has been considerable in the field of vocabulary.

The borrowings from Dutch in this sphere are innumerable, but they are easy to recognise from the way that they conflict with pure Afrikaans phonetics, to the extent that the latter derives from Holland dialects. Over and against *heuning* (honey) and *meule* (mill), we find *koning* and *somer*. It is not always easy to see the reason behind the preference for the 'official' form. Usually the distinguishing principle is quite a simple one. Whereas *herd* (hearth), *kers* (candle) *lantern* and *perd* (horse) are 'authentic' words — in the sense that in Holland dialect lengthened *a* followed by *r* and a dental become *e* —, one also finds forms in *aa*, which come straight from standard Dutch. Unlike the first series, made up of concrete or familiar words, the latter comprise abstract or slightly academic terms (*waard* adj., *waarde*). Curious in this respect are the different words for earth: *aarde* is a recherché term (and quite rare, as *grond* is usually preferred), while *erd* is used specifically of clay. The same applies to intervocalic *d*, where the mutation to *i* does not take place in words borrowed from Dutch like *bode* (messenger), *geleider* (conductor, leader), *hede* (today), *in stede van* (instead of), which belong to formal style. In this area indeed, the influence of the Netherlands has been so strong that with certain common words, which of course existed in dialect form, it was the 'correct' version which finally won the day: *benede* (Holl. *beneje*) 'downstairs', 'below', *hoede* (Holl. *hoeje* = 'hats'), *medelijde* (Holl. *meelij* = 'pity').

In this way Afrikaners, sometimes driven by a kind of snobbery and above all by the desire to enrich their language, have drawn largely on standard Dutch. As Kloeke very graphically puts it, the mother did not die at the birth of her child and has kept a great deal of authority over it, although as it grew up the child's discipline was not all that it might have been.[28]

The short quotation which follows by way of conclusion, is taken from the work of a South African academic,[29] and is quite revealing both in its form (the juxtaposition of the Afrikaans text and its Dutch 'translation' will demonstrate, on some points at least, the peculiarities of phonetics and grammar) and in its content, which enables one to see the complex attitude of the South African towards the Netherlands; a feeling of profound affinity, but at the same time a pride in one's legitimate autonomy.

AFRIKAANS

Ons kan...met sekerheid konstateer dat Afrikaans ontwikkel het uit die Nederlandse dialekte wat vanaf 1652 aan die Kaap gepraat is. Afrikaans en Nederlands is dus suster-tale en gaan altwee terug op die Nederlands van die sewentiende eeu. In sommige opsigte staan Afrikaans selfs nog nader aan daardie Nederlands van die sewentiende eeu as moderne Nederlands.[30] Die taal, letterkunde en die kultuur in die algemeen van Nederland voor 1652 is dus die gemeenskaplike besit van die Nederlandse en die Afrikaanse volke, en ons kan met volle reg Maerlant en Vondel tot ons letterkunde reken.

DUTCH

Wij kunnen...met zekerheid constateren dat het Afrikaans zich ontwikkeld heeft uit de Nederlandse dialecten die vanaf 1652 aan de Kaap gesproken zijn. Afrikaans en Nederlands zijn dus zustertalen en gaan allebei terug op het Nederlands van de zeventiende eeuw. In sommige opzichten staat het Afrikaans nog nader tot dat Nederlands van de zeventiende eeuw dan (het) modern(e) Nederlands. De taal, de letterkunde en de cultuur in het algemeen van het Nederland voor 1652 zijn dus het gemeenschappelijke bezit van het Nederlandse en het Afrikaanse volk, en wij kunnen met het volste recht Maerlant en Vondel tot onze letterkunde rekenen.

(We can...state with certainty that Afrikaans developed from the Dutch dialects which were spoken at the Cape from 1652 onwards. Afrikaans and Dutch are therefore sister-languages and both derive from 17th-century Dutch. In some respects Afrikaans is even closer to that Dutch of the 17th century than modern Dutch. The language, literature and culture in general of the pre-1652 Netherlands are therefore the common heritage of the Dutch and Afrikaans peoples, and we have every right to consider Maerlant and Vondel a part of our literature.)

1 The Coloureds (*Kleurlingen*) are the descendants of the children of miscegenation, in the 17th and 18th centuries, between whites and Hottentots and above all, between whites and Malay slaves.

2 These are taken from C. F. L. Lecoutere, *Inleiding tot de taalkunde en tot de geschiedenis van het Nederlands*, ed. L. Grootaers (Groningen, 1934), and G. Dekker, *Afrikaanse literatuurgeschiedenis* (Kaapstad, 1937).

3 J. L. Pauwels, 'Het Afrikaans, dochtertaal van het Nederlands', in *Verzamelde Opstellen*, p. 59.

4 S. D. E. Boshoff, *Volk en Taal van Suid-Afrika* (Amsterdam, 1921), p. 261.

5 Jan Anthonsz. van Riebeeck (1619–1677), founder of the Cape Colony, governed it until 1665, when he was appointed Governor of Molucca.

6 G. C. Kloeke, *Herkomst en groei van het Afrikaans* (Leiden, 1950).

7 D. B. Bosman, *Oor die ontstaan van Afrikaans* (Amsterdam, 1928[2]).

8 J. Du P. Scholz, *Taalkundige opstellen* (Pretoria, 1963), pp. 232 ff.

9 *Tijdskrif vir Geesteswetenskappe*, VII (1967), p. 387.

10 'Moerdijk' (in fact the name of a village) denotes the demarcation line between North Brabant and the rest of the Netherlands.

11 Op. cit., p. 60. However, this 'family resemblance' may stem not from Afrikaans's direct descent from Flemish but from the fact that the two languages have developed in comparable circumstances. Both have been cut off from Northern Dutch, one by politics, the other by geography, and, moreover, they have both retained a rural quality, the townsfolk having for a long period given preference to French in Flanders and English in South Africa. (This hypothesis is expounded by P. van Hauwermeiren in *Wetenschappelijke Tijdingen*, 45/1 (1975), pp. 16–17.)

12 H. T. Colenbrander, *De afkomst der Boeren* (n.p., 1902).

13 There may also be Malay influence in certain elements of popular syntax, such as the use of the preposition *vir* before the direct object (*ek het vir Jan gesien*), or the dropping of the conjunction *dat* (*ek hoop hij kom vandaag*). A creolisation process is at least probable in the confusion of parts of speech: the use of adverbs for adjectives (*'n reg op kerel*) or adjectives for verbs (*die skape dood bij hope*). But are these phenomena of Malay or Hottentot origin?

14 *Het Afrikaans* (Leiden, 1923[2]).

15 *Studies in Portuguese and Creole, with Special Reference to South Africa* (Johannesburg, 1966).

16 J. L. Pauwels, op. cit., p. 62.

17 For a fuller account, see P. Brachin, 'La "double négation" en afrikaans', *Etudes Germaniques*, 23/3 (1968), pp. 451–463.

18 M. C. Botha/J. Burger, *Praktiese Afrikaanse Grammatika* (Kaapstad, 1923[6]).

19 Ibid.

20 'De dubbele ontkenning in het Afrikaans', *De Nieuwe Taalgids* (1923), pp. 17–23.

21 ''n Paar Afrikaanse eigenaardighede', *De Nieuwe Taalgids* (1923), pp. 298–302.

22 'Over de dubbele ontkenning en nog wat', in *Handelingen van het 6de Vlaamsche Philologencongres* (Antwerpen, 1923), pp. 60–69.

23 'De expletieve ontkenning NIE(T) aan het einde van de zin in het Zuidnederlands en het Afrikaans', appendix to *Het dialect van Aarschot en omgeving* (Leuven, 1958).

24 They had begun very early. In 1685 the Director General of the Dutch East India Company at the Cape, Adriaan van Rheede, noted (without of course having the slightest inkling of the gallons of ink which were later to be spilled over the phrase) that 'the Hottentots are learning to speak our language, but they do so after their own fashion, contorting it to the point of making it incomprehensible, and **our people are imitating them**'.

25 'Iets naders oor die ontkenning in Afrikaans', in *Hertzog-Annale*, Jaarboek II (1955), pp. 29–45.

26 Op. cit., pp. 227 and 234.

27 Ibid., p. 231.

28 On the other hand, borrowings from English are insignificant, particularly since Afrikaners are careful to avoid them and resort when the need arises to neologisms

which are often picturesque: *hysbak* for lift, *woonstel* for flat, and *duikweg* for tunnel.
29 G. Dekker, op. cit., p. 5.
30 The archaic nature of Afrikaans is particularly clear on two points. On the one hand, the lack of a reflexive pronoun (cf. p. 13): *die professor trek HOM* (Du. *zich*) *in sy studeerkamer terug* (The professor retreats into his study). Secondly, in the combination of a finite verb with a positional verb (cf. p. 124): *die ou man SIT oor sy verlede EN MEDITEER* (Du. *zit... te mediteren*) (The old man sits and meditates on his past).

Selected Bibliography

Only fairly non-technical books and articles have been included in the short list below. For more extensive bibliographical information, the reader is referred to the following two admirable studies:

M. C. van den Toorn, *Nederlandse taalkunde* (Groningen, 1976⁶).

G. Geerts, *Voorlopers en varianten van het Nederlands* (Leuven, 1975).

General Studies

W. B. Lockwood, *An Informal History of the German Language* (Cambridge, 1965) (esp. Chapter 11).

O. Vanderputte, *Dutch. The Language of Twenty Million Dutch and Flemish People*, translated by P. Vincent and T. Hermans (Rekkem, 1981²).

E. Kruisinga, *Het Nederlands van nu* (Amsterdam/Antwerpen, 1951²).

P. C. Paardekooper, *A. B. N. en dialect* ('s-Hertogenbosch, 1969³).

History of the Language

C. G. N. de Vooys, *Geschiedenis van de Nederlandse taal* (Groningen, 1975⁵).

A. A. Weijnen, *Het algemeen beschaafd Nederlands historisch beschouwd* (Assen, 1974).

B. Donaldson, *Dutch. A Linguistic History of Holland and Belgium* (Leiden, 1983).

North and South

G. Geerts (ed.), *Taal of taaltje?* (Leuven, 1972).

G. Geerts (ed.), *Aspekten van het Nederlands in Vlaanderen* (Leuven, 1972).

Dutch and German

C. B. van Haeringen, *Nederlands tussen Duits en Engels* (Den Haag, n. d.).

J. Goossens, *Was ist Deutsch — und wie verhält es sich zum Niederländischen?*, 'Nachbarn' 11, Presse- und Kulturabteilung der königlichen Niederländischen Botschaft (Bonn, 1976⁴).

Collections of Articles

C. B. van Haeringen, *Neerlandica* ('s-Gravenhage, 1962²).

C. B. van Haeringen, *Gramarie* (Assen, 1962).

J. L. Pauwels, *Verzamelde opstellen* (Assen, 1965)

K. Heeroma, *Sprekend als nederlandist* (Den Haag, 1968).

C. A. Zaalberg, *Taaltrouw* (Culemborg, 1976).

Album Willem Pée (Tongeren, 1973).

Spel van zinnen (Album A. van Loey) (Brussel, 1975).

Taal- en letterkundig gastenboek voor prof. dr. G. A. van Es (Groningen, 1975).

J. Hoogteijling, *Taalkunde in artikelen* (Groningen, 1968).

M. Klein, *Taalkundig beschouwd. Taalkundige artikelen met inleiding en vragen* (Den Haag, 1980).

Index

The following abbreviations are used: ff = following pages; n = footnote; italics indicate main entry.